THE CHILDREN'S MEDICINE CHEST

THE
CHILDREN'S MEDICINE CHEST

JOHN COPPOLA, M.S., R.PH.

MAIN STREET BOOKS

DOUBLEDAY
NEW YORK LONDON TORONTO SYDNEY AUCKLAND

This book is not intended as a substitute for medical advice of physicians. The reader should regularly consult a physician in matters related to his or her child's health and, particularly, in respect to any symptoms that may require diagnosis or medical attention.

A MAIN STREET BOOK
PUBLISHED BY DOUBLEDAY
A division of Bantam Doubleday Dell Publishing Group, Inc.
1540 Broadway, New York, New York 10036

MAIN STREET BOOKS, DOUBLEDAY, and the portrayal of a building with a tree are trademarks of Doubleday, a division of Bantam Doubleday Dell Publishing Group, Inc.

Library of Congress Cataloging-in-Publication Data

Coppola, John.
    The children's medicine chest / by John Coppola.
        p.   cm.
    "A Main Street book."
    Includes bibliographical references and index.
    1. Pediatric pharmacology—Popular works.   I. Title.
RJ560.C67   1993
615′.1′083—dc20   93-16237
                                                        CIP

ISBN 0-385-46818-0
Copyright © 1993 by John Coppola
All Rights Reserved
Printed in the United States of America
September 1993

10   9   8   7   6   5   4   3   2   1

First Edition

THIS BOOK IS DEDICATED TO ANNE, WHOSE IDEAS, CRITICISMS, AND STEADY ENCOURAGEMENT MADE ITS WRITING POSSIBLE.

CONTENTS

5 MEDICATION MONOGRAPHS

INTRODUCTION

According to numerous surveys, patients who are well informed about their medications, and who follow their doctor's instructions faithfully, will benefit most from those medications. It follows, then, that children will benefit most if parents are more knowledgeable about their children's medications. Although there is an enormous amount of medication information available, the sad truth is that not enough of it is being shared with patients and their families. Many people, including the author, feel this information is absolutely necessary if patients are to receive the greatest benefits from their medications.

A report released in 1989 by the National Council on Patient Information and Education (NCPIE) concluded that many children and teenagers do not benefit maximally from their prescribed medications because they don't use them correctly. This widespread problem, the NCPIE felt, results from the failure of healthcare providers—physicians, pharmacists, nurses, and others—to provide patients and consumers with adequate information about medication taken by children and teenagers in America.

The Children's Medicine Chest attempts to bridge that gap by sharing some of the relevant information with you, the parents. Because your child may be unable to understand this information, you must assume the role of guardian of his or her health. You alone are responsible for making the prudent and timely decisions which *are* the burden of all parents. I hope this book will make your burden lighter.

J.C.

THE CHILDREN'S MEDICINE CHEST

CHAPTER 1

MEDICATION IN CHILDREN: ANOTHER DRUG PROBLEM IN AMERICA!

For most illnesses, medication plays a significant role in curing the disorder and/or alleviating its symptoms. In fact, it's safe to say that medication is probably the treatment of choice for most disorders. And if we consider the medications we purchase over the counter, which, for most of us, far exceed the number of those prescribed for us by our doctors, the use of medication as a treatment method far outstrips all other treatment methods combined. This is why you should be alarmed by a recent report that confirms a significant "drug" problem among children and teenagers in America—a problem not related to what we ordinarily mean by drug addiction or drug abuse.

According to the National Council on Patient Information and Education (NCPIE), the widespread misuse of prescribed medication by children and teenagers has resulted in increased illness, as well as in higher healthcare costs for all Americans.

NCPIE REPORT

The NCPIE—a nonprofit organization composed of 247 organizations representing consumers, government, health agencies, healthcare professionals, health-related groups and manufacturers—is primarily concerned with promoting "the safe and effective use of prescription medicines." One way of doing this is to improve the communication of information about prescription medications between healthcare professionals and their patients.

In May 1989, the NCPIE released a report describing the widespread, inappropriate use of prescribed medication by children and teenagers in America. Because of the report's significance as it relates to the underlying premise of this book, a brief look at its findings may provide a better understanding of the scope of the problem.

The following summary of the NCPIE report includes guidelines for parents, healthcare professionals, and schools for improving medication use among children and teenagers.

A. Types of Improper Medication Use
1. Stopping medication too soon: for example, stopping an antibiotic treatment because your child feels better.
2. Not taking enough medication: for example, forgetting or skipping a dose or not adhering to a consistent medication schedule each day, or during the treatment period, as prescribed.
3. Refusing medication: for example, a child not taking medication because of poor taste, side effects, or "childish behavior," which may be a reflection of the parents' own possible negative attitudes regarding medication.
4. Taking too much medication: for example, giving your child a larger dose than prescribed, or giving an extra dose in order to obtain an "increased" response or to better "control" your child's behavior.

B. Factors Contributing to Medication Misuse in Children and Teenagers
1. Poor communication about medication use between healthcare professionals, parents, and children: Healthcare professionals simply don't share much medication information with patients and family members; and most patients or parents fail to ask appropriate questions of their doctors or pharmacists.
2. Inadequate monitoring of medication-taking, particularly in older children and teenagers.
3. Negative attitudes of parents and children regarding medication: You may feel that medication-taking is unnatural or unhealthy, or that your child might get "hooked on drugs"; and your child, unable to distinguish between legitimate and illegitimate medication use, may have a sense of fear regarding medication-taking.
4. Parents' poor role model regarding medication use: Studies have shown that almost 50% of adults do not take their medication properly; obviously, many adults are not setting good examples for their children.
5. Psychological and social barriers contributing to improper use: Because some medications may alter appearance or produce un-

desirable side effects, which may be perceived as negative by peer groups, some children may not take their medications as prescribed; this is particularly true for older children and teenagers.

6. Lack of involvement by schools with respect to medication use: Schools have yet to play a significant part in the early education of children regarding the positive role of medication in maintaining good health.

C. Guidelines for Parents on Improving Medication Use Among Children

1. Work in partnership with healthcare professionals: Tell your doctor and pharmacist what medications your child is receiving, including over-the-counter medications. Ask questions and, at least, know the following about your child's medication:

    • Name
    • What it is used for
    • Dose and frequency
    • Most common and significant side effects
    • Foods and other medications that your child should avoid while taking the medication
    • Whether your doctor or pharmacist has any of this information in written form so that you may review it at home with your child.

2. Talk to your child about medication and involve him or her in communicating with the doctor or pharmacist: The NCPIE report urges parents to discuss the legitimate use of medication with their children and to encourage them to ask questions of doctors or pharmacists; to participate in the process as much as possible.

3. Talk to your child's teacher and school nurse about his or her medication needs. Let them know that your child needs to receive medication during school hours. Not only is this a way to avoid problems related to missed doses, but it may in fact allow the school nurse to assist your child's physician in assessing the required dosage.

4. Follow good medication practices: Establish safe medication habits for all your family members and be a good role model for your child.

PERIODS OF CHILDHOOD DEVELOPMENT

It has been clearly established that infants are *not* miniature adults, that the child's age and physical development, including height and weight, are important factors when determining medication dosage. Also, infants have limited kidney and liver functions, as well as numerous other physiological differences that must be considered when determining dosage. Following are age groups that identify periods of growth in which most children share common biological and developmental patterns or events:

- Premature infants: infants delivered before full term
- Neonates: birth to 30 days
- Infants: 1 to 12 months
- Toddlers: 1 to 3 years
- Preschoolers: 3 to 5 years
- School-age children: 6 to 12 years
- Adolescents: 13 to 17 years

The use of medication in a child requires special considerations, for it differs significantly from that in an adult. In order to better understand medication behavior in infants and children, and why the same medication acts differently in the same child during different periods of his or her growth, a brief look at some very basic physiology affecting medication action may be helpful in understanding medication behavior.

MEDICATION ABSORPTION

Absorption may be defined as the passing of a medication into the skin or other body tissue. Medications having systemic actions are those which, regardless of their routes of administration, eventually pass through the skin, muscle, or other tissues into the bloodstream. There, the medication is carried throughout the body, where the medication exerts its action on one or more organs or body systems.

Many factors influence medication absorption, such as the patient's age, physical stage of development, and general health; the condition of the site at which the medication is absorbed; and the patient's response or sensitivity to the medication. Other factors affecting absorption are related to the specific medication itself, the acidity (pH) of the medication in the stomach, and the solubility of the medication in the body's fats.

Although medication absorption can occur at almost any part of the body, the routes of administration having the most rapid therapeutic responses are those administered by injection and by inhalation. When a rapid response is desired, as in critical medical emergencies, medication is usually administered directly into the veins by injection. In situations where the patient may be unconscious or semiconscious, or if the patient is an infant, a rectal solution or suppository may be preferred.

Medication intended for children under the age of 5 usually calls for an oral liquid dosage, which is often easier to administer to infants and young children. The oral administration of medications usually requires that they be given on an empty stomach, because foods may delay medication absorption and, in some cases, may prevent absorption altogether. On the other hand, some medications should be administered with meals or shortly thereafter, because they are irritating to the gastrointestinal tract.

Factors affecting medication absorption in newborns and premature infants vary significantly from those affecting it in adults and older children. This is true both for absorption through the skin (topical) and for absorption from the gastrointestinal tract (oral). Because of the incomplete development of the infant's organ systems, and because of a physiology differing from that of adults and older children, absorption requires special considerations. For example, in newborns and infants, medication absorption may be increased because of lower stomach acidity (pH) and because of the increased time it takes for medication to travel through the body (thus allowing more time for absorption to occur).

HAZARDS OF TOPICAL APPLICATION IN INFANTS

For medications applied on the skin (topically), absorption is also greater in infants due to the lack of development of skin tissue. For this reason, therefore, doses for ointments, creams, and lotions must be reduced in infants and young children in order to avoid toxicity resulting from too much medication absorption.

METABOLISM AND ELIMINATION

Most medications are absorbed through the skin or from the gastrointestinal tract and are distributed throughout the body. For medications that are *not* administered by injection or inhalation, a greater time delay occurs before a therapeutic effect is achieved. Once a medication is absorbed, many factors determine how it will act. Newborns and infants have less protein in the blood to bind with medications, and the protein they do have has less binding capacity than that of adults and older children. Increased amounts of unbound medications may achieve a greater, more prolonged effect in infants and newborns, with a potential for increased toxicity.

The removal of most medications from the body is preceded by the breakdown of the medications by enzymes—proteins produced by the body that are necessary for specific chemical reactions. The major organ involved in the metabolism of a medication is the liver, which produces most of the enzymes needed to metabolize (detoxify) the medication in preparation for its elimination. In newborns and infants, the lack of liver development means that there are fewer enzymes being produced to metabolize and remove the medication. Thus the medication remains in the body longer. And the longer a medication remains in the body, the greater the potential for toxicity. This explains why "normal" doses of many medications must be reduced in newborns and infants, as well as in children with impaired kidney or liver functions. This is also why your child's doctor must take special precautions when determining correct medication doses, regardless of the route of administration. There are exceptions to this general rule, however, and some medications must be given in higher than "normal" doses to achieve the desired effect in newborns and infants.

Although most medications are eliminated, or excreted, by the kidneys (in urine), other organs (such as the lungs, skin, and bowels) play a lesser role in medication elimination.

SUMMARY

The normal processes discussed briefly above—absorption, metabolism, and elimination—may be complicated if the child has disorders that alter or interfere with any or all of these processes. For example, immature skin development (which is common in newborns), or open sores or wounds, may significantly increase the absorption of medications applied topically, particularly in premature infants. Gastrointestinal ulcers, mucosal lesions, and either increased or decreased secretion of gastric fluids may also influence medication absorption processes. Other biological deficiencies that play a role in medication behavior include diminished liver and kidney functions (mentioned above) and the absence of specific enzymes necessary for normal body functions.

It's easy to see, therefore, that the way a medication behaves in the body is determined by many different and very complex factors, some of which are related to the properties of the specific medication, and others to the physiology of the child receiving it. Together, these very important considerations determine whether the medication achieves its desired effect or whether the child experiences toxicity. This is why only a doctor should prescribe medication for use in your child. Only a doctor is trained to understand all the complex factors that result in appropriate diagnosis and treatment. Your responsibility as a parent is to provide your doctor with as much information as possible so that he or she will be aware of all the factors we have discussed.

CHAPTER 2

CRITICAL PERIODS FOR BABY

Malformations and developmental problems in children occur most frequently in the period between conception and birth and in the breastfeeding period following delivery. During both periods, and especially for the unborn child during the fetal development period, the inappropriate use of medications by mothers can result in severe consequences.

Once you know you are pregnant, your next step should be to find a doctor who will help you plan for the happy event. Having found one with whom you feel comfortable, you should discuss the use of vitamins; the importance of exercise and proper nutrition; and the use of medications and chemicals (including alcohol and tobacco). You must be able to develop a good "talking" relationship with your doctor at this time in order to get the information you need to ensure a safe delivery, as well as to minimize the potential problems your baby may encounter during these critical periods.

In the remainder of this chapter, we are going to discuss the toxic effects of medications and chemicals on the fetus during pregnancy and on the newborn during the breastfeeding period. These cautions apply both to medications prescribed by a doctor and to over-the-counter (OTC) medications purchased without prescription.

TERATOGENICITY

Teratogenicity may be broadly defined as a physical and/or mental abnormality produced in the fetus by one or more factors—in this case, abnormalities related to the use of medications and chemicals during pregnancy. Although teratogenicity associated with the use of medications is thought to be responsible for only about 5% of all fetal abnormalities, they represent an important category *because they can be prevented.*

Some medications are known to produce harmful effects in the fetus, and many more are believed to be potentially harmful. A tragic but very dramatic example of medication-induced teratogenesis occurred in the 1960s with thalidomide, a medication widely prescribed in Europe as a sedative. Although thalidomide was safe for adults, its effects on the unborn offspring of pregnant women, which were unknown, became horribly clear as more and more babies were born with phocomelia, a physical defect in which the hands and feet are attached close to the body, resembling a seal's flippers.

While thalidomide is a dramatic example of teratogenesis, fetal abnormalities resulting from harmful medication use can be as subtle as minor psychological effects that influence behavior.

Teratogenicity is the result of many complex factors, of which only some are known. Some of the known factors include the medication used, the dose of the medication, and any diseases of the mother, as well as the physiological condition of the fetus, the fetal age, genetic factors, and the age and condition of the placenta.

During pregnancy, medication and essential nutrients enter the fetal circulation via the placenta. Although the developing fetus may be harmed by medications or chemicals throughout the pregnancy period, the fetus is especially vulnerable during the first three months (first trimester) because it lacks the mature organ systems necessary to metabolize medications and eliminate them from the body. During this period, medications that may be safe during the later periods of fetal development may be harmful.

FETAL GROWTH AND DEVELOPMENT

The development of a normal, healthy child is dependent upon many factors, not the least of which is the care taken by prospective mothers during pregnancy. Generally, the healthier the mother is, the better the chances are that baby, too, will be healthy.

While the gestation period lasts about 39 weeks, there are specific biological changes taking place throughout the pregnancy that will determine the condition of the baby at birth. A brief overview of some of these events may aid in understanding the relationship between the use of medications and chemicals during this period and the potential for harming the developing fetus.

The miracle of birth holds many wonders, one of which is the way cells just keep on dividing and multiplying, with some of them forming specific body organs. During the first 2 weeks of pregnancy, the fetal cells are fairly similar—and much less vulnerable to the toxic effects of medications used by mothers. After the second week, however, the heart and central nervous system begin to develop, and continue to develop through the third month (approximately the thirteenth week). From the fourth week, the eyes and ears begin to develop, and continue to do so until birth. At this time, the limbs also begin to develop. The teeth and sexual organs begin their development in the fifth week, continuing until birth.

Although the fetus is less likely to experience toxic effects of medications during the first 2 weeks of life, the following 7 or 8 weeks may produce the most significant abnormalities. During the remaining period of fetal development, the effects of medication toxicity are usually less significant, although serious defects, including stillbirth, can also occur after the first trimester period.

The following table illustrates the periods of growth and development for the various systems of the body, as well as the periods in which these systems are more vulnerable to the toxic (teratogenic) effects of medications and chemicals.

MEDICATIONS AND BREASTFEEDING PROBLEMS

Most medications ingested by nursing women find their way into the mother's milk, usually in very low concentrations. Toxicity for the nursing infant occurs because the newborn is unable to metabolize the medication and eliminate it from the body. During the breastfeeding period, the newborn's organ systems are developing rapidly, but the first weeks following birth are the most critical—the period of greatest risk for the infant. This risk decreases with each passing day, until the infant is weaned.

During the breastfeeding period, nursing mothers should ask their physicians to suggest nonprescription medications that may be safe to use for minor ailments, and they should advise their doctors of all prescription and nonprescription medications they are currently taking. Another source of information about nonprescription medications is your pharmacist, who is familiar with a broad range of alternative products that are both commercially available and safe to use during the breastfeeding period. In either case, don't be shy—ask.

Also ask your physician to advise you of the best time to take

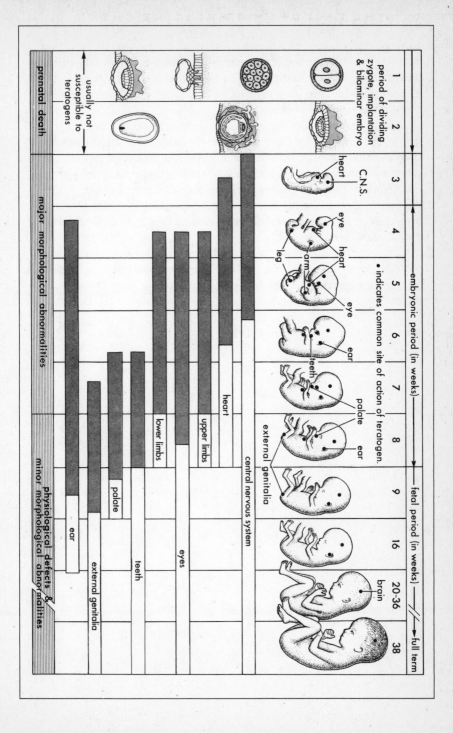

required medication. For a breastfeeding mother, the time a medication is taken may play a significant role in its potential for toxicity in the nursing infant. For example, a dose of medication taken less than 2 hours before breastfeeding may be more harmful than the same dose taken immediately after breastfeeding.

Toxicity is related to the specific properties of the medication, the length of time the medication stays in the body, and the infant's response to the medication. While it may be true that medications that are safe for the mother may be toxic to the nursing infant, the premature infant is especially vulnerable, as is the full-term newborn during the first 30 days following birth, due to insufficient development of the organs essential in the metabolism of medications and in the elimination of them from the body.

A good rule to follow: Breastfeeding mothers should use as few medications as possible, and if medications are absolutely necessary, they should be taken for the briefest period of time possible.

CHAPTER 3

PROBLEM MEDICATIONS DURING PREGNANCY AND BREASTFEEDING

The following list contains the names of medications and chemicals that are known, or thought to be, harmful to the fetus and to the breastfeeding infant. Parents should keep in mind that this is not a complete list, and that the absence of a medication or chemical from this list does not mean that it is not harmful or potentially harmful.

Where the name is identified as a medication group (e.g., salicylates, penicillins, anticonvulsants, etc.), the specific medications belonging to those groups are listed in Appendix II for easy reference. Remember, if in doubt, check with your doctor or pharmacist.

Also included in the comments for each medication is the "pregnancy category" assigned by the Food and Drug Administration (FDA). These categories relate to the documented problems associated with the use of medications during pregnancy. Following are the FDA-assigned pregnancy categories, with a brief explanation for each category:

CATEGORY A: Adequate and well-controlled studies have failed to demonstrate a risk to the fetus during pregnancy.

CATEGORY B: Reproductive studies in animals have failed to demonstrate a risk to the fetus, but there are no adequate and well-controlled studies in pregnant women.

CATEGORY C: Animal studies have demonstrated an adverse effect on the fetus, but there are no adequate and well-controlled studies in pregnant women. Potential benefits of the medication may warrant its use despite potential risks.

CATEGORY D: There is evidence of fetal risk based upon data from investigational or marketing experience, but potential

benefits of the medication may warrant its use despite potential risks.

CATEGORY X: Fetal abnormalities in animals or humans have been
demonstrated, and/or there is evidence of fetal risk
based upon data from investigational or marketing
experience. The risks involved in using the medication clearly outweigh potential benefits.

Where an FDA-assigned category applies to a medication listed below,
the category designation is noted. Brand names are shown in capital
letters.

Acetazolamide (DIAMOX): Studies in rodents have shown skeletal
malformations at high doses. Should not be used during the first
trimester of pregnancy.

Acetohexamide (DYMELOR): Should not be used during pregnancy
unless the benefits-versus-risks suggest its use. May cause low blood
sugar in newborns and in nursing infants. **CATEGORY C.**

Acetophenazine (TINDAL): Use of phenothiazines just prior to delivery may produce prolonged jaundice and other abnormalities in
newborns.

Albuterol (PROVENTIL, VENTOLIN): Animal studies have shown fetal
abnormalities (including cleft palate and other defects); may inhibit
labor; may cause tumors in animal infants when used during
breastfeeding. **CATEGORY C.**

Alcohol (Ethanol, Whiskey): Various studies have shown numerous
and significant fetal abnormalities, including retarded growth and
development, and facial and central nervous system abnormalities
(fetal alcohol syndrome). When used during breastfeeding, alcohol
may retard infant growth and development, may cause blood-clot-
ting deficiencies, and may cause drowsiness and vomiting.

Allopurinol (LOPURIN, ZURINOL, ZYLOPRIM): Animal studies have
shown skeletal abnormalities and fetal death. **CATEGORY C.**

Amantadine (SYMADINE, SYMMETREL): Animal studies have shown
fetal toxicity, as well as vomiting, rash, and urine retention in
breastfeeding animal infants. **CATEGORY C.**

Aminoglutethimide (CYTANDREN): May produce male sex characteristics in female fetuses, and has caused fetal deaths in animal studies. **CATEGORY D.**

Aminophylline (AMOLINE, PHYLLOCONTIN, SOMOPHYLLIN, TRUPHYLLINE): Animal studies have shown fetal abnormalities at very high doses. Breastfeeding animal infants may experience irritability, insomnia, and restlessness. **CATEGORY C.**

Amiodarone (CORDARONE): Animal studies have shown fetal toxicity, as well as diminished growth in breastfeeding newborns. **CATEGORY C.**

Amphetamines (see Appendix II): May produce premature delivery, low birthweight, cardiotoxicity, and withdrawal symptoms in newborns. Breastfeeding infants may be irritable, may be hyperexcited, and may experience poor sleeping habits. **CATEGORY C FOR ALL AMPHETAMINES.**

Anesthetics, Inhalation: Studies have shown that women who work in hospital operating rooms and dental offices, and who are routinely exposed to the use of inhalation anesthetics, may have a higher rate of fetal abnormalities than women who are not so exposed.

Antacids Containing Aluminum (see Appendix II): Chronic use with high doses may cause electrolyte imbalances in fetuses and in newborns. Antacids not containing aluminum have not demonstrated a risk during pregnancy.

Anticancer Medications (Busulfan, Chlorambucil, Cyclophosphamide, Melphalan, Mercaptopurine, Methotrexate, Thioguanine): Should not be used during pregnancy and nursing periods; may suppress fetal and nursing infant's immune system, may retard growth, and may cause cancer. **CATEGORY C OR D FOR ALL.**

Anticoagulants, Oral (see Appendix II): May cause severe malformations of the nose, face, bones, and eyes, as well as other adverse effects, including growth and mental retardation, particularly in the first and third trimesters. Oral anticoagulants should be avoided during pregnancy. May also cause a reduction in clotting factor, resulting in excessive bleeding in nursing infants, particularly in premature infants and neonates.

Anticonvulsants (see Appendix II, under all categories of anticonvulsants): Abnormalities include cleft palate; mental retardation; malformations of the heart, head, and face; diminished growth; and other defects. Higher incidences of abnormalities have been reported in children whose mothers used anticonvulsants during pregnancy, particularly Phenytoin and Phenobarbital. CATEGORY D FOR PARAMETHADIONE; CATEGORY C FOR ETHOTOIN AND PHENYTOIN.

Antidepressants, Tricyclic (see Appendix II): May cause decrease in rate of conception, malformations of the heart, and respiratory system and urinary tract problems when these medications are used just before delivery. Tricyclic antidepressants may also stimulate lactation in nursing mothers. CATEGORY C FOR MOST OF THESE MEDICATIONS.

Antihistamine/Decongestant Combinations (see Appendix II): Breastfeeding infants may be irritable and hyperexcited, particularly premature infants and neonates.

Aspartame (EQUAL, NUTRASWEET): Should not be used by breastfeeding mothers who are genetic carriers of phenylketonuria.

Aspirin: May cause bleeding (hemorrhage), pulmonary hypertension, and heart failure in newborns. Should not be used when breastfeeding, due to the potential for Reye's syndrome and bleeding disorders in infants. CATEGORY D FOR EXTENDED-RELEASE TABLETS.

Atenolol (TENORETIC, TENORMIN): Animal studies have shown fetal toxicity, including abnormal heartbeats, hypotension, hypoglycemia, and respiratory depression. CATEGORY C.

Atropine and Combinations: Although studies have not been performed with these products, fetal toxicities have occurred with some of the ingredients often found in Atropine combination products; may reduce milk production in lactating mothers and may cause drowsiness, diarrhea, and stomach pains in newborns. CATEGORY B FOR ATROPINE; CATEGORY C FOR ATROPINE COMBINATIONS.

Auranofin (RIDAURA): Animal studies have shown fetal abnormalities, including fetal abortions, decrease in fetal weight, and abdominal abnormalities. Should not be used during breastfeeding. CATEGORY C.

Azathioprine (IMURAN): There are some reports of infant mortality in infants in the first trimester of pregnancy. Should not be used during breastfeeding.

Baclofen (LIORESAL): May produce bone defects and reduced birthweight in newborns.

Barbiturates (ALURATE, AMYTAL, BUTISOL, SEMONIL, LOTUSATE, MEBARAL, NEMBUTHAL, Phenobarbital, SECONAL, TUINAL): May cause physical dependence, particularly during the third trimester, and bleeding disorders as well. May cause physical dependence and drowsiness in breastfeeding infants. CATEGORY D FOR ALL BARBITURATES.

Belladonna Combinations: See *Atropine and Combinations* (page 16). CATEGORY C FOR ALL BELLADONNA COMBINATIONS.

Benzodiazepines (see Appendix II): May cause physical dependence and withdrawal symptoms in newborns. The risk of malformations is greatest during the first trimester. May cause weight loss, feeding difficulties, and drowsiness in breastfeeding infants. CATEGORY D FOR ALPRAZOLAM AND HALAZEPAM; CATEGORY X FOR QUAZEPAM, TEMAZEPAM, AND TRIAZOLAM.

Benztropine (COGENTIN): May inhibit lactation in nursing mothers.

Bethanechol (DUVOID, MYOTONECHOL, URECHOLINE): Animal studies have shown this medication to cause uterine contractions in pregnant females. CATEGORY C.

Biperiden (AKINETON): May inhibit lactation in nursing mothers. CATEGORY C.

Bromocriptine (PARLODEL): May inhibit lactation in nursing mothers.

Bumetanide (BUMEX): Animal studies have shown fetal bone abnormalities, growth retardation, and termination of the pregnancy. CATEGORY C.

Caffeine (CAFFEDRINE, DEXITAC, NO DOZ, TREND, QUICK-PEP, VIVARIN, and others, including drug combinations used for pain, antihistamines and decongestants, and cough and cold preparations): A chemical found in coffee, tea, and in many soft drinks, caffeine may cause hyperexcitability, irritability, difficulty sleeping, skeletal abnormalities, low birthweight, and increased fetal loss.

Calcium Carbonate (ALKA-MINTS, ALKETS, AMITONE, BISODOL, CALCILAC, CALCITREL, CALGLYCINE, CHOOZ, DICARBOSIL, DI-GEL, EQUILET, GUSTALAC, MARBLEN, NORALAC, PAMA NO. 1, SPASTOSED, TITRACID, TITRALAC, TUMS, TUMS E-X): Chronic use of high doses may result in electrolyte imbalances in the newborn.

Captopril (CAPOTEN, CAPOZIDE): May cause fetal growth retardation, reduce blood pressure (hypotension), and produce cranial malformations. CATEGORY C.

Carbamazepine (EPITOL, TEGRETOL): Small head, low birthweight, spina bifida, and defects of the head, face, and fingernails have been reported in newborns. May also reduce growth in breastfeeding infants. CATEGORY C.

Carbidopa (ingredient found in SINIMET): Animal studies have shown skeletal malformations and suppressed fetal growth in offspring. May inhibit lactation.

Carbimazole (NEO-MERCAZOLE): May cause goiter in nursing infants.

Castor Oil (ALPHAMUL, EMULSOIL, FLEET FLAVORED CASTOR OIL, NEOLOID): May cause premature labor.

Cellulose Sodium Phosphate (CALCIBIND): Do not use during pregnancy; will reduce the body's absorption of calcium needed in fetal bone formation. CATEGORY C.

Chloral Hydrate (AQUACHLORAL, NOCTEC): Chronic use may result in physical dependence and withdrawal symptoms in newborns. May cause sedation in nursing infants.

Chlorambucil (LEUKERAN): May cause fetal urinary tract abnormalities. Should not be used during breastfeeding.

Chloramphenicol (CHLOROMYCETIN, MYCHEL): May cause bone marrow depression if used near term or during breastfeeding.

Chloroquine (ARALEN): May cause toxicity of the central nervous system, affecting sight and hearing functions. The threat of malaria may be more dangerous to the mother and fetus than the potential risks of using this medication during pregnancy. May cause serious adverse effects in nursing infants.

Chlorpropamide (DIABINESE, GLUCAMIDE): See *Acetohexamide* (page 14).

Chlorthalidone (HYGROTON, THALITONE): See *Diuretics, Thiazide* (page 21).

Cholestyramine (QUESTRAN): May prevent the absorption of vitamins and nutrients required for fetal growth and development.

Cimetidine (TAGAMET): Animal studies have shown decreased male hormone levels. May inhibit lactation, gastric acidity, and medication metabolism. **CATEGORY B.**

Clofazimine (LAMPRENE): Animal studies have shown an increase in stillbirth, diminished skull development and survival in newborns, and skin discoloration in nursing animals. **CATEGORY C.**

Clofibrate (ATROMID-S): Not recommended for use during pregnancy or breastfeeding periods due to the fact that cholesterol is required for normal fetal and infant development. **CATEGORY C.**

Clomiphene (CLOMID): Animal studies have shown fetal toxicity, and abnormalities and fetal death in humans have been reported.

Clonidine (CATAPRES, CATAPRES-TTS): Animal studies have shown that this medication may cause termination of the pregnancy. **CATEGORY C.**

Clotrimazole (MYCELEX): Animal studies have shown fetal abnormalities, including decrease in litter size and decrease in the number of surviving young. **CATEGORY B.**

Cocaine: A prescription medication used primarily as local anesthetic in surgery; an illegal "street drug" used to produce brief but intense euphoria. Cocaine increases the possibility of spontaneous abortion and premature labor; retards fetal growth; and may produce abnormalities of the heart, head, and urinary tract in the newborn. The use of cocaine during pregnancy has also resulted in central nervous system defects in newborns, which may persist for several months. May cause dependence in breastfeeding infants. **CATEGORY C.**

Codeine and Combinations: Codeine is used alone to relieve pain, or in combination with other drugs to relieve pain; to treat diarrhea; and to stop cough. The use of narcotics during pregnancy may produce physical dependency and withdrawal symptoms in newborns and nursing infants. **CATEGORY C FOR CODEINE.**

Colchicine (in COL-BENEMID): Studies have shown Colchicine to stop cell division in animals and to decrease spermatogenesis in humans. **CATEGORY D.**

Colestipol (COLESTID): Although no studies have been performed, Colestipol may prevent absorption of vitamins and nutrients required for fetal growth and development.

Contraceptives, Oral: May cause changes in breastmilk of lactating mothers, as well as breast enlargement in nursing female infants. **CATEGORY X FOR ALL.**

Corticosteroids (see Appendix II): May cause cleft palate, water balance defects, skeletal abnormalities, absence of tongue, decreased mouth size, and other abnormalities. If used during breastfeeding, these drugs may retard growth in newborns.

Cyclosporine (SANDIMMUNE): Animal studies have shown fetal toxicity, including fetal death at almost twice the normal adult dose. Should not be used during breastfeeding period. **CATEGORY C.**

Danazol (DANOCRINE): May produce masculinization in the female fetus and nursing infant. Do not use during pregnancy or nursing periods.

Diltiazem (CARDIZEM): Animal studies have shown severe fetal toxicity, including skeletal defects, reduced survival rates, and fetal deaths. **CATEGORY C.**

Diphenoxylate and Atropine (DIPHENATOL, LATROPINE, LOFENE, LOMANATE, LOMOTIL, LONOX, LO-TROL, LOW-QUEL, NORMIL): Animal studies have shown retarded growth in female fetuses, as well as reduced fertility. **CATEGORY C.**

Disopyramide (NORPACE, NORPACE CR): Has been reported to cause uterine contractions in women before term.

Diuretics, Thiazide: May produce jaundice, a decrease in blood platelets, and other toxicity in newborns; and may inhibit lactation in nursing mothers. **CATEGORY B FOR DIURIL, HYGROTON, ESIDRIX, HYDRODIURIL, AND ZAROLOXYN; CATEGORY C FOR NATURETIN, EXNA, ANHYDRON, ENDURON, AND NAQUA; CATEGORY D FOR SALURON.**

Docusate/Mineral Oil (LIQUI-DOSS): Mineral Oil may decrease the absorption of vitamins and nutrients required for fetal growth and development.

Dronabinol (MARINOL): Animal studies have shown decreased weight gains in pregnant mothers, as well as increased fetal death. Should not be used during breastfeeding. **CATEGORY B.**

Enalapril (VASERETIC, VASOTEC): Animal studies have shown fetal toxicity, including decrease in fetal weight. **CATEGORY C.**

Ephedrine (EPHED II): See *Albuterol* (page 14).

Epinephrine (ADRENALIN, ASTHMAHALER, ASTHMA NEFRIN, BRONITIN, BRONKAID, DEY-DOSE, MEDIHALER-EPI, MICRONEFRIN, PRIMATENE, RACEPINEHRINE, S-2 INHALANT, VAPONEFRIN): See *Albuterol* (page 14).

Ergostat: Do not use during pregnancy. May cause uterine contractions, reduced oxygen to the fetus, and brain hemorrhage. May also suppress lactation and cause diarrhea, vomiting, and convulsions in nursing infants. **CATEGORY X FOR ERGOTAMINE AND ERGOTAMINE COMBINATIONS.**

Erythromycin: The estolate form (ERYTHROZONE, ILOSONE) has been associated with reversible liver toxicity in pregnant women.

Erythromycin and Sulfisoxazole (PEDIAZOLE): Animal studies have shown fetal toxicity, including jaundice and fetal death from Sulfisoxazole; may also cause jaundice in breastfeeding animal infants. CATEGORY C.

Estrogens: The use of estrogens during pregnancy may result in serious fetal abnormalities, including malformations, reproductive abnormalities, and cancer in females. Estrogens may also inhibit lactation, decrease the quality of the milk, and cause problems in the bone development of nursing infants. CATEGORY X FOR ALL.

Ethacrynic Acid (EDECRIN): Animal studies have shown decreases in fetal weight. CATEGORY B.

Ethambutol (MYAMBUTOL): Animal studies have shown numerous problems involving fetal skeletal malformations, cleft palate, harelip, and other abnormalities.

Etoposide (VEPESID): Animal studies have shown serious fetal toxicities (mainly associated with injection use), including skeletal abnormalities, decreased fetal weight, fetal and maternal death. Do not use during the first trimester of pregnancy. May cause cancer in nursing animal infants. CATEGORY D.

Etretinate (TEGISON): Fetal abnormalities observed in humans include significant skeletal malformations of the head, face, fingers and toes, arms, legs and hips, plus other abnormalities. Abnormalities have been observed in children whose mothers stopped using the medication more than 2 years prior to the birth of an affected child. Women using this medication should use contraceptive measures. May also cause abnormal bone development in nursing infants, as well as other serious adverse effects. CATEGORY X.

Flecainide (TAMBOCOR): Animal studies have shown fetal abnormalities, as well as embryonic toxicity. CATEGORY C.

Flucytosine (ANCOBON): May cause fetal abnormalities. CATEGORY C.

Fluoxymesterone (ANDROID-F, HALOTESTIN, ORA-TESTRYL, TESTOLIN): May cause masculinization of female fetuses; avoid use during pregnancy. May also cause abnormal bone development in nursing infants. CATEGORY X (FOR ALL ANDROGENS).

Furosemide (LASIX): Animal studies have shown increased kidney toxicity in fetuses. **CATEGORY C.**

Gemfibrozil (LOPID): Animal studies have shown increased fetal deaths, as well as tumors in nursing animal offspring. **CATEGORY B.**

Glipizide (GLUCOTROL): See *Acetohexamide* (page 14).

Glyburide (DIABETA, MICRONASE): See *Acetohexamide* (page 14.)

Glycopyrrolate (ROBINUL, ROBINUL FORTE): See *Atropine and Combinations* (page 16).

Heroin: An illegal "street drug" that may produce physical dependency and withdrawal symptoms in newborns. May also produce or prolong dependency in nursing infants.

Hydroxychloroquine (PLAQUENIL): May cause severe central nervous system defects, including ear damage, deafness, hemorrhaging from the eyes, and retinal pigmentation. Deaths have been reported in nursing infants.

Hydroxyurea (HYDREA): May cause serious toxicity to both the fetus and nursing infants, including cancer.

Indomethacin (INDOCIN, INDOCIN-SR, INDO-LEMMON, IN-DOMETACIN, ZENDOLE): Animal studies have shown serious fetal abnormalities and fetal death; may produce convulsions in nursing animal infants.

Isotretinoin (ACCUTANE): Serious fetal toxicity has resulted from the use of this medication, including malformations of the heart and middle ear, as well as abnormalities in fluid balance. May cause poor bone development in nursing infants. **CATEGORY X.**

Ketoconazole (NIZORAL): May cause serious neurological effects in nursing infants, including convulsions and muscle spasms. Breastfeeding should not be started for at least 72 hours after the last dose of Ketoconazole. **CATEGORY C.**

Lindane (G-WELL, KWELL, KWILDANE, SCABENE): May be toxic in nursing infants, especially in premature infants and neonates. **CATEGORY B.**

Lithium (CIBALITH-S, ESKALITH, LITHANE, LITHOBID, LITHONATE, LITHOTABS): Reports in humans suggest an increased incidence of goiter and cardiovascular malformations in newborns, and lithium toxicity in nursing infants. **CATEGORY D.**

Lomustine (CEENU): May cause cancer and other serious adverse effects in nursing infants; avoid use during breastfeeding period.

Lysergic Acid Diethylamide (LSD): An illegal "street drug" hallucinogenic properties whose fetal effects are unknown.

Marijuana: An illegal "street drug" used to produce euphoria. It is used experimentally in cancer patients to relieve the nausea and vomiting associated with chemotherapy; may cause learning defects and other abnormalities in infants whose mothers are chronic users.

Meclofenamate (MECLOMEN): Animal studies have shown this medication to interfere with normal bone and skeletal development in offspring.

Medroxyprogesterone (CURRETAB, PROVERA): See *Fluoxymesterone* (page 22).

Meprobamate (EQUAGESIC, EQUANIL, EQUAZINE-M, ME-PROGESIC, MEPROSPAN, MICRAININ, MILTOWN, NEURA-MATE, NEURATE, SEDABAMATE, TRANMEP, TRANQUIGESIC): There have been reports of fetal malformations in women who used this medication during the first trimester of pregnancy. May cause sedation in nursing infants.

Methimazole (TAPAZOLE): May interfere with thyroid function in the fetus and in nursing infants. **CATEGORY D.**

Methsuximide (CELONTIN): Although there have been no reports of problems, fetal toxicity has been reported with other anticonvulsants.

Methyldopa (ALDOMET, ALDOCLOR, ALDORIL): May cause temporary growth retardation in the third trimester and may stimulate lactation in nursing mothers. **CATEGORY B.**

Methyltestosterone (ANDROID, ESTRATEST, METANDREN, ORETON METHYL, TESTRED, TYLOSTERONE): May cause masculinization of female fetuses. Avoid use during pregnancy and the period of lactation. **CATEGORY X.**

Methysergide (SANSERT): See *Ergostat* (page 21).

Metronidazole (FEMAZOLE, FLAGYL, METIZOLE, METRO, METYRL): May cause blood disorders and appetite loss in nursing infants. **CATEGORY B.**

Mexiletine (MEXITIL): Animal studies have shown termination of the pregnancy. May cause serious adverse effects in nursing animal infants.

Nalidixic Acid (NEGRAM): May cause hemolytic anemia in breastfeeding infants who have a specific enzyme deficiency.

Nicotine (NICORETTE, tobacco): Problems relating to toxicity in newborns appear to be related to the number of cigarettes smoked per day by the pregnant mother. Symptoms of toxicity include decreased birthweight and height, increased spontaneous abortions, increased incidence of malformations, the risk of sudden infant death syndrome (SIDS), and diminished long-term performance in reading ability and in mental and physical performance tests. May cause respiratory irritation and increased infections, vomiting, diarrhea, and rapid heart rate for nursing infants; may also inhibit lactation.

Nitrofurantoin (FURADANTIN, FURALAN, FURAN, MACRODANTIN, NITROFAN): May cause decreased sperm count in male newborns and hemolysis in nursing infants, particularly in infants who have G6PD deficiency.

Norethindrone (MICRONOR, NORLUTIN, NOR-Q-D): May cause masculinization of the female fetus. Avoid use during pregnancy. **CATEGORY X.**

Norfloxacin (NOROXIN): Animal studies have shown embryonic loss, plus nausea and vomiting, in mothers; and cartilege damage in nursing offspring. **CATEGORY C.**

Opiates (Codeine, DARVON, DARVON-N, DEMEROL, DILAUDID, LEVO-DROMORAN, Methadone, Morphine): May cause sedation or prolonged habituation and physical dependency, particularly in premature infants and neonates. **CATEGORY C FOR MOST.**

Penicillins (see Appendix II): May cause diarrhea and fungal infections, and make nursing infants sensitive to penicillins. **CATEGORY B FOR MOST.**

Pentazocine (TALWIN, TALWIN COMPOUND, TALWIN-NX, TOLACEN): Animal studies have shown fetal abnormalities.

Phenobarbital (BARBITA, LUMINAL, SOLFOTON): May decrease blood oxygen, reduce weight gain, decrease responsiveness, and cause excessive sleeping in nursing infants. **CATEGORY D.**

Phenothiazines (COMPAZINE, MELLARIL, PERMITIL, PROLIXIN, SERENTIL, SPARINE, STELAZINE, THORAZINE, TINDAL, TRILAFON): Limited studies have shown fetal abnormalities, including jaundice, and both exaggerated and decreased reflex activity. Phenothiazines should not be used during the first trimester and during the last 2 weeks of pregnancy. Nursing infants may experience drowsiness, malformations, and undesirable central nervous system effects; and nursing mothers, increased lactation.

Phenylbutazone (AZOLID, BUTAGEN, BUTAZOLIDIN): May cause blood disorders in nursing infants. **CATEGORY C.**

Phenytoin (DILANTIN, DIPHENYLAN): May cause blood disorders in nursing infants. **CATEGORY C.**

Praziquantel (BILTRICIDE): Animal studies have shown increased rates of fetal abortion. Do not breastfeed while using this medication, which should be stopped at least 72 hours before breastfeeding is resumed.

Primidone (APO-PRIMIDONE, MYIDONE, MYSOLINE, SERTAN): Although there are no reports of fetal toxicity, it has been observed with other anticonvulsants. (See also *Anticonvulsants*, page 16). May cause drowsiness in infants.

Procarbazine (MATULANE): Animal studies have shown fetal toxicity, including malformations and premature births. Do not use during pregnancy and nursing periods.

Progestins (AMEN, AYGESTIN, NORLUTATE, NORLUTIN, PROVERA): See Norethindrone. May stimulate lactation in nursing mothers. **ALL PROGESTINS ARE CATEGORY D OR X.**

Propoxyphene (DARVOCET-N, DARVON, DARVON-N, DOLENE, DOLENE-AP, DOLOXENE, PROPACET, SK-65): May cause physical addiction and withdrawal symptoms in newborns.

Propranolol (INDERAL, INDERAL LA, INDERIDE, INDERIDE LA, IPRAN): There are some reports of low blood sugar (hypoglycemia), respiratory depression, and slow heart rate (bradycardia) in newborns. **CATEGORY C.**

Propylthiouracil: May cause goiter, hypothyroidism, and fetal death, and may suppress thyroid function in infants. **CATEGORY X.**

Quinine (QUINAAM, QUINDAN, QUINE, QUINITE, STREMA): Has caused hearing loss in newborns, and it may cause abnormalities of the central nervous system and extremities. **CATEGORY X.**

Reserpine and Combinations (DEMI-REGROTON, DIUPRES, DI-URESE-R, DIURIGEN WITH RESERPINE, DIUTENSEN-R, HYDROMOX R, HYDROPINE, HYDROPINE H.P., HYDROPRES, HYDROSINE, HYDROTENSIN, MALLOPRES, METATENSIN, NA-QUIVAL, REGROTON, RENESE-R, SALAZIDE, SALUTENSIN, SALUTENSIN-DEMI, SERPASIL, SERPASIL-ESIDRIX): May cause increased respiratory secretions, nasal congestion, loss of appetite, and decrease of oxygen in the blood of newborns. May also cause nasal congestion, increased respiratory secretions, decreased appetite, and decreased blood oxygen in nursing infants, as well as excessive discharge of milk in nursing mothers.

Rifampin (RIFADIN, RIFAMATE, RIMACTANE): Animal studies have shown fetal toxicity, including postnatal hemorrhage in newborns, cleft palate, and bone abnormalities. **CATEGORY C.**

Salicylates (see Appendix II): Studies performed in animals have shown that salicylates produce birth defects in the first and third trimesters and may complicate delivery. (See also *Aspirin*, page 16.)

Sulfonamides (see Appendix II): May cause anemia in nursing infants who have a G6PD deficiency, and other skeletal malformations. **CATEGORY C FOR SULFAMETHOXAZOLE AND SULFISOXAZOLE.**

Tamoxifen (NOLVADEX): Fetal abortions, vaginal bleeding, and fetal deaths have been reported. Avoid breastfeeding while on this medication, which may cause cancer in nursing infants. **CATEGORY D.**

Tetracyclines (see Appendix II): May produce permanent discoloration of teeth and diminished skeletal growth in the fetus. May also cause permanent discoloration of the teeth in nursing infants. **CATEGORY D.**

Trimethobenzamide (TEGAMIDE, TIGAN): Has produced stillbirths.

Valproic Acid (DEPAKENE, DEPAKOTE, Myproic Acid): Human and animal studies have shown severe fetal abnormalities, primarily involving the spinal cord. These medications have caused spina bifida and other serious defects when used during the first trimester of pregnancy in humans. Expectant mothers should consult their obstetricians very early in their pregnancies to determine if they have neural tube defects. **CATEGORY D.**

Vitamin A: Fetal abnormalities may include urinary tract malformations as well as retarded growth of the fetus. **CATEGORY X.**

Vitamin D (Calcifediol, Calcitriol, Dihydrotachysterol, Ergocalciferol): Fetal toxicity in animals has been shown. In humans, parathyroid suppression, mental retardation, and heart damage have been documented. **CATEGORY C FOR CALCITRIOL.**

CHAPTER 4

THE MEDICINE CHEST AND POISON EMERGENCIES

The average home is a virtual "supermarket" of products that are potentially hazardous, particularly to children. In addition to the many toys, tools, furniture, and appliances that are often the cause of household accidents, other hazards exist. According to the American Association of Poison Control Centers, more than 2 million poisonings occur each year in the United States. Most occur in the home, with approximately 47%, or more than 1 million, occurring in children under 3 years of age, and 62% in children under 6. Poisonings are the third most common cause of death in the home, with an estimated treatment cost of $8 billion annually. Almost 10% of all emergency room visits are related to poisonings, and they account for 5% to 10% of all hospital admissions.

THE MEDICINE CHEST

Every home should have certain basic medical supplies on hand in case you or your child has some minor medical accident, such as a cut, muscle pull, or burn. While it's better to have as few medications as possible around the house, especially where there are young children, some first aid supplies are necessary for minor emergencies.

Remember, you should use the medications listed below only to provide temporary relief in minor medical situations or, in the case of medical emergencies, until you are able to obtain expert medical assistance.

Analgesics/antipyretics: Medication used to relieve mild to moderate pain caused by headache, muscle sprains, or bruises, and to reduce fever caused by colds or flu, etc. Acetaminophen, Aspirin, and Ibuprofen are good choices (for examples of specific brands of these products, see Chapter 5). Caution: The use of Aspirin in treating high fever produced by flu or chickenpox may result in Reye's syndrome, a serious disorder in infants, children, and adolescents. In these situations, Acetaminophen or Ibuprofen is recommended:

- Tablets or capsules may be used for older children and adults.
- Chewable tablets are available for fussy children.
- Acetaminophen drops or liquid may be more convenient for infants and younger children.

Anesthetic, local: Medication that relieves pain or itching when applied on the skin or to the mucous membranes. Pain or itching may result from cuts, scratches, burns, rash, sore throat, etc. Do not use for sunburn, as it may lead to sensitization. For examples of specific products that may be used from this group, see Chapter 5 under the general drug monograph for anesthetics (page 48).

Antibacterial, local: Medication for minor scratches, cuts, or other minor wounds. One of the over-the-counter antibacterial creams or ointments containing Bacitracin will suffice and can be recommended by your pharmacist.

Antidiarrheal: Medication used to stop diarrhea, such as a product containing Loperamide, or Kaolin/Pectin.

Antiseptic: Hydrogen Peroxide (4- to 8-ounce bottle) for minor skin wounds. (Do not confuse with peroxide used in hair coloring.) Fresh Hydrogen Peroxide should "bubble" when placed on the skin. If the solution does not bubble, it should be replaced. Another good, all-purpose antiseptic is povidone iodide (e.g., BETADINE). Cover should be replaced tightly and bottle stored in a dark place.

Bandages, adhesive: To cover minor cuts, scratches, and abrasions.

Bandages, elastic: To wrap sprained wrists, ankles, and knees.

Band-Aids: To cover and protect minor cuts, scratches, and abrasions.

Cathartic/laxative: Medication that will stimulate or produce a bowel movement (correct constipation). Milk of Magnesia is a good example for adults, and a pediatric rectal enema for infants and younger children may be used after consultation with your pediatrician. In accidental poisoning, sorbitol is preferred over saline cathartics due to its superiority as a cathartic and its better taste.

Charcoal, activated: Prevents toxic substances from being absorbed and aids in their elimination from the body.

Cough preparations: Medication used for coughs caused by colds, flu, or allergies. The list of cough preparations is a long one, with products containing one or several ingredients, depending upon the "type" of cough—dry, productive, allergic, etc. While many preparations are effective in stopping coughs, one or more products containing as few ingredients as possible are probably better when dealing with children's medication. Two products that should do the trick are Guaifenesin and Dextromethorphan. Both are available without a prescription and are competitively priced.

Cup, eye: To flush (irrigate) the eye with saline solution to remove a foreign particle.

Decongestant, nasal: Medication used to open a "stuffy" nose, to aid breathing. Plain Pseudoephedrine is an effective decongestant; available as a pediatric liquid or tablets.

Earwax remover: Medication used to soften earwax so that it can be removed by flushing gently with a soft, rubber ear syringe.

Ice pack: To use on sprains and swollen muscles and joints.

Ipecac, Syrup of: Medication used to induce vomiting in accidental poisoning.

Pads, gauze: Various sizes to cover and protect minor cuts, scratches, burns, and abrasions.

POISONING

In an article appearing in *Florida Pharmacist Today*,* Drs. Jay Schauben and Joseph Spillane stated that each year, we bring almost 400 products into our homes that are potentially toxic; of these, medications account for 16 to 30. In addition to the various prescription and nonprescription medications, we also purchase potentially harmful products such as household cleaners and detergents, insecticides, cosmetics and personal-care products, Nicotine products, toxic plants, caustic chemicals, and solvents.

If your child swallows any of these products, he or she may not require emergency treatment or even medical attention, but you should at least know where to call to speak to someone who can provide expert assistance regarding ingestion of potentially toxic substances (see Appendix IV). While it's "easier said than done," the best advice is to remain calm so that accurate and complete information can be provided when calling the poison control center, the emergency room, or your physician, and so that you can be ready to follow the instructions given.

PREPARING FOR POISON EMERGENCIES

For most accidental poisonings, it is desirable to remove the toxic substance from the body as quickly as possible. Although there are several medications that may be effective in blocking absorption of the toxic substance, none is more effective than Syrup of Ipecac, which should be kept in every home medicine chest. When used correctly, Syrup of Ipecac may minimize the effects of the poison until your child is able to receive appropriate medical attention by competently trained medical personnel.

Syrup of Ipecac is a quick and effective medication for inducing vomiting. It should be used only when indicated, and only if your child is fully conscious, so that he or she will not aspirate (breathe) vomit into the lungs. *Never attempt to induce vomiting if your child is semiconscious or unconscious, or is having seizures. Also, vomiting should not be induced if your child has swallowed an acid or alkali, or a product that contains a petroleum distillate.* The labeling for commercial products that contain these will provide appropriate cautionary information, including accidental poisoning instructions.

* Schauben, J., and Spillane, J., "Poisoning: An Overview for Pharmacists," *Florida Pharmacist Today* 54, no. 3 (March 1990): 6–14.

Dosage guidelines for Syrup of Ipecac given orally are as follows:

- Adults and children over 12: 15–30 milliliters (1–2 table-spoonsful), followed immediately by 1 glass of water (240 milliliters); may be repeated in 20 minutes if vomiting does not occur.
- Children 1–12 years: 15 milliliters (1 tablespoonful), followed by ½ to 1 glass of water (120–240 milliliters).
- Children 6 months to 1 year: 5–10 milliliters (1–2 teaspoonsful).
- Children to 6 months: Use only as directed by a physician.

Note: The dose may be repeated in 30 minutes if vomiting has not occurred. Obtain medical attention as soon as possible.

CAUTION: DO NOT CONFUSE SYRUP OF IPECAC WITH IPECAC FLUIDEXTRACT, WHICH ALSO CONTAINS IPECAC BUT IS APPROXIMATELY 14 TIMES STRONGER THAN THE SYRUP.

POTENTIALLY TOXIC SUBSTANCES

The following is not a complete list of all potentially toxic substances found in a home, but it represents the products most commonly found. When bringing a product into the home, you should always read the label thoroughly to determine whether the product contains potentially toxic substances and, if so, the steps to be taken if the product is accidentally swallowed.

Acetone (nail polish remover, cleaners, and solvents): Use Syrup of Ipecac (see page 32) or warm salt water to induce vomiting, only if administered shortly after ingestion and only if child is conscious. Obtain medical treatment as soon as possible.

Acids, mineral (sulfuric, hydrochloric or muriatic, phosphoric, and hydrofluoric) (found in car batteries, pool chemicals, etching solvents, etc.):

- Internal: Administer large amounts of milk, ice cream, or antacids, which serve to coat the throat and gastrointestinal tract to protect against the destructive effects of the acids; do not induce vomiting.

- External or in the eyes: Flush with large amounts of water. Obtain medical treatment as soon as possible.

Acids, organic (glacial acetic, lactic, oxalic [solid], and trichloroacetic): Obtain medical treatment as soon as possible. If immediate medical attention is not available, administer milk, ice cream, or antacids to coat the gastrointestinal tract and neutralize some of the acid.

Alcohol (ethanol) (found in beverages, colognes, perfumes, elixirs, and other medication products): Use Syrup of Ipecac (see page 32) or warm salt water to induce vomiting, only if administered shortly after ingestion and only if child is conscious.

Alcohol, rubbing (isopropyl alcohol): See entry just above.

Alcohol, wood (methanol): Use Syrup of Ipecac (see page 32) or warm salt water to induce vomiting, only if administered shortly after ingestion and only if child is conscious. Obtain medical treatment as soon as possible.

Alkalis (sodium and potassium hydroxides [lye], ammonia products, dishwashing detergents, and water softeners):

- Internal: Administer large amounts of milk and water; do not induce vomiting.
- External or in the eyes: Flush with large amounts of water. Obtain medical treatment as soon as possible.

Aniline dyes (laundry markers): Use Syrup of Ipecac (see page 32) or warm salt water to induce vomiting. Obtain medical treatment as soon as possible.

Antifreeze (ethylene glycol): Use Syrup of Ipecac (see page 32) or warm salt water immediately after ingestion to induce vomiting if child is conscious. Obtain medical treatment as soon as possible.

Antiseptics, germicides, disinfectants, fungicides, deodorants, hair conditioners, and fabric softeners:

- Internal: Administer Syrup of Ipecac (see page 32) or warm salt water to induce vomiting.

- External: Flush with large amounts of water.
Obtain medical treatment as soon as possible.

Detergents and laundry soaps, shampoos, and household cleansers:

- Internal: Give milk, ice cream, or antacids.
- External: Flush with large amounts of water.
Obtain medical treatment as soon as possible.

Glues, degreasers, and insecticides: Give milk, ice cream, or antacids. Obtain medical treatment as soon as possible.

Mothballs, mothflakes, diaper and toilet bowl deodorizers: Give milk, ice cream, or antacids. Obtain medical treatment as soon as possible.

Nicotine (cigarettes, cigars, and chewing tobacco): Use Syrup of Ipecac (see page 32) or warm salt water to induce vomiting if child is conscious. Obtain medical treatment as soon as possible.

Petroleum distillates (furniture polish, gasoline, kerosene, lighter fluids, mineral oil, mineral spirits, paint thinners, etc.): Give milk, ice cream, or antacids. Do not induce vomiting. Obtain medical treatment as soon as possible.

POTENTIALLY TOXIC PLANTS

The plants known to be poisonous are relatively few, and in the United States few deaths result from swallowing poisonous plants. While not all plants are poisonous, many can produce illness having seriously painful or uncomfortable symptoms. In addition, as with medications, people may react differently after swallowing the same plants. For those who are hypersensitive, severe reactions may result; for others, only mild symptoms. Further, not all parts of a poisonous plant are toxic to humans, although most plants can make you sick if you swallow enough of them.

If you know that your child has ingested a plant that may be poisonous, or if your child comes to you and tells you that he or she has eaten a plant and feels sick, or if you find your child semiconscious or unconscious next to a partially eaten plant, contact your nearest regional poison control center for assistance (see Appendix IV for the one nearest you). Try to determine how much of the plant your child may have swallowed. Also, obtain some of the plant so that you are able to describe it; or if necessary, take it with you if your child must go to the emergency room for treatment.

The following is a list of some of the more common plants found in or around the home. This is not a complete list. Before bringing a new plant into the home, or before having one planted on your property, you should try to determine its toxicity.

Apple (*Malus*): Seeds may cause cyanide poisoning, which is usually mild and will not require induced vomiting.

Apricot (*Prunus*): Twigs, foliage, and pits may cause cyanide poisoning, which requires the use of Syrup of Ipecac (see page 00) or warm salt water to induce vomiting.

Azalea, or rhododendron (*Rhododendron*): All parts of the plant, found in most parts of the country except the Southwest, are toxic and can cause nausea, vomiting, difficulty breathing, decrease in blood pressure, and coma. Treatment requires induced vomiting—with Syrup of Ipecac (see page 32) or warm salt water—and medical treatment.

Baneberry (*Actaea*): Found in many areas of the United States, it has white or red berries. The juice may cause blistering (vesication). If baneberry is swallowed, vomiting should be induced with Syrup of Ipecac (see page 32) or warm salt water, and medical treatment obtained.

Be-still-tree (*Thevetia peruviana*): This beautiful shrub or small tree is found in Florida, Hawaii, Texas, and possibly in other warm climate areas. All parts of the plant are poisonous, particularly the nut. For symptoms and treatment, see *Foxglove* (page 38).

Bird of paradise, or Poinciana (*Poinciana gilliesii*): Found throughout the South and elsewhere as a pot plant, poinciana has scarlet stamens shooting up from yellow flowers. The green pod contains a severe gastrointestinal irritant, which can cause nausea, vomiting, and diarrhea. Treatment is not usually required unless large amounts are swallowed or unless the symptoms are severe.

Bittersweet, or woody nightshade (*Solanum dulcamara*): This climbing vine with shiny red berries is found in the Eastern, the North Central, and the Pacific coastal states. It is probably the most commonly swallowed of the plant poisons. Swallowing small amounts usually results in stomach cramps, diarrhea, or constipation. Induced vomiting is not necessary unless large amount is swallowed, resulting in drowsiness, muscle weakness, and paralysis. To induce vomiting, use Syrup of Ipecac (see page 32) or warm salt water.

Blue flag, or iris (*Iris versicolor*): Blue flag is found throughout the United States. For symptoms and treatment, see *Hyacinth* (page 38).

Box (*Buxus sempervirens*): This hedge plant is found throughout the United States; the leaves are very poisonous. Induced vomiting— with Syrup of Ipecac (see page 32) or warm salt water—may be required if several leaves are swallowed.

Buttercup (*Ranunculus*): All parts of this common plant, found throughout the United States, are poisonous; the juice may cause blistering in the mouth, severe gastrointestinal distress, and diarrhea. Induce vomiting with Syrup of Ipecac (see page 32) or warm salt water.

Caladium (*Caladium*): All parts of this large-leafed houseplant are poisonous, containing oxalate crystals, which are irritating to the mouth and gastrointestinal tract. Give demulcents like milk, ice cream, or antacids. Medical treatment is usually not required unless a large amount has been swallowed and symptoms are severe.

Castor bean, or palma christi, or castor-oil plant (*Ricinus communis*): Found mostly in California and Florida, this garden plant has shiny, dark or mottled beans that are extremely poisonous. If swallowed, they can cause gastrointestinal hemorrhage, as well as liver and kidney damage, and can be fatal. Induce vomiting with Syrup of Ipecac (see page 32) or warm salt water. Obtain medical treatment as quickly as possible.

Christmas holly (*Ilex*): The red berries can cause nausea, vomiting, and diarrhea, but treatment is usually not required unless several are swallowed. Induce vomiting with Syrup of Ipecac (see page 32) or warm salt water.

Common nightshade: For symptoms and treatment, see *Bittersweet, or woody nightshade* (page 36).

Crocus, or autumn or meadow saffron (*Colchicum autumnale*): The seeds produce the medication Colchicine, used in treating gout. Found in gardens throughout the country, the plant is poisonous in all its parts, especially the seeds and bulbs, and can cause nausea, burning of the throat and mouth, muscle weakness, diarrhea, and breathing difficulties (respiratory depression). Induce vomiting with Syrup of Ipecac (see page 32) or warm salt water. Obtain medical treatment as soon as possible.

Daffodil, or jonquil, or narcissus (*Narcissus*): Found throughout the country, the plant is at its most toxic in the bulb. For symptoms and treatment, see *Hyacinth* (see below).

Dumb cane (*Dieffenbachia sequine*): This houseplant contains oxalate crystals. For symptoms and treatment, see *Caladium* (page 37).

Elephant's ear (*Colocasia antiquorum*): This large-leafed house plant contains oxalate crystals. For symptoms and treatment, see *Caladium* (page 37).

Foxglove (*Digitalis purpurea*): Used as a garden plant throughout the United States, and found wild in the Pacific coastal states, this plant's cardiac glycosides are important in treating various heart disorders. All of the plant is poisonous, particularly the seeds and leaves, and can cause nausea, abdominal cramps, diarrhea, irregular heartbeats, mental confusion, and convulsions. Induce vomiting with Syrup of Ipecac (see page 32) or warm salt water. Obtain medical treatment.

Hyacinth (*Hyacinthus orientalis*): Hyacinth is found throughout the United States. The bulb is the most poisonous part of the plant, which can cause severe gastrointestinal distress and vomiting. Give milk, ice cream, or antacids. Medical treatment is usually not required unless symptoms are severe.

Hydrangea (*Hydrangea*): This plant is found commonly throughout much of the United States; the leaves, bulbs, branches, and flowers contain cyanide. For symptoms and treatment, see *Apricot* (page 36).

Iris, or blue flag: For symptoms and treatment see *Hyacinth* (see above).

Jerusalem cherry (*Solanum pseudo-capsicum*): The bright red berries of this common houseplant are poisonous. For symptoms and treatment, see *Bittersweet, or woody nightshade* (page 36).

Lantana, or red sage, or bunchberry (*Lantana camara*): Found commonly in Southern gardens or in indoor pots, the plant is poisonous in all its parts, particularly the unripened berries, which are potentially lethal in small quantities. Symptoms of accidental poisoning include nausea, vomiting, diarrhea, muscle weakness, stomach pains, difficulty breathing, visual difficulties, hypersensitivity to sunlight (photosensitivity), respiratory depression, and circulatory collapse. Induce vomiting with Syrup of Ipecac (see page 32) or warm salt water. Obtain medical attention quickly.

Lily of the valley (*Convallaria majalis*): A common garden flower that grows wild in many Eastern states, it has bright red berries and bell-shaped white flowers. All parts of the plant are poisonous and contain cardiac glycosides similar to those of foxglove. For symptoms and treatment, see *Foxglove* (page 38).

Mistletoe, American (*Phorandendron flavescens*): The white berries can cause severe gastrointestinal distress and significant rise in blood pressure, which may require induced vomiting—with Syrup of Ipecac (see page 32) or warm salt water—and medical treatment.

Monkshood (*Aconitum napellus*): This plant with helmet-shaped flowers is found throughout the United States, except the South. It is a popular garden plant whose leaves, seeds, and roots are poisonous. Symptoms of poisoning include a tingling or burning sensation beginning in the mouth and extending throughout the body, muscle weakness, slow pulse, vomiting, diarrhea, breathing difficulty, convulsions, and cardiac arrest. Induce vomiting immediately with Syrup of Ipecac (see page 32) or warm salt water. Obtain medical attention as soon as possible.

Morning glory (*Convolvulus arrenis*): The toxic seeds can cause gastrointestinal distress, mental confusion, and blurred vision. Obtain medical treatment as soon as possible.

Mushrooms (various species): They are found throughout the United States. Although not all mushrooms are poisonous, some are extremely toxic. If your child has accidentally swallowed a mushroom that is not known to be edible, induce vomiting with Syrup of Ipecac (see page 32) or warm salt water. Obtain medical attention immediately. If possible, try to identify the mushroom and obtain a sample for identification if your child must be taken to an emergency facility for further treatment.

Narcissus: For symptoms and treatment, see *Hyacinth* (page 38).

Nutmeg (*Myristica fragrans*): The toxic seeds can cause drowsiness, dizziness, delirium, abdominal cramps, thirst, numbness, and coma. Obtain medical attention as soon as possible.

Oleander (*Nerium oleander*): Found wild in the South and as a houseplant elsewhere, oleander is a perfumy shrub containing several cardiotoxic substances. For symptoms and treatment, see *Foxglove* (page 38). Ingestion requires hospitalization and close observation.

Philodendron (*Philodendron scandus*): All parts of this large-leafed plant are toxic. For symptoms and treatment, see *Caladium* (page 37).

Poinsettia (*Euphorbia pulcherrima*): The leaves, stems, and flowers of this favorite Christmastime plant are poisonous if swallowed. The milky-white sap can be very irritating and may cause severe vomiting and diarrhea. If sap gets on the skin or in the eyes, flush well with water to prevent irritation. If one bite of the leaf is swallowed, rinse the mouth well with water and give ice cream, milk, or antacids to minimize the gastrointestinal irritation. If an unknown amount is swallowed, induce vomiting (if vomiting has not occurred) with Syrup of Ipecac (see page 32) or warm salt water. Obtain medical treatment.

Poison hemlock (*Conium maculatum*): Found throughout the United States, this plant resembles a wild carrot, or Queen Anne's lace. Symptoms of ingestion include nausea, vomiting, weakness, slow pulse, and difficulty breathing. Induce vomiting with Syrup of Ipecac (see page 32) or warm salt water. Obtain medical treatment as quickly as possible.

Rhododendron (*Rhododendron*): For symptoms and treatment, see *Azalea, or rhododendron* (page 36).

Star-of-Bethlehem (*Ornithogalum umbellatum*): Found commonly throughout the Northeastern and North Central states, the plant is low-growing, with starlike white flowers. It is thought to contain digitalis glycosides, particularly in the bulb and leaves. Swallowing of small amounts may be treated by use of Syrup of Ipecac (see page 32) or warm salt water, which will induce vomiting. The swallowing of large amounts may require medical treatment after vomiting has been induced. For symptoms, see *Foxglove* (page 38).

CHAPTER 5

MEDICATION MONOGRAPHS

HOW TO USE THE MONOGRAPHS

The medication monographs that follow are listed in alphabetical order, by *brand name,* such as AMOXIL, TYLENOL, etc., or by *group name,* such as antihistamines, cough and cold combinations, etc. The only exceptions are medications that are better known by their *generic names* than their brand names (examples are Aspirin, Tetracycline, Benzocaine, Ampicillin, Amoxicillin, Theophylline, Quinidine, Quinine, etc.). For these medications, the monographs are listed by generic name first. For medications listed by either brand or generic names, the information follows the outline shown below. For medications listed by group names, the beginning discussion applies to all medications in the group, followed by a brief discussion of each medication in that group.

Following is a brief discussion of the information to be found in each section of the monographs.

GROUP NAME: The group name is a name given to medications sharing common actions, uses, or other characteristics that allow them to be considered together as a group. Examples of group names are "penicillins," which include Amoxicillin, Ampicillin, etc.; and "salicylates," which include Aspirin, Buffered Aspirin, etc. The monograph discussion for medication groups is actually two monographs: The first is a general discussion of all the medications listed in the medication group; the second presents brief discussions of each specific medication in the group. *For this reason, therefore, it is very important that parents read the general discussion for the medication group, plus the abbreviated* *discussion of the specific medication that applies to their child, in order to have all the information they need.*

BRAND NAME(S):   This is the name given to a medication that is registered (as a trademark) by the manufacturer and cannot be used by another company or person. Brand names are shown in capital letters. The brand name listed for the monograph is the one that is most commonly used or prescribed for that generic medication. Where applicable, other brands of the generic medication also appear in parenthesis. To the right of the brand name, you may find the letters "Rx," "OTC," or both, which signify that the medication requires a prescription (Rx) or may be purchased over the counter (OTC) without a prescription.

GENERIC NAME: The generic name is the common name of a medication. Generic names may denote single or multiple-ingredient products. Examples are Acetaminophen; Acetaminophen/Aspirin; Chlorpheniramine; Sulfamethoxazole/Trimethoprim, etc. To the right of the generic name, you may find the letters "Rx," "OTC," or both, which signify that the medication requires a prescription (Rx) or may be purchased over the counter (OTC) without a prescription.

USES AND INDICATIONS: This section describes the types of illnesses or symptoms that are treated by the medications being discussed in the monographs.

ADVERSE EFFECTS: Adverse, or side, effects of medications are effects that are undesirable. Side effects may be mild and require no action; or they may be troublesome and require a decrease in dosage and/or frequency of the medication. Some side effects may be severe enough that the medication must be stopped altogether and another prescribed instead.

WARNINGS AND PRECAUTIONS: This section provides information that often enables a doctor to determine whether or not a child should be placed on a certain medication; or in some cases, how the medication should be used in children with specific medical problems. Examples are children with kidney or liver disorders who may require adjustments (decreases) in dosages and/or dose frequencies in order to avoid toxic buildup of the medication in the body; children who lack certain enzymes needed to metabolize certain medications; and children with diabetes or heart problems, in which case certain medications should either be avoided or used with caution. These are some of the many considerations your doctor must make in determining the right medication and the right dosage for your child.

MEDICATION AND FOOD INTERACTIONS: This section includes information about the interactions between two medications, or between a medication and food, and the result of the interaction on one or both medications. In some cases, the effect of the medication may be decreased or canceled entirely; in others, the effect may be increased or prolonged. The interaction may also increase the toxicity of one or both medications.

DOSAGE GUIDELINES: This section offers suggested pediatric doses. Please keep in mind that the exact dose for your child can be determined only after many factors are considered, and only your child's doctor has all the information necessary to make this determination.

The following table relates to the terms used in the administration of medications, particularly as they relate to medication dosages. In order to help you in understanding the terminology used in the "Dosage Guidelines" sections of the monographs for oral medications, the following table of information is provided. Most oral medications found in the monograph sections are listed either in micrograms, milligrams, grams, or as a liquid measure, e.g., milliliter, teaspoonful (5 milliliters), tablespoonful (15 milliliters), or ounce.

2.5 milliliters =	½ teaspoonful	1 kilogram =	2.2 pounds
5 milliliters =	1 teaspoonful	10 kilograms =	22 pounds
7.5 milliliters =	1½ teaspoonsful	20 kilograms =	44 pounds
10 milliliters =	2 teaspoonsful	30 kilograms =	66 pounds
15 milliliters =	1 tablespoonful	40 kilograms =	88 pounds
30 milliliters (or 1 ounce) =	2 tablespoonsful	1,000 milligrams =	1 gram

COMMENTS: Included in this section may be information regarding use, storage, special handling, or other important or useful data.

MEDICATION MONOGRAPHS

The information found in the medication monographs is adapted from several sources, but two in particular: *USP DI: Drug Information for the Healthcare Professional,* published by the United States Pharmacopeial Convention, Inc.; and *Drug Facts and Comparisons,* published by the Facts and Comparisons Division of J. B. Lippincott Company, with most of the information coming from *USP DI.* Widely used by pharmacists and physicians, both references are updated annually. The United States Pharmacopeial Convention, Inc., which publishes *USP DI,* is comprised of scientific and healthcare practitioners from across the United States and abroad, and has specialty advisory panels, as well as individual healthcare practitioners who provide medication information. These healthcare practitioners, as well as related scientists, represent all facets of the healthcare picture in America, including consumers, manufacturers, physicians, pharmacists, nurses, the elderly, research scientists, healthcare scientists, and nutritionists. Therefore, the information found in *USP DI* regarding dosages is very useful for two reasons: First, the information represents the judgments of many pediatricians; and second, the information is based on actual clinical experiences with infants and children.

GROUP NAME

AMPHETAMINES

1. AMPHETAMINE. 2. DEXTROAMPHETAMINE (DEXEDRINE).
3. METHAMPHETAMINE (DESOXYN).

USES AND INDICATIONS

Amphetamines are central nervous system stimulants and are used in treating attention deficit disorders in children. Amphetamines increase muscle activity and mental alertness without producing drowsiness.

ADVERSE EFFECTS

The adverse effects of amphetamines that require medical attention include irregular heartbeats; chest pain; uncontrolled movements of the head, arms, and legs; and skin rash or hives. Other adverse effects that may require medical attention if they are bothersome or become more severe include irritability or nervousness, trouble sleeping, blurred vision, constipation or diarrhea, dizziness, dry mouth, headache, excessive sweating, stomach cramps, weight loss, and nausea or vomiting.

WARNINGS AND PRECAUTIONS
Use amphetamines with caution in children with hypertension, glaucoma, or hyperthyroidism.

MEDICATION AND FOOD INTERACTIONS
- Sodium Bicarbonate, citrates (see Appendix II), and calcium- and magnesium-containing antacids (see Appendix II) may increase the toxic effects of amphetamines.
- Insulin may increase the risk of too much sugar in the blood when used with amphetamines.
- Amphetamines may delay the absorption and effect of Phenobarbital and DILANTIN.
- The effects of both amphetamines (see Appendix II) and thyroid hormones (see Appendix II) may be increased when used together.

COMMENTS
Amphetamines are classified as Schedule II Controlled Substances, and their distribution and use are strictly regulated by federal and state laws. As a group, amphetamines share similarities in their actions and uses, but there are variations in their dosages. As a general rule, amphetamines should be taken during the day and shortly before meals to minimize stomach upset. Evening doses may interfere with the child's ability to sleep. Also, dosage guidelines for the treatment of attention deficit disorders may be very flexible, and some physicians modify therapy to permit children to "skip" taking doses on weekends and holidays, as well as during summer vacations and spring and winter school breaks.

Children on long-term amphetamine therapy should be monitored closely to avoid medication dependence and/or medication-related behavior problems. They should also be monitored for growth suppression. Children should be periodically seen by their pediatricians to determine the need for continued amphetamine use.

Following are abbreviated monographs for the amphetamines, which should be used only as directed by a physician.

GENERIC NAME
1. AMPHETAMINE   Rx
See also general information on amphetamines on page 45.

DOSAGE GUIDELINES
- Tablets:
  Children to 3 years: Use is not recommended.
  Children 3–5 years: By mouth, 2.5 milligrams (½ tablet) daily,
    then increase in increments of 2.5 milligrams (½ tablet) per day
    at weekly intervals until desired effect is obtained.
  Children 6 years or older: By mouth, 5 milligrams (1 tablet) 1–2
    times daily, then increase in increments of 5 milligrams (1 tab-
    let) per day at weekly intervals until desired effect is obtained.

BRAND NAME(S)
2. DEXEDRINE   Rx
See also general information on amphetamines on page 45.

GENERIC NAME
DEXTROAMPHETAMINE

DOSAGE GUIDELINES
- Long-acting capsules, elixir, and tablets:
  For dosage, see 1. *Amphetamine* (above). The long-acting capsule
    may be used for once-a-day dosage.

BRAND NAME(S)
3. DESOXYN   Rx
See also general information on amphetamines on page 45.

GENERIC NAME
METHAMPHETAMINE

DOSAGE GUIDELINES
- Tablets and long-acting tablets:
  Children to 6 years: Use is not recommended.
  Children 6 years or older: By mouth, 2.5–5 milligrams (½ to 1
    tablet) 1–2 times daily initially, then may be increased in incre-
    ments of 5 milligrams (1 tablet) per day at weekly intervals until
    the desired effect is obtained. The long-acting forms of 10 milli-

grams and 15 milligrams may be administered in the morning, but they should not be used in children under 12 years.

GROUP NAME
ANESTHETICS, LOCAL OR TOPICAL

1. Benzocaine (AMBESOL, CHLORASEPTIC, ORAJEL, NUM-ZIT).
2. Dibucaine (NUPERCAINAL). 3. Dyclomine (SUCRETS). 4. Lidocaine (XYLOCAINE).

The anesthetics discussed here include only those products that are applied to the skin, mucous membranes, and eyes. In general, anesthetics are drugs used to relieve pain and itching, and they are often combined with other medications, such as anti-infectives and corticosteroids. While most anesthetic products require a doctor's prescription, many are sold over the counter and are freely available to the general consumer.

USES AND INDICATIONS
Some of the specific conditions calling for these products include teething, sore mouth and gums, sore throat, rectal pain and itching, and skin disorders associated with pain or itching.

ADVERSE EFFECTS
Adverse effects of anesthetics are related to patient hypersensitivity, excessive dosage, and excessive systemic absorption, resulting in various toxic effects. In addition, adverse effects may be determined by the specific drug, the dosage form used, the amount of drug used, and the part of the body being treated. Some adverse effects include the following:
- Ophthalmic: stinging, burning, excessive tearing, sensitivity to light, and corneal inflammation and erosion.
- Mucosal and topical: skin rash; contact dermatitis; hives; redness; itching; stinging or burning sensation; swelling of the skin, mouth, or throat; and tenderness of the affected area.
- Central nervous system: blurred or double vision, dizziness, trembling or shaking, ringing in the ears, convulsions, anxiety, excitement, restlessness, drowsiness, unconsciousness, and respiratory arrest.

- Cardiovascular: Excessive sweating, slow heart rate, decreased blood pressure, and cardiac arrest.
- Other: bloody urine, increased urination (sometimes painful), and, in rare instances, convulsions in children (from XYLOCAINE), and serious blood disorders in infants and children (from AMBESOL or ORAJEL) when used for teething pain.

WARNINGS AND PRECAUTIONS

- Local anesthetic products should not be used in children who may be allergic to products containing para-aminobenzoic acid derivatives or paraben preservatives.
- Local anesthetics should be applied sparingly and should not be used for prolonged periods. If the condition does not improve within the period prescribed by the physician, or the time specified in the product's labeling instructions, advise your doctor.
- While a small amount of medication applied to the eyes may be absorbed systemically, anesthetics applied to the skin or mucous membranes may be readily absorbed and may produce toxic effects, particularly in newborns and small infants.

MEDICATION AND FOOD INTERACTIONS

Primarily for topical anesthetics used on the mucous membranes: The effectiveness of sulfonamides (see Appendix II) may be decreased when used concurrently with AMBESOL and related products.

BRAND NAME(S)
1. ORAJEL   OTC
(Other brands: **AMBESOL, CHLORASEPTIC, NUM-ZIT**) See also general information on anesthetics, local or topical, on page 48.

GENERIC NAME
BENZOCAINE

USES AND INDICATIONS

Benzocaine is a local anesthetic product used for teething, sore throat, and minor skin abrasions. It is also an active ingredient in combination products used topically to relieve pain.

WARNINGS AND PRECAUTIONS

- The excessive use of ORAJEL to relieve the pain and discomfort of teething in infants can result in a serious blood disorder called methemaglobinemia—a chemical reaction in which oxygen is strongly bound to red blood cells and is not available to provide oxygen to body cells and tissues.
- Apply or spray to the affected area sparingly. Do not use for prolonged periods.

DOSAGE GUIDELINES

- Jelly (7.5%):
  Apply the 7.5% jelly around the affected gums as needed for teething pain. Do not use any longer than necessary; use sparingly.
- Lotion:
  Children to 2 years: Use is not recommended.
  Children 2 years and older: Apply to affected area 3–4 times daily as needed.
- Lozenges (5 milligrams):
  Pediatric: Dissolve one 5-milligram lozenge slowly in the mouth for sore throat; may be repeated at 1-hour intervals as needed.
- Aerosol solution, cream, and ointment:
  Children to 2 years: Use is not recommended.
  Children 2 years and older: Spray or apply to affected area as needed.

BRAND NAME(S)
2. NUPERCAINAL   OTC
See also general information on anesthetics, local or topical, on page 48.

GENERIC NAME
DIBUCAINE

USES AND INDICATIONS
NUPERCAINAL is used to relieve the pain and discomfort of hemorrhoids, as well as other rectal disorders associated with pain or itching.

DOSAGE GUIDELINES
- Cream and ointment:
  - Pediatric: Apply to affected area as necessary. Do not use more than 7.5 grams of the cream or 15 grams of the ointment per day in children.

BRAND NAME(S)
3. SUCRETS   OTC
See also general information on anesthetics, local or topical, on page 48.

GENERIC NAME
DYCLOMINE

USES AND INDICATIONS
SUCRETS is used to relieve the pain or discomfort of sore or scratchy throat, as well as mouth pain.

DOSAGE GUIDELINES

- Lozenges (1.2 milligrams):
  Children to 3 years: Dosage has not been established.
  Children 3 years and older: Dissolve one 1.2-milligram lozenge slowly in the mouth for sore throat; may be repeated at 2-hour intervals as needed.

BRAND NAME(S)
4. XYLOCAINE   Rx
See also general information on anesthetics, local or topical, on page 48.

GENERIC NAME
LIDOCAINE

USES AND INDICATIONS
XYLOCAINE is used topically to relieve nose, mouth, and throat pain, and in painful skin disorders.

DOSAGE GUIDELINES
- Ointment:
  Children to 2 years: Dosage has not been established.
  Children 2 years and older: Apply to the affected area as needed.

GROUP NAME
ANTACIDS

1. ALUMINUM CARBONATE (BASALJEL). 2. ALUMINUM HYDROXIDE (ALTERNAGEL, AMPHOJEL). 3. ALUMINUM HYDROXIDE/MAGNESIUM CARBONATE (GAVISCON [LIQUID]). 4. ALUMINUM HYDROXIDE/MAGNESIUM TRISILICATE (GAVISCON [TABLETS]). 5. ALUMINUM/MAGNESIUM HYDROXIDE (ALUDROX, AMPHOJEL, CREAMALIN, MAALOX). 6. ALUMINUM/ MAGNESIUM HYDROXIDE WITH SIMETHICONE (AMPHOJEL PLUS, DI-GEL, GELUSIL, MAALOX PLUS, MYLANTA-II). 7. ALUMINUM/MAGNESIUM WITH CALCIUM CARBONATE (CAMALOX). 8. CALCIUM CARBONATE/MAGNESIUM HYDROXIDE (BISODOL, DI-GEL, ROLAIDS SODIUM FREE). 9. MAGALDRATE (RIOPAN). 10. MAGALDRATE/SIMETHICONE (RIOPAN PLUS). 11. MAGNESIUM HYDROXIDE (PHILLIPS' MILK OF MAGNESIA). 12. MAGNESIUM TRISILICATE WITH ALUMINUM/MAGNESIUM HYDROXIDES (MAGNATRIL).

USES AND INDICATIONS
Chemically, antacids are basic, inorganic salts that form alkaline solutions when dissolved. Their ability to neutralize stomach acids by decreasing the acidity of gastric secretions makes these medications useful in providing temporary relief from the pain and discomfort of peptic ulcers, heartburn, sour stomach, and indigestion. The usefulness of antacids is based upon their ability to neutralize hydrochloric acid, and the most potent antacids are, in decreasing order, Calcium Carbonate, Sodium Bicarbonate, and magnesium and aluminum salts. Other indications for antacids include prevention of kidney stones; treatment of excessive calcium and phosphates; and diarrhea. The following general information should be kept in mind regarding antacids:

- Liquid antacids are suspensions and should be shaken well before using.
- Antacid tablets should be chewed thoroughly before swallowing.
- Antacids may interact with many other medications to alter their

effects; therefore, they should be administered at least 1 hour after other medications are given.

- The sodium content of some antacids is high and may affect children with high blood pressure (check the label).
- Due to antacids' potential for interaction with other medications, parents should advise their child's physician of other medications their child is currently taking, including over-the-counter products.

ADVERSE EFFECTS

The following adverse effects may occur with antacids containing the specific active ingredients identified below:

- Antacids containing aluminum, calcium, or Sodium Bicarbonate may cause severe constipation and swelling (water retention) of the feet or lower legs.
- The long-term use of antacids containing calcium or Sodium Bicarbonate may result in headache, nausea or vomiting, loss of appetite, muscle weakness, and the frequent urge to urinate.
- The prolonged use of, or ingestion of, large doses of antacids containing aluminum may result in swelling of the hands and feet.

WARNINGS AND PRECAUTIONS

- Do not use calcium-containing antacids in children with hypercalcemia.
- Do not use aluminum- and magnesium-containing antacids in children with kidney disorders.
- Antacids may mask the symptoms of appendicitis or of gastrointestinal or rectal-bleeding disorders.
- The laxative effects of magnesium-containing antacids may aggravate ulcerative colitis. They may also cause excessive loss of body electrolytes due to diarrhea.
- Aluminum- and calcium-containing antacids may cause constipation and depletion of body phosphorous.
- Do not use antacids in children with intestinal obstruction disorders or stomach cramps.

MEDICATION AND FOOD INTERACTIONS

- Aluminum-containing antacids may decrease the absorption of fat-soluble vitamins, especially Vitamin A.

- Hypermagnesemia may result when magnesium-containing antacids and Vitamin D are taken together.
- Aluminum- and calcium-containing antacids may decrease the absorption of fluorides.
- Hypercalcemia may result in children taking calcium-containing antacids and large quantities of milk or Vitamin D.
- Calcium-, magnesium-, and Sodium Bicarbonate–containing antacids may decrease the effectiveness of Aspirin-type medications.
- Aluminum- and magnesium-containing antacids may decrease the effectiveness of DILANTIN.
- Calcium- and magnesium-containing antacids may decrease the effectiveness of PANCREASE.
- Aluminum-containing antacids may decrease the effectiveness of NYDRAZID.
- Antacids may decrease the effectiveness of iron preparations.
- Aluminum- and magnesium-containing antacids may decrease the effectiveness of LANOXIN.
- Calcium-, magnesium-, and Sodium Bicarbonate–containing antacids may increase the toxicity of Quinidine and amphetamines (see Appendix II).

DOSAGE GUIDELINES

Following are dosage guidelines for some commonly used antacids, listed by generic name.

1. **Aluminum Carbonate** (BASALJEL): OTC
   - Oral suspension: By mouth, 5–15 milliliters (1–3 teaspoonsful) every 3–6 hours; or 1 and 3 hours after meals and at bedtime; or as directed by a physician.
2. **Aluminum Hydroxide** (ALTERNAGEL, AMPHOJEL): OTC ·
   - Oral suspension:
     Infants to 1 year: Use only as directed by a physician.
     Children: By mouth, 5–15 milliliters (1–3 teaspoonsful) every 3–6 hours; or 1 and 3 hours after meals and at bedtime; or as directed by a physician.
     Note: A whitish color in the stool should not cause alarm.
3. **Aluminum Hydroxide/Magnesium Carbonate** (GAVISCON [liquid]): OTC
   See 5. *Aluminum/Magnesium Hydroxide* for dosage information.

4. **Aluminum Hydroxide/Magnesium Trisilicate** (GAVISCON [tablets]): OTC
   See 5. *Aluminum/Magnesium Hydroxide* for dosage information.
5. **Aluminum/Magnesium Hydroxide** (ALUDROX, AMPHOJEL, CREAMALIN, MAALOX): OTC
   - Oral suspension:
     Infants: Do not use except as directed by a physician.
     Children: By mouth, 5–15 milliliters (1–3 teaspoonsful) every 3–6 hours, or 1 and 3 hours after meals and at bedtime; or as directed by a physician.
6. **Aluminum/Magnesium Hydroxide with Simethicone** (AMPHOJEL PLUS, DI-GEL, GELUSIL, MAALOX PLUS, MYLANTA-II): OTC
   See 5. *Aluminum/Magnesium Hydroxide* for dosage information.
7. **Aluminum/Magnesium with Calcium Carbonate** (CAMALOX): OTC
   - Oral suspension: By mouth, 5–15 milliliters (1–3 teaspoonsful) every 3–6 hours; or 1 and 3 hours after meals and at bedtime; or as directed by a physician.
8. **Calcium Carbonate/Magnesium Hydroxide** (BISODOL, DI-GEL, ROLAIDS SODIUM FREE): OTC
   - Chewable tablets and oral suspension:
     Children to 6 years: Use is not recommended.
     Children over 6 years: By mouth, 1–2 tablets or 5–10ml (1–2 teaspoonsful) as needed; or as directed by a physician.
9. **Magaldrate** (RIOPAN): OTC
   - Oral suspension: By mouth, 5–15 milliliters (1–3 teaspoonsful) every 3–6 hours; or 1 and 3 hours after meals and at bedtime; or as directed by a physician.
10. **Magaldrate/Simethicone** (RIOPAN PLUS): OTC
    See 9. *Magaldrate* for dosage information.
11. **Magnesium Hydroxide** (PHILLIPS' MILK OF MAGNESIA): OTC
    - Oral suspension:
      Children to 1 year: Use is not recommended.
      Children 1–6 years: By mouth, 2.5–5 milliliters (½–1 teaspoonful); or as directed by a physician.
      Children over 6 years: By mouth, 1 tablet up to 4 per day; or as directed by a physician.
12. **Magnesium Trisilicate with Aluminum/Magnesium Hydroxides** (MAGNATRIL): OTC
    See 5. *Aluminum/Magnesium Hydroxide* for dosage information.

COMMENTS

Antacids should be used for short periods in children. If symptoms persist or become severe, parents should seek medical attention. Avoid prolonged use in infants or children, unless as directed by a physician. All antacid suspensions should be shaken well before using, and the tablets chewed before swallowing.

GROUP NAME
ANTHELMINTICS

1. Mebendazole (VERMOX). 2. Niclosamide (NICLOCIDE).
3. Praziquantel (BILTRICIDE). 4. Pyrantel (ANTIMINTH).
5. Quinacrine (ATABRINE). 6. Thiabendazole (MINTEZOL).

USES AND INDICATIONS

Anthelmintics are anti-infective medications used in treating parasitic infections caused by worms such as roundworms, hookworms, pinworms, tapeworms, threadworms, whipworms, and flukes. These parasites are often present in foods that have spoiled or been inadequately cooked, as well as in the soil in areas where human hygiene practices are poor or absent. Some meats that may contain these parasites are beef, fish, and pork. Pork products, in particular, should be well cooked before being eaten.

ADVERSE EFFECTS

The adverse effects typical of most of the more commonly used anthelmintics include nausea, vomiting, stomach cramps, fever, diarrhea, and rash with itching. Other adverse effects may include dizziness, drowsiness, rectal itching, loss of appetite, constipation, excessive sweating, palpitations, and water retention.

WARNINGS AND PRECAUTIONS

- In case of overdose, a rapid-acting laxative or an enema may be administered to empty the gastrointestinal tract. Do not induce vomiting.
- Most anthelmintics may be taken with fluids during a light meal.
- For most parasitic infections, strict hygiene should be practiced; night clothing, bed linen, and towels and face cloths should be changed regularly and thoroughly cleaned in boiling water.

- For pinworm infections, all family members should be treated at the same time.
- Chewable tablets may be crushed before swallowing.
- In treating hookworm and whipworm infections in children, parents may be required to administer supplemental iron for up to 6 months if the child develops anemia before or during treatment.
- Oral suspensions should be shaken well before use.

BRAND NAME(S)
1 . VERMOX   Rx
See also general information on anthelmintics on page 56.

GENERIC NAME
MEBENDAZOLE

USES AND INDICATIONS
VERMOX is used in the treatment of pinworms, hookworms, roundworms, and whipworms. It is also used as a secondary medication in combating tapeworm infections.

WARNINGS AND PRECAUTIONS
- VERMOX should be used cautiously in children who have liver disorders.
- Children on high-dose therapy should have complete blood cell counts taken during the first month of treatment, and weekly thereafter.

MEDICATION AND FOOD INTERACTIONS
TEGRETOL may decrease the effectiveness of VERMOX in high-dose treatment.

DOSAGE GUIDELINES
- Chewable tablets:
  Children to 2 years: Dosage has not been established.
  Children 2 years and older:
  - Roundworms, whipworms, and hookworms: By mouth, 100 milligrams in the morning and evening for 3 days; may be repeated in 2–3 weeks if necessary.
  - Pinworms: By mouth, 100 milligrams as a single dose; may be repeated in 2–3 weeks if necessary.
  - Tapeworms: By mouth, 200–400 milligrams 3 times daily for 3

days, then increase to 400–500 milligrams 3 times daily for 10 days.

BRAND NAME(S)
2. NICLOCIDE   Rx
See also general information on anthelmintics on page 56.

GENERIC NAME
NICLOSAMIDE

USES AND INDICATIONS
NICLOCIDE is used in treating tapeworm infections.

DOSAGE GUIDELINES
*   Chewable tablets:
    *   Beef and fish tapeworms:
        Children to 24 pounds: Use is not recommended.
        Children 24–75 pounds: By mouth, 1 gram as a single dose.
        Children over 75 pounds: By mouth, 1.5 grams as a single dose the first day, then 1 gram daily for 6 days; may be repeated in 1–2 weeks if necessary.
    *   Dwarf tapeworms:
        Children to 24 pounds: Use is not recommended.
        Children 24–75 pounds: By mouth, 1 gram as a single dose the first day, then 500 milligrams daily for 6 days; may be repeated in 1–2 weeks if necessary.
        Children over 75 pounds: By mouth, 1.5 grams as a single dose the first day, then 1 gram daily for 6 days; may be repeated in 1–2 weeks if necessary.

COMMENTS
To administer to a young child, the chewable tablets may be crushed, and some water added to make a paste.

BRAND NAME(S)
3. BILTRICIDE   Rx
See also general information on anthelmintics on page 56.

GENERIC NAME
PRAZIQUANTEL

Uses and Indications
BILTRICIDE is used in treating tapeworm infections and flukes.

Warnings and Precautions

- BILTRICIDE should not be used for eye infections caused by parasites.
- Tablets should be swallowed whole with liquid during meals.

Dosage Guidelines
- Tablets: Children to 4 years: Use is not recommended.
  Children 4 years and older:
  - Fluke infestations: By mouth, 20–30 milligrams for each 2.2 pounds of body weight 3 times daily for 1–3 days; repeat if necessary.
  - Tapeworms: By mouth, 10–25 milligrams for each 2.2 pounds of body weight as a single dose.

BRAND NAME(S)
4 . ANTIMINTH   Rx
See also general information on anthelmintics on page 56.

GENERIC NAME
PYRANTEL

Uses and Indications
ANTIMINTH is used in treating roundworms, pinworms, hookworms, and other intestinal parasites.

Warnings and Precautions

- If any of the following symptoms occur, seek medical help as soon as possible: skin rash, difficulty breathing, muscle spasms, lightheadedness, and coma.
- Use with caution in children with liver disorders.

Dosage Guidelines
- Oral suspension:
  - Roundworms and pinworms:
    Children to 2 years: Use is not recommended.
    Children 2 years and older: By mouth, 11 milligrams for each

2.2 pounds of body weight as a single dose; repeat in 2–3 weeks if necessary.

- Hookworms (the doses shown below should be given for 3 consecutive days):
  Children to 26 pounds: Use is not recommended.
  Children 26–51 pounds: By mouth, 125–250 milligrams as a single dose.
  Children 52–99 pounds: By mouth, 250–500 milligrams as a single dose.
  Children 100–149 pounds: By mouth, 500–750 milligrams as a single dose.

COMMENTS
ANTIMINTH should be shaken well before use.

BRAND NAME(S)
5. ATABRINE   Rx
See also general information on anthelmintics on page 56.

GENERIC NAME
QUINACRINE

USES AND INDICATIONS
ATABRINE is used in treating tapeworm infections and giardiasis (intestinal parasites).

ADVERSE EFFECTS
The adverse effects of ATABRINE are those common to other anthelmintics. Parents should obtain medical attention if their child exhibits any of the following symptoms: mood changes, hallucinations, nightmares, nervousness or irritability, severe nausea or vomiting, severe stomach cramps, irregular heartbeat, severe diarrhea, fainting, restlessness, difficulty sleeping, or convulsions.

WARNINGS AND PRECAUTIONS

- ATABRINE should be used with caution in children with psoriasis or liver disorders.
- The yellow coloring of the skin, eyes, or urine is not a harmful reaction of ATABRINE but merely its dyelike characteristic.
- ATABRINE should be taken after meals, with water, tea, or fruit juice.

- In treating giardiasis, parents should exercise strict hygiene for all household members, including hand-washing before eating and after using the bathroom; boiling of drinking water for at least 10 minutes (or using other adequate disinfectant measures); and avoiding uncooked foods such as salads, fruit, etc.
- In long-term therapy with ATABRINE, children should receive periodic eye examinations.

DOSAGE GUIDELINES
- Tablets:
  - Dwarf tapeworm:
    Children to 4 years: Use is not recommended.
    Children 4–8 years: By mouth, ½ tablespoonful of Sodium Sulfate as a laxative the night before, then 200 milligrams of ATABRINE the next morning. Then give 100 milligrams of ATABRINE after breakfast for the next 3 days.
    Children 8–10 years: By mouth, ½ tablespoonful of Sodium Sulfate as a laxative the night before, then 300 milligrams of ATABRINE the next day. Then give 100 milligrams of ATABRINE after breakfast for the next 3 days.
    Children 11–14 years: By mouth, ½ tablespoonful of Sodium Sulfate as a laxative the night before, then 400 milligrams of ATABRINE the next day. Then give 100 milligrams of ATABRINE after breakfast for the next 3 days.
  - Other tapeworm infections:
    Children to 5 years: Use is not recommended.
    Children 5–10 years: By mouth, 400 milligrams in 3–4 divided doses 10 minutes apart. Give with 300-milligram doses of Sodium Bicarbonate to minimize nausea and vomiting.
    Children 11–14 years: By mouth, give 600 milligrams in 3–4 divided doses 10 minutes apart. Give with 300-milligram doses of Sodium Bicarbonate to minimize nausea and vomiting.
  - Giardiasis:
    Children: By mouth, 7 milligrams daily for each 2.2 pounds of body weight, divided into 3 doses and given after meals for 5 days, not to exceed 300 milligrams daily.

COMMENTS
The bitter taste of ATABRINE may be masked by crushing the tablet and mixing it with honey, jam, or chocolate syrup.

BRAND NAME(S)
6. MINTEZOL   Rx
See also general information on anthelmintics on page 56.

GENERIC NAME
THIABENDAZOLE

USES AND INDICATIONS
MINTEZOL is used in the treatment of infections caused by round-worms, threadworms, pinworms, hookworms, whipworms, and porkworms, as well as for larva migrans (creeping eruption).

ADVERSE EFFECTS
In addition to the adverse effects common to most anthelmintics, others include fever, chills, achy joints and muscles, ringing or buzzing in the ears, lower back pain, bed-wetting, skin peeling or blistering, and blurred or yellow vision.

WARNINGS AND PRECAUTIONS

- MINTEZOL should be used with caution in children with liver or kidney disorders.
- MINTEZOL may cause an unusual odor in the urine, which is not medically significant and should not cause alarm.
- Treatment with MINTEZOL should be stopped if allergic reactions, such as rash or other skin reactions, occur.
- MINTEZOL suspension should be shaken well before use.

DOSAGE GUIDELINES
- Chewable tablets and oral suspension:
  Larva migrans: By mouth, 25 milligrams for each 2.2 pounds of body weight twice daily for 2–5 days for patients under 150 pounds. The oral suspension may be applied to the skin lesions (larva burrows) 2–4 times daily for up to 14 days.
  Threadworm, whipworm, roundworm, and hookworm infections: By mouth, 25 milligrams for each 2.2 pounds of body weight twice daily for 2 days in uncomplicated infections, or 5–7 days in severe infections.
  Porkworm infections: By mouth, 25 milligrams for each 2.2 pounds of body weight twice daily for 2–7 days.

Pinworms: By mouth, 25 milligrams for each 2.2 pounds of body weight twice daily for 1 day.

GROUP NAME

ANTICONVULSANTS, BARBITURATE

1. MEPHOBARBITAL (MEBARAL). 2. PHENOBARBITAL (BARBITA, SOLFOTON).

USES AND INDICATIONS
Barbiturate anticonvulsants are central nervous system depressants. They are used in children to treat epilepsy and other seizure disorders.

ADVERSE EFFECTS
The major adverse effects of barbiturate anticonvulsants are those resulting from central nervous system depression.

- Central nervous system: drowsiness, lethargy, headache, mental depression, vertigo, joint pain, mood alterations, impairment of judgment, loss of muscle coordination, sedation, confusion, and a hangover feeling.
- Hypersensitivity: rash, fever, itching, increased sensitivity to sunlight, jaundice, and hepatitis (which has resulted in some fatalities).
- Blood: decrease in blood cells, easy bruising or bleeding.
- Other: nausea, vomiting, diarrhea, and constipation.

WARNINGS AND PRECAUTIONS

- Barbiturate anticonvulsants should not be used, or should be used with extreme caution, in children with mental illness.
- Barbiturate anticonvulsants should be used cautiously in children with kidney disorders.
- Discontinue barbiturate anticonvulsants at the earliest signs of fever, headache, inflammation of the lining of the mouth, conjunctivitis, or runny nose.
- Barbiturate anticonvulsants are contraindicated in children with breathing disorders.

- Children on long-term therapy with barbiturate anticonvulsants should receive complete blood counts periodically.

MEDICATION AND FOOD INTERACTIONS

- The depressant effects may be significantly increased when barbiturate anticonvulsants are used with other central nervous system depressants, such as alcohol-containing products, antihistamines (see Appendix II), benzodiazepines (see Appendix II), and tricyclic antidepressants (see Appendix II).
- Barbiturate anticonvulsants may decrease the effectiveness of corticosteroids (see Appendix II).
- Phenobarbital may decrease the effectiveness of GRIFULVIN and VIBRAMYCIN.

BRAND NAME(S)
1. MEBARAL   Rx
See also general information on barbiturate anticonvulsants on page 63.

GENERIC NAME
MEPHOBARBITAL

USES AND INDICATIONS
MEBARAL is used in the treatment of both grand mal and petit mal seizures.

DOSAGE GUIDELINES
- Tablets:
  Children to 5 years: By mouth, 16–32 milligrams 3–4 times daily.
  Children 5 years and older: By mouth, 32–64 milligrams 3–4 times daily.

COMMENTS
MEBARAL may be used as an alternate to Phenobarbital therapy, as a replacement for other anticonvulsants, or in combination with other anticonvulsants. When MEBARAL is used as a replacement medication, the dose should gradually be increased while the other medication is gradually decreased. Abrupt withdrawal may result in seizures.

GENERIC NAME
2. PHENOBARBITAL   Rx
See also general information on barbiturate anticonvulsants on page 63.

BRAND NAME(S)
BARBITA (and SOLFOTON)

USES AND INDICATIONS
Phenobarbital is used in the long-term treatment of epilepsy and seizure disorders.

DOSAGE GUIDELINES
- Capsules, elixir, oral solution, and tablets: By mouth, 1–6 milligrams daily for each 2.2 pounds of body weight as a single dose, or in divided doses as prescribed by your child's doctor.

GROUP NAME
ANTICONVULSANTS, BENZODIAZEPINES

1. CLONAZEPAM (KLONOPIN). 2. CLORAZEPATE (TRANXENE). DIAZEPAM (VALIUM, VAZEPAM).

BRAND NAME(S)
1. KLONOPIN   Rx

GENERIC NAME
CLONAZEPAM

USES AND INDICATIONS
KLONOPIN is used in treating epileptic disorders, including various forms of grand mal and petit mal seizures, simple and complex partial seizures, and mixed seizures.

DOSAGE GUIDELINES
- Tablets:
  Children to 10 years or 66 pounds: By mouth, 10–50 micrograms daily for each 2.2 pounds of body weight in 2–3 divided doses initially, then may be increased by 250–500 micrograms every 3 days until the seizures are controlled, or until a maintenance dose of 100–200 micrograms daily for each 2.2 pounds of body weight is reached.

COMMENTS

As with all anticonvulsants, changes in dosages (both increases and decreases) should be made gradually, and abrupt withdrawal should be avoided due to the possibility of increased seizure episodes. In replacement therapy, KLONOPIN should gradually be increased while the other anticonvulsant medication is gradually decreased.

For more information regarding other uses and indications, adverse effects, warnings and precautions, and medication and food interactions, see the general monograph for benzodiazepines (page 115).

BRAND NAME(S)
2. TRANXENE   Rx

GENERIC NAME
CLORAZEPATE

USES AND INDICATIONS

The primary use for TRANXENE is in epilepsy.

DOSAGE GUIDELINES

- Capsules and tablets:
  Children to 9 years: Dosage has not been established.
  Children 9–12 years: By mouth, 7.5 milligrams twice daily initially, then may be increased at 1-week intervals in increments of 7.5 milligrams until the seizures are controlled, not to exceed 60 milligrams daily in divided doses as prescribed by your child's doctor.

COMMENTS

Changes in dosage of TRANXENE should be made gradually in order to avoid the possibility of increased seizure episodes.

For more information regarding other uses and indications, adverse effects, warnings and precautions, and medication and food interactions, see the general monograph for benzodiazepines (page 115).

BRAND NAME(S)
3. VALIUM (and VAZEPAM)   Rx

GENERIC NAME
DIAZEPAM

USES AND INDICATIONS
VALIUM is used in treating epilepsy and seizure disorders.

DOSAGE GUIDELINES
- Oral solution and tablets:
  Children to 6 months: Use is not recommended.
  Children 6 months and older: By mouth, 1–2.5 milligrams 3–4 times daily, then may gradually be increased as required.

COMMENTS
For more information regarding other uses and indications, adverse effects, warnings and precautions, and medication and food interactions, see the general monograph for benzodiazepines (page 115).

GROUP NAME
ANTICONVULSANTS, DIONE

1. PARAMETHADIONE (PARADIONE). 2. TRIMETHADIONE (TRIDIONE).

USE AND INDICATIONS
The dione anticonvulsants are used in treating petit mal seizures that are resistant to other anticonvulsant therapy.

ADVERSE EFFECTS

The major adverse effects include:
- Ophthalmic: double vision; glare caused by bright light.
- Allergic: itchy skin and swollen lymph glands.
- Blood: sore throat; fever; bleeding of the gums, nose, or vagina; and purple spots on skin.
- Gastrointestinal: nausea, vomiting, stomach pain.
- Other: muscle weakness, tiredness, confusion, loss of appetite, dizziness, hair loss, difficulty sleeping, and weight loss.

WARNINGS AND PRECAUTIONS

- Dione anticonvulsants should be used cautiously in children with liver or kidney disorders.
- Children on dione anticonvulsant therapy should be monitored routinely for blood, kidney, and liver functions.

- Dione anticonvulsants should be used cautiously in children with a history of eye or blood disorders.

MEDICATION AND FOOD INTERACTIONS

The following may increase the depressant effects of dione anticonvulsants and the potential for seizures: alcohol-containing products, HALDOL, and CYLERT.

BRAND NAME(S)
1. PARADIONE   Rx

See also general information on dione anticonvulsants on page 67.

GENERIC NAME
PARAMETHADIONE

USES AND INDICATIONS

PARADIONE is used in treating petit mal seizures in children.

DOSAGE GUIDELINES

- Capsules:
  Children to 2 years: By mouth, 100 milligrams 3 times daily.
  Children 2–6 years: By mouth, 200 milligrams 3 times daily.
  Children 6 years and over: By mouth, 300 milligrams 3 times daily.

BRAND NAME(S)
2. TRIDIONE   Rx

See also general information on dione anticonvulsants on page 67.

GENERIC NAME
TRIMETHADIONE

USES AND INDICATIONS

TRIDIONE is used in treating petit mal seizures in children.

DOSAGE GUIDELINES

- Capsules:
  Children to 2 years: By mouth, 100 milligrams 3 times daily.
  Children 2–6 years: By mouth, 200 milligrams 3 times daily.
  Children 6 years and over: By mouth, 300 milligrams 3–4 times daily.

GROUP NAME
ANTICONVULSANTS, HYDANTOIN

1. ETHOTOIN (PEGANONE). 2. MEPHENYTOIN (MESANTOIN).
3. PHENYTOIN (DILANTIN).

USES AND INDICATIONS

The hydantoin anticonvulsants appear to function primarily in the motor cortex region of the brain, where they alter the electrolyte chemistry of sodium and calcium. The hydantoins are used in treating major seizure disorders, including grand mal and psychomotor disorders. Mephenytoin is usually reserved for treating seizure disorders that are not alleviated by less toxic anticonvulsants, and for treating Jacksonian seizures, in which the muscles alternately contract and relax.

ADVERSE EFFECTS

As with other anticonvulsants, the hydantoins are also associated with many adverse effects, including serious cardiac, blood, liver, and dermatological reactions. The following adverse effects are listed in summary form by organ or body system:

- Central nervous system: mental confusion, dizziness, slurred speech, double vision, fatigue, depression, irritability, loss of muscle coordination, headache, tremors, numbness, drowsiness, and inability to sleep.
- Dermatological: rash (sometimes accompanied by fever) and lupus erythematosus.
- Gastrointestinal: nausea, vomiting, and constipation or diarrhea.
- Blood: anemias (which usually respond to folic acid treatment) and serious disorders associated with significant reduction in blood components (which can be fatal).
- Liver: jaundice, hepatitis, and destruction of the liver (which can be fatal).
- Gums: gingival hyperplasia, which is an increase in the number of cells of the gums. It may be reduced by maintaining good oral hygiene (frequent brushing and gum massage, plus regular dental-

care visits). Children are particularly susceptible to these effects, which occur more frequently with DILANTIN.
- Other: enlargement of the lips, coarsening of facial skin, hyperglycemia, conjunctivitis, sensitivity to light, water retention, weight gain, chest pains, and excessive hair growth.

WARNINGS AND PRECAUTIONS

- Hydantoin anticonvulsants should be used with extreme caution in children who are hypersensitive to other hydantoins; children with liver or kidney disorders; children with diabetes, cardiac disease, blood disorders, or thyroid disease; and children with low blood pressure.
- Children on hydantoins should be closely monitored by their doctors.
- The abrupt withdrawal of hydantoins may cause seizure episodes; therefore, withdrawal or an increase in dosage should be accomplished gradually over an extended period of time.

MEDICATION AND FOOD INTERACTIONS

- The following drugs may increase the effects of hydantoins by slowing their metabolism: ZYLOPRIM, CHLOROMYCETIN, TAGAMET, VALIUM, NYDRAZID, MONISTAT, succinimide anticonvulsants (see Appendix II), and sulfonamides (see Appendix II).
- The following may decrease the effects of hydantoins by increasing their metabolism and elimination from the body: Theophylline and TEGRETOL.
- The following may decrease the effects of hydantoins by inhibiting their absorption from the gastrointestinal tract: antacids (see Appendix II), Calcium Gluconate, and dairy products.
- The following may have reduced effects when used with hydantoins due to their increased metabolism: corticosteroids (see Appendix II), VIBRAMYCIN, HALDOL, and Quinidine.
- The effectiveness of LASIX is decreased when used with hydantoins.

BRAND NAME(S)
1. PEGANONE   Rx
See also general information on hydantoin anticonvulsants on page 69.

GENERIC NAME
ETHOTOIN

USES AND INDICATIONS
PEGANONE is often used in place of DILANTIN in patients experiencing gum disorders.

DOSAGE GUIDELINES
- Tablets: By mouth, up to 750 milligrams daily initially, in divided doses as specified by your doctor, then may gradually be adjusted until the seizures are controlled.

BRAND NAME(S)
2. MESANTOIN   Rx
See general information on hydantoin anticonvulsants on page 69.

GENERIC NAME
MEPHENYTOIN

DOSAGE GUIDELINES
- Tablets: By mouth, 25–50 milligrams daily initially, then may be increased by an additional 50 milligrams daily at 1-week intervals until the seizures are controlled.

COMMENTS
MESANTOIN has a higher incidence of adverse blood effects than do other hydantoins; should be used only after other, less toxic anticonvulsants have been tried and found ineffective.

BRAND NAME(S)
3. DILANTIN   Rx
See also general information on hydantoin anticonvulsants on page 69.

GENERIC NAME
PHENYTOIN

USES AND INDICATIONS
DILANTIN is used as an anticonvulsant in treating major seizure disorders.

DOSAGE GUIDELINES

- Chewable tablets and oral suspension: By mouth, 5 milligrams daily for each 2.2 pounds of body weight, divided into 2–3 doses; then may gradually be adjusted to 300 milligrams daily. The maintenance dose is 4–8 milligrams daily for each 2.2 pounds of body weight, divided into 2–3 doses.
- Extended-action capsules and prompt-acting capsules: By mouth, up to 750 milligrams daily initially, divided into 2–3 doses; then may gradually be adjusted until the seizures are controlled.

COMMENTS

Because Phenytoin products manufactured by different companies may have clinically significant therapeutic differences, parents should ask their pharmacist to provide the same brand of Phenytoin each time they renew their child's prescription.

GROUP NAME
ANTICONVULSANTS, SUCCINIMIDE

1. ETHOSUXIMIDE (ZARONTIN). 2. METHSUXIMIDE (CELONTIN).
3. PHENSUXIMIDE (MILONTIN).

USES AND INDICATIONS

The succinimides, particularly ZARONTIN and MILONTIN, are among the first line of medications used in treating petit mal seizures. CELONTIN is used only after other, less toxic anticonvulsants have been tried and found to be ineffective.

ADVERSE EFFECTS

As with other anticonvulsants, the succinimides have significant adverse effects, and their use in children must be carefully monitored, both by physicians and parents. Adverse effects include:

- Blood: abnormal decrease in blood components (which can be fatal).

- Gastrointestinal: nausea, vomiting, diarrhea, constipation, stomach cramps, loss of appetite, and weight loss.
- Central nervous system: drowsiness, dizziness, irritability, nervousness, blurred vision, sensitivity to light, loss of muscle coordination, insomnia, tiredness, hiccoughs, nearsightedness, and behavioral changes.
- Dermatological: itching, rash, abnormal hair growth, lupus erythematosus, skin eruptions, and baldness.
- Psychological: mental slowness, depression, sleep disturbances (including night terrors), inability to concentrate, confusion, and hypochondria.
- Urinary: frequent urination; bloody discharge.
- Other: muscle weakness, swelling of the tongue and gums, and swelling of the eyes.

WARNINGS AND PRECAUTIONS

- As with other anticonvulsants, the dosage of succinimides should be increased or decreased gradually. The withdrawal of these medications may increase seizure episodes.
- Succinimides should be gradually withdrawn at the first signs of aggressive behavior or depression.
- Succinimides should be used with extreme caution in children who have impaired liver or kidney functions, or who have blood disorders.
- Taking these medications with food or milk may minimize possible stomach irritation.
- Children receiving these or other anticonvulsants should be closely monitored by periodic testing: blood counts, testing of liver and kidney functions, and urinalysis.
- Parents should be alert to the toxic signs of these medications and should advise their physicians immediately if they occur.

MEDICATION AND FOOD INTERACTIONS

- TEGRETOL, Phenobarbital, and DILANTIN may decrease the effectiveness of succinimides.
- The use of products that contain alcohol or other central nervous system depressants may increase the depressant effects of both medications when used with succinimides.

BRAND NAME(S)
1. ZARONTIN   Rx
See general information on succinimide anticonvulsants on page 72.

GENERIC NAME
ETHOSUXIMIDE

DOSAGE GUIDELINES
* Capsules and syrup:
  Children to 6 years: By mouth, 250 milligrams once daily initially,
    then may be increased by an additional 250 milligrams daily at
    4–7 day intervals until the seizures are controlled, or until a
    total daily dose of 1 gram is reached.
  Children 6 years and older: By mouth, 250 milligrams twice daily
    initially, then may be increased by an additional 250 milligrams
    daily at 4–7 day intervals until the seizures are controlled, or
    until a total daily dose of 1.5 grams is reached.

BRAND NAME(S)
2. CELONTIN   Rx
See also general information on succinimide anticonvulsants on page
72.

GENERIC NAME
METHSUXIMIDE

DOSAGE GUIDELINES
* Capsules: By mouth, 300 milligrams once daily initially, then may
  be increased by an additional daily dose of up to 300 milligrams at
  1-week intervals until the seizures are controlled, or until a total
  daily dose of 1.2 grams is reached.

BRAND NAME(S)
3. MILONTIN   Rx
See also general information on succinimide anticonvulsants on page
72.

GENERIC NAME
PHENSUXIMIDE

DOSAGE GUIDELINES

- Capsules: By mouth, 500 milligrams twice daily initially, then may be increased by an additional 500 milligrams daily at 1-week intervals until the seizures are controlled, or until a total daily dose of 3 grams is reached.

COMMENTS

MILONTIN may harmlessly color the urine pink or reddish-brown.

GROUP NAME

ANTICONVULSANTS, MISCELLANEOUS

1. CARBAMAZEPINE (TEGRETOL). 2. PHENACEMIDE (PHENURONE). 3. PRIMIDONE (MYIDONE, MYSOLINE). 4. VALPORIC ACID DERIVATIVES (DEPAKENE, DEPAKOTE).

BRAND NAME(S)
1. TEGRETOL   Rx

GENERIC NAME
CARBAMAZEPINE

USES AND INDICATIONS

TEGRETOL is used primarily in the treatment of epilepsy and psychomotor and grand mal seizure disorders, as well as mixed seizures. Due to the potential toxicity of this medication, TEGRETOL should be used only after other anticonvulsants have been tried and found to be ineffective.

ADVERSE EFFECTS

There are significant adverse effects associated with the use of TEGRETOL, and parents should be aware of these in order to detect signs of possible toxicity in their children as soon as possible. If you observe the following side effects, seek medical help as soon as possible:

- Most frequent side effects: nausea, vomiting, dizziness, and drowsiness.

- Liver: jaundice, destruction of liver, and hepatitis (which can be fatal).
- Central nervous system: dizziness, drowsiness, confusion, headache, blurred vision, fatigue, speech disturbances, depression, ringing in the ears, paralysis, behavior changes, and abnormal involuntary movements.
- Blood: abnormal reduction in blood components (which can be fatal).
- Gastrointestinal: nausea, vomiting, diarrhea, constipation, loss of appetite, abdominal pains, swelling of the tongue or gums, and dryness of the mouth.
- Urinary tract: frequent urination, kidney failure, urinary retention, and hypertension.
- Cardiovascular: abnormal rise or fall in blood pressure, water retention, abnormal heartbeats, and blood clots. Some of these side effects can be fatal.
- Dermatological: itching, rash, sensitivity to light, excessive sweating, lupus erythematosus, baldness, and alterations in skin pigmentation.
- Bone and muscle: pain in the joints and muscles, leg cramps, and softening of the bones.
- Ophthalmic: double vision and other vision changes, abnormal involuntary eye movements, and conjunctivitis.
- Lungs: fever, pneumonia, and difficulty breathing.

WARNINGS AND PRECAUTIONS

- TEGRETOL should not be used in children who have bleeding disorders.
- TEGRETOL should be used with caution in children with glaucoma or with cardiac, liver, or kidney disorders.
- If nausea or vomiting occur, give with food.
- Children taking TEGRETOL should be closely monitored to prevent or minimize the potential for serious adverse effects, and periodic testing for TEGRETOL serum levels should be performed by your doctor.

MEDICATION AND FOOD INTERACTIONS

- Erythromycin may increase the toxic effects of TEGRETOL.
- TEGRETOL may increase the liver-toxic effects of TYLENOL.

- TEGRETOL may decrease the effectiveness of COUMADIN, DI-LANTIN, CELONTIN, and DEPAKENE or DEPAKOTE when used together.
- The toxicity of both TEGRETOL and NYDRAZID may be increased when used together.
- TEGRETOL may decrease the effectiveness of Theophylline.

DOSAGE GUIDELINES
- Chewable tablets, oral suspension, and tablets:

    Children to 6 years: By mouth, 10–20 milligrams daily for each 2.2 pounds of body weight in 2–3 divided doses initially, then may be increased by up to 100 milligrams daily at weekly intervals until the seizures are controlled. Maximum daily dose should not exceed 400 milligrams in 3–4 divided doses.

    Children 6–12 years: By mouth, 100 milligrams twice daily the first day, then may be increased by 100 milligrams daily at weekly intervals until the seizures are controlled. Maximum daily maintenance dose should not exceed 1 gram in 3–4 divided doses.

BRAND NAME(S)
2. PHENURONE   Rx

GENERIC NAME
PHENACEMIDE

USES AND INDICATIONS
PHENURONE is used in epilepsy in treating complex partial (psychomotor) seizures that do not respond to other anticonvulsants. PHENURONE may be used alone or in combination with other anticonvulsants.

ADVERSE EFFECTS
As with other anticonvulsants, the adverse effects of PHENURONE may be serious, and parents should be alert for early signs of toxicity. These include changes in behavior, aggressiveness, appetite and weight loss, hepatitis (which can be fatal), abnormal decrease in blood components (including aplastic anemia, which can be fatal), skin rash, fatigue, muscle pain, headaches, insomnia, dizziness, drowsiness, loss of muscle coordination, tingling or numbness, abdominal pain, and unusual bleeding or bruising.

WARNINGS AND PRECAUTIONS

- Use with caution when giving PHENURONE with other anticonvulsants that have similar adverse effects.
- Use PHENURONE only after other, less toxic anticonvulsants have been tried and found to be ineffective.
- Use with caution in children who have a history of behavioral disorders.
- Use PHENURONE with extreme caution in children who have blood, liver, or kidney disorders.
- The abrupt withdrawal of PHENURONE, or rapid change in dosage, may cause seizure episodes.

MEDICATION AND FOOD INTERACTIONS

- The use of PHENURONE with PEGANONE may produce paranoia in children.
- The toxic effects of PHENURONE are increased when used with other anticonvulsants that have similar toxicity.

DOSAGE GUIDELINES

- Tablets:
  Children to 5 years: Use is not recommended.
  Children 5–10 years: By mouth, 250 milligrams 3 times daily initially; then, if necessary, may be increased in increments of 250 milligrams at 1-week intervals until the seizures are controlled. The maximum total daily dose should not exceed 2.5 grams given in divided doses.

COMMENTS

PHENURONE may be used in conjunction with other anticonvulsants or as a replacement for one or more anticonvulsants. When used as a replacement for other anticonvulsant therapy, the dose of PHENURONE should gradually be increased as the other drug is gradually decreased.

BRAND NAME(S)
3. MYSOLINE (and MYIDONE)   Rx

GENERIC NAME
PRIMIDONE

Uses and Indications

MYSOLINE is used in the treatment of epilepsy, either as a single agent or in combination with other anticonvulsants. It is used in grand mal epilepsy and in psychomotor and cortical focal seizures. It may control grand mal seizures that are unresponsive to other anticonvulsants.

In the body, MYSOLINE is reduced to form two by-products, both of which have their own anticonvulsant properties. One of these by-products, Phenobarbital, is an important medication used in the treatment of epilepsy.

Adverse Effects

The adverse effects of MYSOLINE include loss of muscle coordination, vertigo, nausea, vomiting, loss of appetite, anemia (which often responds to the administration of FOLVITE), fatigue, changes in behavior, hyperexcitability, paranoia, abnormal involuntary eye movements, double vision, drowsiness, skin eruptions, rash, wheezing, and tightness in the chest. Children may be especially prone to the hyperexcitability and restlessness caused by MYSOLINE.

Warnings and Precautions

- MYSOLINE should be used with caution in children who have a history of abnormal blood pigmentation or of liver, kidney, or respiratory disorders (asthma, emphysema, etc.).
- Children on MYSOLINE therapy should be periodically tested for complete blood cell counts, as well as MYSOLINE and Phenobarbital drug levels.
- Increases or decreases in the doses of MYSOLINE should be made gradually. Abrupt withdrawal may result in seizure episodes.

Medication and Food Interactions

- MYSOLINE may decrease the effectiveness of the following: TYLENOL, COUMADIN, corticosteroids (see Appendix II), tricyclic antidepressants (see Appendix II), VIBRAMYCIN, SYNTHROID, and Quinidine.
- Central nervous system depressants, antihistamines (see Appendix II), antihistamine/decongestant combinations (see Appendix II), benzodiazepines (see Appendix II), and products containing alcohol may increase the toxic effects of both drugs when used with MYSOLINE.
- The use of DEPAKENE or DEPAKOTE with MYSOLINE may in-

crease the effects of MYSOLINE while decreasing the effects of DEPAKENE or DEPAKOTE.

• MYSOLINE may increase the body's need for Ascorbic Acid and for Vitamins D and B_{12}.

• RITALIN may increase the toxic effects of MYSOLINE.

DOSAGE GUIDELINES
• Chewable tablets, oral suspension, and tablets:

Children to 8 years: By mouth, 50 milligrams at bedtime for 3 days, then may be increased to 50 milligrams twice daily for 3 days, and then may be increased to 100 milligrams twice daily for 3 days. On the tenth day, a dose of 125–250 milligrams (or 10–25 milligrams for each 2.2 pounds of body weight) may be given in divided doses as prescribed by a physician, and the dose may be adjusted until the seizures are controlled.

Children 8 years and older: By mouth, 100–125 milligrams once daily at bedtime for 3 days, then may be increased to 100–125 milligrams twice daily for 3 days, and then may be increased to 100–125 milligrams 3 times daily for 3 more days. On the tenth day, a dose of 250 milligrams 3 times daily may be given, and then the dose may be adjusted until the seizures are controlled. The usual maintenance dose is 250 milligrams 3–4 times daily; higher maintenance doses may be necessary but should not exceed 2 grams daily in 4 divided doses.

BRAND NAME(S)
4. DEPAKOTE   Rx
(Other brand: **DEPAKENE**)

GENERIC NAME
VALPROIC ACID DERIVATIVES

USES AND INDICATIONS
DEPAKOTE is used in various epileptic disorders, both as a single-agent treatment and as an adjunct in combination with other anticonvulsants for the treatment of simple and complex grand mal and petit mal seizures, myoclonic seizures, and mixed seizures. DEPAKOTE is also used in preventing recurrent seizures resulting from high fevers in children.

ADVERSE EFFECTS

The adverse effects of DEPAKOTE may be categorized as follows:

- Gastrointestinal: nausea, vomiting, diarrhea, constipation, abdominal cramps, increased appetite with weight gain, or loss of appetite with weight loss.
- Dermatological: rash, hair loss, and small nonraised purplish-red spots on the skin (hemorrhages).
- Bone and muscle: muscle weakness.
- Blood: unusual bleeding or bruising, anemia, and bone marrow suppression.
- Liver: severe liver toxicity (which can be fatal).
- Central nervous system: drowsiness, dizziness, loss of muscle coordination, tremors, double vision, abnormal involuntary eye movements, depression, psychotic behavior, difficulty speaking, emotional upset, aggressiveness, and hyperactivity.

MEDICATION AND FOOD INTERACTIONS

- TEGRETOL may decrease the effectiveness of DEPAKOTE.
- DEPAKOTE may increase the toxicity of hydantoins.

DOSAGE GUIDELINES

- Capsules, enteric coated tablets, and syrup:
  Children to 1 year: Use is not recommended.
  Children 1–12 years:
  - Used alone: By mouth, 15–45 milligrams daily for each 2.2 pounds of body weight initially, then may be increased at 1-week intervals by 5–10 milligrams daily for each 2.2 pounds of body weight until the seizures are controlled.
  - Used in combination therapy: By mouth, 30–100 milligrams daily for each 2.2 pounds of body weight initially, then may be increased at 1-week intervals by 5–10 milligrams daily for each 2.2 pounds of body weight until the seizures are controlled.

GROUP NAME
ANTIDEPRESSANTS, TRICYCLIC   Rx

1. AMITRIPTYLINE (AMITRIL, ELAVIL, EMITRIP, ENDEP). 2. DESIPRAMINE (NORPRAMIN, PERTOFRANE). 3. IMIPRAMINE (TOFRANIL).

USES AND INDICATIONS
In children, the tricyclic antidepressants are used in treating attention deficit disorders and bed-wetting.

ADVERSE EFFECTS
The most common adverse effect of tricyclics is sedation. Parents should immediately report any observed side effects, which may include:

- Cardiovascular: dizziness when standing, faintness, abnormal heartbeats (either slow or rapid).
- Central nervous system: confusion, lack of concentration, disorientation, hallucinations, nervousness, anxiety, agitation, restlessness, panic, inability to sleep, nightmares, drowsiness, fatigue, headache, and dizziness.
- Neurological: numbness of the extremities, tingling, loss of coordination, hyperactivity, shaking, seizures, ringing in the ears, and inability to speak.
- Atropine-like (anticholinergic): dry mouth, blurred vision, feeling of increased pressure in the eyes, dilated pupils, constipation, and difficulty urinating.
- Allergic: rash, itching, increased fluid retention (may include swelling of the face and tongue), fever, and sensitivity to light.
- Gastrointestinal: nausea and vomiting, loss of appetite, diarrhea, unusual taste sensation, swollen or black tongue, increased salivation, and stomach cramps.
- Endocrine: increased breast size in females and males.
- Other: nasal congestion, excessive appetite, weight gain or loss, flushing, chills, tearing of the eyes, increase in body temperature, and hair loss.

WARNINGS AND PRECAUTIONS

Tricyclic medications should be used with extreme caution in children who have seizure disorders; who have heart, kidney, or liver disorders; who have hyperthyroid disorders; who are taking thyroid medication; or who have a history of urinary retention.

MEDICATION AND FOOD INTERACTIONS

The following interactions apply to tricyclics as a group. While they are not all-inclusive, they are the more significant interactions observed clinically.

- Tricyclics increase the drying effects of SYMMETREL, antihistamines (see Appendix II), TEGRETOL, HALDOL, RITALIN, and Quinidine.
- Tricyclics may increase the effects of COUMADIN.
- Tricyclics may decrease the effectiveness of anticonvulsants (see Appendix II).
- TAGAMET may increase the toxic effects of tricyclic medications.
- RITALIN may increase the toxic effects of tricyclic medications; it may also have a decreased effect when used with tricyclic medications.
- Thyroid hormones (see Appendix II) may produce adverse heart effects.

BRAND NAME(S)
1. ELAVIL   Rx
(Other brands: **AMITRIL, EMITRIP, ENDEP**)
See also general information on tricyclic antidepressants on page 82.

GENERIC NAME
AMITRIPTYLINE

USES AND INDICATIONS

In children, ELAVIL is used in treating attention deficit disorders and bed-wetting.

ADVERSE EFFECTS

Drowsiness is greater with ELAVIL than with other tricyclic medications.

DOSAGE GUIDELINES
- Syrup:
  - Attention deficit disorders:
    Children to 12 years: Use is not recommended.
    Children 12 years and older: 0.3–2.0 milligrams per 2.2 pounds of body weight, administered orally in divided doses as prescribed by a physician, over 24 hours.
  - Bed-wetting:
    Children to 6 years: By mouth, 10 milligrams daily at bedtime.
    Children 6 years and older: By mouth, 10 milligrams daily at bedtime initially, then may be increased as necessary to 25 milligrams at bedtime.
- Tablets:
  Children to 6 years: Use is not recommended.
  Children 6–12 years: By mouth, 10–30 milligrams daily in 2 divided doses.

BRAND NAME(S)
2. NORPRAMIN (and PERTOFRANE)   Rx
See also general information on tricyclic antidepressants on page 82.

GENERIC NAME
DESIPRAMINE

USES AND INDICATIONS
In children, NORPRAMINE is used in treating attention deficit disorders.

DOSAGE GUIDELINES
- Capsules and tablets:
  Children to 6 years: Use is not recommended.
  Children 6–12 years: By mouth, 10–30 milligrams daily in divided doses as prescribed by a physician.

BRAND NAME(S)
3. TOFRANIL   Rx
See also general information on tricyclic antidepressants on page 82.

GENERIC NAME
IMIPRAMINE

USES AND INDICATIONS

In children, TOFRANIL is used in treating attention deficit disorders and bed-wetting.

DOSAGE GUIDELINES

- Tablets:
  - Attention deficit disorders:
    Children to 6 years: Use is not recommended.
    Children 6–12 years: By mouth, 10–30 milligrams daily in 2 divided doses.
  - Bed-wetting: By mouth, 25 milligrams 1 hour before bedtime. If this dose does not work, dose may be increased to 50 milligrams 1 hour before bedtime for children under 12 years, and to 75 milligrams 1 hour before bedtime for children over 12 years.

GROUP NAME
ANTIDIARRHEAL PREPARATIONS

1. BISMUTH SUBSALICYLATE (PEPTO-BISMOL). 2. KAOLIN/PECTIN (KAOPECTATE). 3. LOPERAMIDE (IMODIUM, IMODIUM A-D).

USES AND INDICATIONS

The antidiarrheal preparations act to prevent or treat diarrhea by both local and systemic actions. Some are available only with a doctor's prescription, and some may be purchased over the counter in pharmacies. Because of their diverse actions, cautions, and side effects, antidiarrheal medications are discussed individually below.

BRAND NAME(S)
1. PEPTO-BISMOL   OTC

GENERIC NAME
BISMUTH SUBSALICYLATE

USES AND INDICATIONS

PEPTO-BISMOL is used in treating heartburn, abdominal cramps, and diarrhea. It is often used in the prevention and treatment of traveler's diarrhea.

ADVERSE EFFECTS

The major adverse effects of PEPTO-BISMOL are constipation, ringing in the ears, dark or grayish stools, and fever.

WARNINGS AND PRECAUTIONS

- Do not use in children who are allergic to Aspirin-like products.
- PEPTO-BISMOL may cause constipation in small children and infants.
- If child has a fever, or if diarrhea persists for more than 2 days, contact your child's doctor.

MEDICATION AND FOOD INTERACTIONS

PEPTO-BISMOL may decrease the absorption and effectiveness of tetracyclines (see Appendix II).

DOSAGE GUIDELINES

- Chewable tablets:
  Children to 3 years: Use is not recommended.
  Children 3–6 years: Chew or dissolve ⅓ tablet in mouth every 30 minutes to 1 hour, up to 8 doses in 24 hours, as necessary.
  Children 6–9 years: Chew or dissolve ⅔ tablet in mouth every 30 minutes to 1 hour, up to 8 doses in 24 hours, as necessary.
  Children 9–12 years: Chew or dissolve 1 tablet in mouth every 30 minutes to 1 hour, up to 8 doses in 24 hours, as necessary.
- Oral suspension:
  Children to 3 years: Use is not recommended.
  Children 3–6 years: By mouth, 5 milliliters (1 teaspoonful) every 30 minutes to 1 hour, up to 8 doses in 24 hours, as necessary.
  Children 6–9 years: By mouth, 10 milliliters (2 teaspoonsful) every 30 minutes to 1 hour, up to 8 doses in 24 hours, as necessary.
  Children 9–12 years: By mouth, 15 milliliters (1 tablespoonful) every 30 minutes to 1 hour, up to 8 doses in 24 hours, as necessary.

COMMENTS

The oral suspension of PEPTO-BISMOL should be shaken well before using.

BRAND NAME(S)
2. KAOPECTATE   OTC

GENERIC NAME
KAOLIN/PECTIN

USES AND INDICATIONS

KAOPECTATE, relatively unabsorbed by mouth, is used to remove bacteria and toxins from the gastrointestinal tract while reducing the loss of water and salts that results from diarrhea.

ADVERSE EFFECTS

The major adverse effect of KAOPECTATE is constipation, particularly in children.

WARNINGS AND PRECAUTIONS

- Diarrhea may cause significant loss of fluid and salts in small infants and children.
- If diarrhea continues more than 48 hours, contact your child's doctor.

MEDICATION AND FOOD INTERACTIONS

KAOPECTATE may decrease the absorption of LINCOCIN and LANOXIN.

DOSAGE GUIDELINES

- Oral suspension:
  Children to 3 years: Dosage must be individualized for the patient.
  Children 3–6 years: By mouth, 15 milliliters (1 tablespoonful) of the concentrate, or 15–30 milliliters (1–2 tablespoonsful) of the regular-strength suspension, after each loose bowel movement.
  Children 6–12 years: By mouth, 30 milliliters (2 tablespoonsful) of the concentrate, or 60 milliliters (4 tablespoonsful) of the regular-strength suspension, after each loose bowel movement.
  Children 12 years and older: By mouth, 45 milliliters (3 tablespoonsful) of the concentrate, or 60 milliliters (4 tablespoonsful) of the regular-strength suspension, after each loose bowel movement.

COMMENTS

Oral suspensions of KAOPECTATE, to be shaken well before use, should be administered after each loose bowel movement until the diarrhea is controlled.

BRAND NAME(S)
3. IMODIUM (and IMODIUM A-D) Rx

GENERIC NAME
LOPERAMIDE

USES AND INDICATIONS
IMODIUM, used in treating both acute and chronic diarrhea, acts directly on the smooth muscles of the intestinal walls to slow intestinal movement. It also prevents the fluid and salt loss that occurs with diarrhea.

ADVERSE EFFECTS
The major adverse effects of IMODIUM include abdominal cramps, dry mouth, constipation, nausea, vomiting, skin rash, and drowsiness.

OVERDOSAGE: The symptoms of overdosage include central nervous system depression, constipation, nausea, vomiting, and stomach cramps. If these symptoms are observed, call your doctor.

WARNINGS AND PRECAUTIONS

- IMODIUM should be used cautiously in children who are dehydrated or who have electrolyte disorders, and it is not recommended for use in children under 2 years of age or in children who have chronic diarrhea.
- IMODIUM is not recommended in children with ulcerative colitis and in children with liver disorders.
- If diarrhea persists for more than 2 days, contact your child's doctor.

DOSAGE GUIDELINES
- Capsules and oral solution:
  By mouth, 80–240 micrograms daily for each 2.2 pounds of body weight in 2–3 divided doses.

  Or:
  Children to 2 years: Use is not recommended.
  Children 2–5 years: By mouth, 1 milligram 3 times daily as needed.
  Children 5–8 years: By mouth, 2 milligrams twice daily as needed.

Children 8–12 years: By mouth, 2 milligrams 3 times daily as needed.

GROUP NAME
ANTIFUNGAL AGENTS

1. CLIOQUINOL (VIOFORM). 2. CLIOQUINOL/HYDROCORTISONE (VIOFORM-HC). 3. CLOTRIMAZOLE (LOTRIMIN, MYCELEX). 4. FLUCYTOSINE (ANCOBON). 5. GRISEOFULVIN (FULVICIN P/G, FULVICIN U/F, GRIFULVIN V, GRISACTIN, GRISACTIN ULTRA, AND OTHERS). 6. NYSTATIN (MYCOSTATIN, NILSTAT). 7. NYSTATIN/ TRIAMCINOLONE (MYCO II, MYCOBIOTIC II, MYCOGEN II, MYCOLOG II, MYCO-TRIACET, MYTREX, AND OTHERS). 8. TOLNAFTATE (AFTATE, GENASPORE, NP-27, TINACTIN, TING, ZEASORB-AF).

USES AND INDICATIONS
Antifungal medications are used in treating infections caused by fungi (fungal organisms are often difficult to treat) and yeast. Some antifungal medications are also active against bacteria and protozoa.

BRAND NAME(S)
1. VIOFORM   OTC

GENERIC NAME
CLIOQUINOL

USES AND INDICATIONS
VIOFORM is used in treating fungal infections of the skin and nails, athlete's foot, and minor bacterial skin infections.

ADVERSE EFFECTS
The major adverse effects of VIOFORM are skin rash, itching, and other skin irritations.

WARNINGS AND PRECAUTIONS

- Children who are allergic to iodine or iodine-containing preparations may also be hypersensitive to VIOFORM.
- Use is not recommended in children under 2 years.

- VIOFORM may interfere with the diagnostic test for thyroid function.
- VIOFORM may stain skin and clothing yellow.

DOSAGE GUIDELINES
- Cream and ointment:
  Children to 2 years: Use is not recommended.
  Children over 2 years: Apply to the affected area 2–4 times daily.

BRAND NAME(S)
2. VIOFORM-HC   Rx

GENERIC NAME
CLIOQUINOL/HYDROCORTISONE

USES AND INDICATIONS
VIOFORM-HC is used in treating atopic dermatitis, contact dermatitis, eczema, anogenital itching, and minor skin infections with inflammation.

The use of VIOFORM-HC in children under 2 years is not recommended, and the treatment period in children over 2 years should not exceed 2 weeks. For additional information, see *1. VIOFORM* (page 89).

DOSAGE GUIDELINES
- Cream, lotion, and ointment:
  Children to 2 years: Use is not recommended.
  Children over 2 years: Apply to the affected area 2–4 times daily.

COMMENTS
VIOFORM-HC lotion should be shaken well before use. The cream and ointment are available in strengths that contain 0.5% and 1% Hydrocortisone.

BRAND NAME(S)
3. LOTRIMIN (and MYCELEX)   Rx

GENERIC NAME
CLOTRIMAZOLE

USES AND INDICATIONS

LOTRIMIN is used in treating athlete's foot, ringworm, jock itch, and other related fungal infections.

ADVERSE EFFECTS

The major adverse effects of LOTRIMIN are related to the dosage form: nausea, vomiting, stomach cramps, and diarrhea for the oral dosage form; and hypersensitivity reactions, e.g., skin rash, itching, burning, peeling, and skin eruptions, for the topical dosage forms.

DOSAGE GUIDELINES

- Cream and ointment:
  Apply to affected skin area twice daily, morning and evening.
- Oral troches:
  Children to 4 years: Use is not recommended.
  Children over 4 years: Dissolve 1 troche slowly in mouth 5 times a day for at least 14 days. Children who are taking medications that suppress the body's natural defense mechanisms (e.g., corticosteroids) may require a longer treatment period.

BRAND NAME(S)
4. ANCOBON   Rx

GENERIC NAME
FLUCYTOSINE

USES AND INDICATIONS

ANCOBON is used in treating fungal infections of the lungs and urinary tract, fungal meningitis, and widespread infections caused by fungi. ANCOBON produces its antifungal effect by interfering with the production of essential substances in fungi.

ADVERSE EFFECTS

The following adverse effects of ANCOBON may require medical attention: mental confusion, hallucinations, sore throat, fever, skin rash, unusual weakness, and bleeding or bruising. Other, less serious adverse effects include nausea, vomiting, diarrhea, headache, and dizziness or drowsiness.

WARNINGS AND PRECAUTIONS

- ANCOBON should be used with caution in children with liver or kidney disorders or with blood disorders (bone marrow depression).
- Testing for blood, kidney, and liver functions should be performed during therapy with ANCOBON.
- In children with impaired kidney function, a change in dosage and dosage frequency may be required.

MEDICATION AND FOOD INTERACTIONS

The potential toxicity of ANCOBON on the kidney, liver, or blood may be increased if used with other medications that have similar adverse effects.

DOSAGE GUIDELINES

- Capsules: By mouth, 12.5–37.5 milligrams for each 2.2 pounds of body weight every 6 hours.

BRAND NAME(S)
5. GRIFULVIN V   Rx
(Other brands: **FULVICIN P/G, FULVICIN U/F, GRISACTIN, GRISACTIN ULTRA,** and others)

GENERIC NAME
GRISEOFULVIN

USES AND INDICATIONS

GRIFULVIN V is used in treating systemic infections caused by fungi. It acts as an antifungal agent by interfering with the cells' reproductive function.

ADVERSE EFFECTS

The following adverse effects of GRIFULVIN V may require medical attention: mental confusion, skin rash, itching, soreness of the tongue or mouth, and sensitivity to sunlight. Other, less serious effects include nausea, vomiting, diarrhea, headache, dizziness, unusual tiredness, stomach pain, and difficulty sleeping.

WARNINGS AND PRECAUTIONS

- GRIFULVIN V should be used with caution in children with lupus, porphyria, or liver disorders.
- Alcohol-containing products should not be used in children taking GRIFULVIN V.
- GRIFULVIN V should be taken with meals, or shortly after meals, to avoid upset stomach.

MEDICATION AND FOOD INTERACTIONS

- GRIFULVIN V used with alcohol-containing products may cause excessive sweating, flushing, and rapid heartbeats.
- GRIFULVIN V may decrease the effectiveness of COUMADIN.
- The use of MYSOLINE may decrease the effects of GRIFULVIN V.
- There may be increased sensitivity to sunlight when GRIFULVIN V is used with other medications having a similar effect.

DOSAGE GUIDELINES
- Capsules, oral suspension, and tablets:
  - Microsize products (FULVICIN U/F, GRIFULVIN V, GRISAC-TIN):
  Children to 31 pounds: Use is not recommended.
  Children 31–51 pounds: By mouth, 62.5–125 milligrams every 12 hours, or 125–250 milligrams once a day.
  Children over 51 pounds: By mouth, 125–250 milligrams every 12 hours, or 250–500 milligrams once a day.
  - Ultramicrosize tablets (FULVICIN P/G, GRISACTIN ULTRA):
  Children to 2 years: Dose has not been established.
  Children 31–51 pounds: By mouth, 31.25–82.5 milligrams every 12 hours, or 62.5–165 milligrams once a day.
  Children over 51 pounds: By mouth, 62.5–165 milligrams every 12 hours, or 125–330 milligrams once a day.

COMMENTS
GRIFULVIN V oral suspension should be shaken well before use.

BRAND NAME(S)
6. MYCOSTATIN (and NILSTAT) Rx

GENERIC NAME
NYSTATIN

USES AND INDICATIONS

MYCOSTATIN is an antifungal agent used in the treatment of various fungal and yeast infections of the skin and vaginal areas, as well as systemic infections caused by these organisms.

ADVERSE EFFECTS

The adverse effects of MYCOSTATIN include skin rash, nausea, vomiting, diarrhea, and stomach pains.

WARNINGS AND PRECAUTIONS

- The use of MYCOSTATIN lozenges should be avoided in children under 5 years of age.
- When treating candidiasis in infants and small children, occlusive dressings, such as diapers or rubber pants, should not be worn over the medication.

DOSAGE GUIDELINES

- Cream, ointment, and topical powder: Apply to the affected area of the skin 2–3 times daily.
- Lozenges:
  Children to 5 years: Use is not recommended.
  Children 5 years and older: Dissolve 1–2 lozenges slowly in the mouth 4–5 times daily for up to 14 days. Do not chew or swallow the lozenge before it has dissolved.
- Oral suspension (the oral suspension may be used for systemic infections, in which case the suspension is swallowed; or for treating fungal infections of the mouth or tongue, in which case the suspension may be swished around in the mouth for several seconds and then spit out, or as directed by the physician):
  Premature and small infants: By mouth, 100,000 units 4 times daily.
  Older infants: By mouth, 200,000 units 4 times daily.
  Children: By mouth, 500,000 units 4 times daily.
- Oral tablets:
  Premature and small infants: Use oral suspension.
  Children: By mouth, 500,000 units 4 times daily.

COMMENTS

MYCOSTATIN oral suspensions should be shaken well before using, and the lozenges stored in a refrigerator.

BRAND NAME(S)
7. MYCOLOG II   Rx
(Other brands: **MYCO II, MYCOBIOTIC II, MYCOGEN II, MYCO-TRIACET, MYTREX,** and others)

GENERIC NAME
NYSTATIN/TRIAMCINOLONE

USES AND INDICATIONS

MYCOLOG II is used in treating fungal infections accompanied by inflammation.

DOSAGE GUIDELINES

- Cream: Apply to the affected area of the skin twice daily, morning and evening.
- Ointment: Apply to the affected area of the skin 2–3 times daily.

BRAND NAME(S)
8. TINACTIN   OTC
(Other brands: **AFTATE, GENASPORE, NP-27, TING, ZEASORB-AF**)

GENERIC NAME
TOLNAFTATE

USES AND INDICATIONS

TINACTIN is used in treating athlete's foot and jock itch.

ADVERSE EFFECTS

The adverse effects of TINACTIN are mainly skin rash and other skin irritations. The aerosol may produce a stinging sensation.

WARNINGS AND PRECAUTIONS

- Use is not recommended for children under 2 years.
- Contact with the eyes should be avoided.

DOSAGE GUIDELINES

- Aerosol powder, aerosol solution, cream, gel, topical powder, topical solution, and topical spray solution:
  Children to 2 years: Use is not recommended.
  Children 2 years and older: Spray or apply to affected area twice daily.

COMMENTS

The aerosol powder and solution should be shaken well before use. Treatment should be continued for 2 weeks after the symptoms have disappeared to prevent reinfection.

GROUP NAME
ANTIHISTAMINES

1. BROMPHENIRAMINE (DIMETANE). 2. CHLORPHENIRAMINE (ALLER-CHLOR, CHLOR-TRIMETON, PEDIACARE ALLERGY FORMULA). 3. CYPROHEPTADINE (PERIACTIN). 4. DIMENHYDRINATE (DRAMAMINE, MOTION-AID). 5. DIPHENHYDRAMINE (BENADRYL, BENYLIN COUGH). 6. DIPHENYLPYRALINE (HISPRIL). 7. DOXYLAMINE (UNISOM NIGHTTIME SLEEP AID). 8. HYDROXYZINE (ATARAX, VISTARIL). 9. PROMETHAZINE (PHENERGAN). 10. PYRILAMINE (DORMAREX). 11. TRIMEPRAZINE (TEMARIL). 12. TRIPELENNAMINE (PBZ). 13. TRIPROLIDINE (ACTIDIL, ALLERACT).

USES AND INDICATIONS

Antihistamines act by blocking the effects of histamine, a natural chemical found in cells throughout the body. It is released when a foreign substance comes in contact with, or is introduced into, the body. When released, histamine produces a "histamine reaction," the effects of which range from mild symptoms, such as itching, rash, and watery eyes, to a severe anaphylactic reaction, which may result in shock, collapse of blood circulation, and, possibly, death. When a child experiences an allergic reaction to dust, to pollen, or to a medication, the symptoms experienced are the result of a histamine reaction. In theory, any child may be allergic to any medication.

As a medication group, antihistamines are among the most widely used of all pharmacological products. They are used in single-ingredient products and in combination with other medications. Antihistamines are used in many clinical situations, including allergies, hay fever, itching, rash, nausea, vomiting, insect bites, motion sickness, coughs and colds, and watery eyes and runny nose. Antihistamines share several common characteristics: They block the effects of histamine; they dry secretions; they exhibit antinauseant effects; and they produce sedation. Often, the choice as to which antihistamine to use is determined by which of these effects is most desired—for example, the use of an antihistamine with a high "drying" effect for a runny nose; or one with a strong antinauseant effect for nausea and vomiting; or one with strong antihistamine properties for itchy eyes and rash.

The table below lists the antihistamines by their generic names and gives their significant properties as antihistamines. The properties are identified by the terms "none" (no effect), "low" (little effect), "moderate" (moderate effect), and "high" (significant effect). For more information, see also *Antihistamine/Decongestant Combinations* (page 105) and *Cough and Cold Preparations* (page 148).

ANTIHISTAMINE	ANTIHISTAMINE PROPERTIES	ANTICHOLINERGIC PROPERTIES	ANTINAUSEANT PROPERTIES	SEDATIVE PROPERTIES
Brompheniramine	high	moderate	none	low
Chlorpheniramine	moderate	moderate	none	low
Cyproheptadine	moderate	moderate	none	low
Diphenhydramine	moderate	high	high	high
Diphenhylpyraline	moderate	moderate	none	low
Promethazine	high	high	high	high
Pyrilamine	moderate	low	none	low
Trimeprazine	high	high	high	moderate
Tripelennamine	moderate	low	none	moderate
Triprolidine	high	moderate	none	low

ADVERSE EFFECTS
The major adverse effects of antihistamines are sedation and dry mouth.

WARNINGS AND PRECAUTIONS

- Antihistamines should not be used in children who have previously been allergic to an antihistamine, or in newborn or premature infants.
- They should be used with caution in children with cardiac disorders, glaucoma, hyperthyroidism, or bronchial asthma.

MEDICATION AND FOOD INTERACTIONS

Potential interactions with antihistamines (see Appendix II) are numerous. In general, antihistamines should not be administered with other depressant-type medications, including alcohol-containing products and tricyclic antidepressants (see Appendix II). The use of these medications together will increase the depressant effects of both medications. Infants and young children may be particularly sensitive to the toxic effects of these medications.

DOSAGE GUIDELINES

Following are dosage guidelines for some commonly used antihistamines, listed by generic name.

1. **Brompheniramine** (DIMETANE): Rx, OTC
   - Elixir and tablets:
     Children to 2 years: By mouth, 0.5 milligram for each 2.2 pounds of body weight in 3–4 divided doses as needed.
     Children 2–6 years: By mouth, 1 milligram every 4–6 hours as needed.
     Children 6–12 years: By mouth, 2 milligrams every 4–6 hours as needed.
     Children 12 years and older: By mouth, 4 milligrams every 4–6 hours as needed.

2. **Chlorpheniramine** (ALLER-CHLOR, CHLOR-TRIMETON, PEDIACARE ALLERGY FORMULA): Rx and OTC:
   - Chewable tablets, syrup, and tablets:
     Children to 6 years: Use is not recommended.
     Children 6–12 years: By mouth, 2 milligrams 3–4 times daily as needed.
   - Extended-release capsules and tablets:
     Children to 12 years: Use is not recommended.
     Children 12 years and older: By mouth, 8 milligrams every 12 hours as needed.

3. **Cyproheptadine** (PERIACTIN): Rx
- Syrup and tablets:
  Children to 2 years: By mouth, 125 micrograms for each 2.2 pounds of body weight every 8–12 hours as needed.
  Children 2–6 years: By mouth, 2 milligrams every 8–12 hours as needed, not to exceed 12 milligrams daily.
  Children 6–14 years: By mouth, 4 milligrams every 8–12 hours as needed, not to exceed 16 milligrams daily.

4. **Dimenhydrinate** (DRAMAMINE, MOTION-AID): OTC
- Chewable tablets, elixir, syrup, and tablets:
  Children to 2 years: Use is not recommended.
  Children 2–6 years: By mouth, 12.5–25 milligrams every 6–8 hours as needed, not to exceed 75 milligrams daily.
  Children 6–12 years: By mouth, 25–50 milligrams every 6–8 hours as needed, not to exceed 150 milligrams daily.
- Suppositories:
  Children to 6 years: Use is not recommended.
  Children 6–8 years: By rectum, 12.5–25 milligrams every 8–12 hours as needed.
  Children 8–12 years: By rectum, 25–50 milligrams every 8–12 hours as needed.
  Children 12 years and older: By rectum, 50 milligrams every 8–12 hours as needed.

5. **Diphenhydramine** (BENADRYL, BENYLIN COUGH): Rx, OTC
- Capsules, elixir, syrup, and tablets:
  – Antihistamine:
    Premature infants and newborns: Use is not recommended.
    Children up to 20 pounds: By mouth, 6.25–12.5 milligrams every 4–6 hours as needed.
    Children over 20 pounds: By mouth, 12.5–25 milligrams every 4–6 hours as needed.
  – Nausea and vomiting or motion sickness: By mouth, 1–1.5 milligrams for each 2.2 pounds of body weight every 4–6 hours as needed, not to exceed 300 milligrams daily.

6. **Diphenylpyraline** (HISPRIL): Rx
- Extended-release capsules:
  Children to 6 years: Use is not recommended.
  Children 6 years and older: By mouth, 5 milligrams once daily as needed.

7. Doxylamine (UNISOM NIGHTTIME SLEEP AID): OTC
- Tablets:
  Children to 6 years: Use is not recommended.
  Children 6–12 years: By mouth, 6.25–12.5 milligrams every 4–6 hours as needed.

8. Hydroxyzine (ATARAX, VISTARIL): Rx
- Capsules, tablets, and oral suspension:
  Antianxiety and sleep aid: By mouth, 0.6 milligram for each 2.2 pounds of body weight as a single dose.
  Antihistamine and for vomiting:
  - Capsules:
    Children to 6 years: By mouth, 30–50 milligrams daily in divided doses.
    Children 6–12 years: By mouth, 50–100 milligrams daily in divided doses.
  - Oral suspension, syrup, and tablets:
    Children to 6 years: By mouth, 12.5 milligrams every 6 hours as needed.
    Children 6 years and older: By mouth, 12.5–25 milligrams every 6 hours as needed.

9. Promethazine (PHENERGAN): Rx
Not recommended in premature infants and neonates.
- Syrup and tablets:
  Antihistamine: By mouth, 125 micrograms for each 2.2 pounds of body weight every 4–6 hours, or 0.5 milligram for each 2.2 pounds of body weight at bedtime as needed; or 6.25–12.5 milligrams 3 times daily, or 25 milligrams at bedtime as needed.
  Nausea and vomiting: By mouth, 0.25–0.5 milligram for each 2.2 pounds of body weight every 4–6 hours as needed, or 12.5–25 milligrams every 4–6 hours as needed.
  Motion sickness: By mouth, 0.5 milligrams for each 2.2 pounds of body weight every 12 hours as needed, or 12.5–25 milligrams every 12 hours as needed.
  Sleep aid: By mouth, 0.5–1 milligram for each 2.2 pounds of body weight at bedtime as needed; or 12.5–25 milligrams at bedtime as needed.
- Suppositories:
  Antihistamine: By rectum, 125 micrograms for each 2.2 pounds of body weight every 4–6 hours, or 0.5 milligram for each 2.2

pounds of body weight at bedtime as needed; or 6.25–12.5 milligrams 3 times daily, or 25 milligrams at bedtime as needed.

Nausea and vomiting: By rectum, 250–500 micrograms for each 2.2 pounds of body weight every 4–6 hours as needed; or 12.5–25 milligrams every 4–6 hours as needed.

Motion sickness: By rectum, 0.5 milligram for each 2.2 pounds of body weight every 12 hours as needed; or 12.5–25 milligrams every 12 hours as needed.

Sleep aid: By rectum, 0.5–1 milligram for each 2.2 pounds of body weight at bedtime as needed; or 12.5–25 milligrams at bedtime as needed.

10. Pyrilamine (DORMAREX): OTC
  • Capsules and tablets:
  Children to 6 years: Use is not recommended.
  Children 6 years and older: By mouth, 12.5–25 milligrams every 8 hours as needed.

11. Trimeprazine (TEMARIL): Rx
  • Extended-release capsule:
  Children to 6 years: Use is not recommended.
  Children 6 years and older: By mouth, 5 milligrams once daily as needed.
  Syrup and tablets:
  Premature infants and neonates: Use is not recommended.
  Children 6 months to 3 years: By mouth, 1.25 milligrams at bedtime, or 2.5 milligrams 3 times daily as needed.
  Children 3 years and older: By mouth, 2.5 milligrams at bedtime, or 2.5 milligrams 3 times daily as needed.

12. Tripelennamine (PBZ): Rx
  • Elixir and tablets:
  Premature infants and neonates: Use is not recommended.
  Infants and Children: By mouth, 1.25 milligrams for each 2.2 pounds of body weight every 6 hours as needed, not to exceed 300 milligrams daily.

13. Triprolidine (ACTIDIL, ALLERACT): Rx, OTC
  • Syrup and tablets:
  Premature infants and neonates: Use is not recommended.
  Children 4 months to 2 years: By mouth, 312 micrograms every 6–8 hours as needed.

Children 2–4 years: By mouth, 625 micrograms every 6–8 hours as needed.

Children 4–6 years: By mouth, 937 micrograms every 6–8 hours as needed.

Children 6–12 years: By mouth, 1.25 milligrams every 6–8 hours as needed.

GROUP NAME

ANTIHISTAMINE/ DECONGESTANT/ ANALGESIC COMBINATIONS

1. CHLORPHENIRAMINE/PHENYLEPHRINE WITH ACETAMINOPHEN (ADVANCED FORMULA DRISTAN). 2. CHLORPHENIRAMINE/PHENYLPROPANOLAMINE WITH ACETAMINOPHEN (ALLEREST HEADACHE STRENGTH, CORICIDIN 'D' DECONGESTANT, CORICIDIN DEMILETS, SINAREST, TYLENOL COLD MEDICATION). 3. CHLORPHENIRAMINE/PSEUDOEPHEDRINE WITH ACETAMINOPHEN (CHILDREN'S COTYLENOL, CODIMAL, MAXIMUM STRENGTH TYLENOL ALLERGY SINUS). 4. CHLORPHENIRAMINE/ PHENYLPROPANOLAMINE WITH ASPIRIN (SINE-OFF SINUS MEDICINE).

USES AND INDICATIONS

The combinations of antihistamines, decongestants, and analgesics are used in treating the temporary symptoms associated with colds, flu, and nasal and sinus congestions, including runny or stuffy nose, headache, and the aches and pains that accompany flu.

For more information regarding uses and indications, adverse effects, warnings and precautions, and medication and food interactions, see the general monograph for antihistamines (page 96) and that for antihistamine/decongestant combinations (page 105).

DOSAGE GUIDELINES

The following products are listed by brand or proprietary names.

1. ADVANCED FORMULA DRISTAN (Chlorpheniramine/ Phenylephrine with Acetaminophen): OTC
- Coated caplets and tablets:
  Children to 6 years: Use is not recommended.

Children 6–12 years: By mouth, 1 caplet or tablet every 4 hours as needed.

2. **ALLEREST HEADACHE STRENGTH** (Chlorpheniramine/Phenyl-propanolamine with Acetaminophen): OTC
   • Tablets:
   Children to 6 years: Use is not recommended.
   Children 6–12 years: By mouth, 1 tablet every 4 hours as needed.

   CORICIDIN 'D' DECONGESTANT (Chlorpheniramine/Phenyl-propanolamine with Acetaminophen): OTC
   • Tablets:
   Children to 6 years: Use is not recommended.
   Children 6–11 years: By mouth, 1 tablet every 4 hours as needed.

   CORICIDIN DEMILETS (Chlorpheniramine/Phenylpropanol-amine with Acetaminophen): OTC
   • Chewable tablets:
   Children to 6 years: Use is not recommended.
   Children over 6 years: By mouth, chew 2 tablets every 4 hours as needed.

   SINAREST (Chlorpheniramine/Phenylpropanolamine with Acet-aminophen): OTC
   • Tablets:
   Children to 6 years: Use is not recommended.
   Children 6–12 years: By mouth, 1 tablet every 4 hours as needed.

   TYLENOL COLD MEDICATION (Chlorpheniramine/Phenylpro-panolamine with Acetaminophen): OTC
   • Effervescent tablets:
   Children to 6 years: Use is not recommended.
   Children 6–11 years: By mouth, 1 tablet dissolved in water every 4 hours.

3. **CHILDREN'S COTYLENOL** (Chlorpheniramine/Pseudoephedrine with Acetaminophen): OTC
   • Oral solution (alcohol-free):
   Children to 2 years: Use is not recommended.
   Children 2–5 years: By mouth, 5 milliliters (1 teaspoonful) every 4–6 hours as needed.

Children 6–11 years: By mouth, 10 milliliters (2 teaspoonsful) every 4–6 hours as needed.
• Chewable tablets:
Children to 2 years: Use is not recommended.
Children 2–5 years: By mouth, 2 tablets every 4–6 hours as needed.
Children 6–11 years: By mouth, 4 tablets every 4–6 hours as needed.

CODIMAL (Chlorpheniramine/Pseudoephedrine with Acetaminophen): OTC
• Capsules and coated tablets:
Children to 6 years: Use is not recommended.
Children 6–12 years: By mouth, 1 capsule or tablet every 4–6 hours as needed.

MAXIMUM   STRENGTH   TYLENOL   ALLERGY   SINUS (Chlorpheniramine/Pseudoephedrine with Acetaminophen): OTC
• Tablets:
Children to 6 years: Use is not recommended.
Children 6–12 years: By mouth, 1 tablet every 4–6 hours as needed.

4. SINE-OFF SINUS MEDICINE (Chlorpheniramine/Phenylpropanolamine with Aspirin): OTC
• Tablets:
Children to 6 years: Use is not recommended.
Children 6–12 years: By mouth, 1 tablet every 4 hours as needed.

COMMENTS

Antihistamine combinations should be used only for short periods and only if they are needed to relieve the symptoms of colds, flu, or nasal and sinus congestion. If symptoms persist for more than 2–3 days, this may mean that a more serious condition exists and that your child should be seen by a doctor.

GROUP NAME

Antihistamine/ Decongestant Combinations

1. Brompheniramine/Phenylpropanolamine (BROMATAP, DIMETAPP).
2. Brompheniramine/Pseudoephedrine (BROMFED, BROMFED-PD, DRIXORAL). 3. Carbinoxamine/Pseudoephedrine (CARBODEC, CARDEC-S, RONDEC). 4. Chlorpheniramine/Pseudoephedrine (CO-PYRONIL 2 PEDIATRIC, DECONAMINE, DORCOL CHILDREN'S COLD FORMULA, DURA-TAP PD, FEDAHIST, KRONOFED-A JR., PEDIACARE COLD FORMULA, RYNA, SUDAFED PLUS, T-DRY JUNIOR). 5. Diphenhydramine/Pseudoephedrine (BENYLIN DECONGESTANT). 6. Phenylephrine/Brompheniramine (DIMETANE DECONGESTANT). 7. Phenylephrine/Chlorpheniramine (COLTAB CHILDREN'S, NOVAHISTINE). 8. Phenylephrine/Chlorpheniramine with Pyrilamine (R-TANNATE, RYNATAN). 9. Phenylephrine/ Phenylpropanolamine with Pyrilamine/Chlorpheniramine (HISTALET FORTE). 10. Phenylpropanolamine/Chlorpheniramine (ALLEREST, A.R.M. MAXIMUM STRENGTH, CORSYM, DEMAZIN, GENAMIN, MYMINIC, NORAMINIC, SNAPLETS-D, TRIAMINIC ALLERGY, TRIAMINIC CHEWABLES, TRIAMINIC COLD, TRIND).
11. Phenylpropanolamine/Pheniramine with Pyrilamine (TRIAMINIC ORAL INFANT DROPS). 12. Phenylpropanolamine/Phenylephrine with Phenyltoloxamine/Chlorpheniramine (AMARIL D, NALDECON, NEW-DECONGEST, TRI-PHEN-CHLOR). 13. Phenylpropanolamine/ Phenyltoloxamine with Pyrilamine/Pheniramine (POLY-HISTINE-D PED). 14. Promethazine/Phenylephrine (PHENERGAN VC, PROMETH PLAIN). 15. Triprolidine/Pseudoephedrine (ACTIFED).

Uses and Indications

Antihistamine/decongestant combinations are used to provide temporary relief from the sneezing, nasal congestion, and nasal discharge often associated with allergies and the common cold. Decongestants constrict the nasal vessels and, combined with the action of the antihistamine component, provide a drying effect in the nose.

ADVERSE EFFECTS

Many physicians question the value of many of the antihistamine/ decongestant combinations. They feel that using single-ingredient products is more effective and produces fewer undesirable effects, particularly in infants and small children.

The potential adverse effects include irregular heartbeats; tiredness or weakness; sore throat and fever; bleeding or bruising; severe dryness of the mouth, nose, or throat; tightness of the chest; difficulty breathing; drowsiness; seizures; difficulty sleeping; hallucinations; flushing; headache; trembling or shaking; muscle spasms in the neck or back; restlessness; blurred vision; confusion; loss of appetite; ringing in the ears; and rash.

WARNINGS AND PRECAUTIONS

Antihistamine/decongestant combinations should be avoided or used with caution in children, particularly those with acute asthma, heart disease, glaucoma, diabetes, high blood pressure, or hyperthyroidism. They should not be used in premature infants and newborns. For more information, see general monographs for antihistamines (page 96) and cough and cold preparations (page 148).

MEDICATION AND FOOD INTERACTIONS

- Antihistamine/decongestant combinations used concurrently with other central nervous system depressants may increase the sedative effects of both medications; these include other antihistamines (see Appendix II), tricyclic antidepressants (see Appendix II), and benzodiazepines (see Appendix II).
- Phenylpropanolamine, Pseudoephedrine, and Phenylephrine may increase the cardio-toxic effects of LANOXIN.
- Phenylpropanolamine and Pseudoephedrine may increase the effects of central nervous system stimulant medications, e.g., amphetamines (see Appendix II).

For more information regarding interactions, see general monographs for antihistamines (page 96) and cough and cold preparations (page 148).

DOSAGE GUIDELINES

The following products are listed by generic name.

1. **Brompheniramine/Phenylpropanolamine** (BROMATAP, DIME-
   TAPP): OTC
   - Elixir:
     Children 1–6 months: By mouth, 1.25 milliliters 3–4 times daily
       as needed.
     Children 7 months–2 years: By mouth, 2.5 milliliters 3–4 times
       daily as needed.
     Children 2–4 years: By mouth, 3.75 milliliters 3–4 times daily as
       needed.
     Children 4–12 years: By mouth, 5 milliliters (1 teaspoonful) 3–4
       times daily as needed.
     Children 12 years and older: See adult dose.
   - Extended-release capsules:
     Children to 6 years: Use is not recommended.
     Children 6 years and older: By mouth, 1 capsule every 12 hours
       as needed.

2. **Brompheniramine/Pseudoephedrine** (BROMFED, BROMFED-PD,
   DRIXORAL): Rx, OTC
   - Syrup:
     Children to 6 years: Must be individualized for patients.
     Children 6–12 years: By mouth, 5 milliliters (1 teaspoonful) every
       4–6 hours as needed.
   - Tablets:
     Children to 6 years: Must be individualized for patient.
     Children 6–12 years: By mouth: ½ tablet every 4 hours as
       needed.

3. **Carbinoxamine/Pseudoephedrine** (CARBODEC, CARDEC-S,
   RONDEC): Rx
   - Oral solution and syrup:
     Children 1–3 months: By mouth, 0.25 milliliter 4 times daily as
       needed.
     Children 3–6 months: By mouth, 0.5 milliliter 4 times daily as
       needed.
     Children 6–9 months: By mouth, 0.75 milliliter 4 times daily as
       needed.

Children 9–18 months: By mouth, 1.0 milliliter 4 times daily as needed.

Children 18 months to 6 years (syrup only): By mouth, 2.5 milliliters (½ teaspoonful) 4 times daily as needed.

- Tablets:

Children to 6 years: Use is not recommended.

Children 6 years and older: By mouth, 1 tablet 4 times daily as needed.

4. **Chlorpheniramine/Pseudoephedrine** (CO-PYRONIL 2 PEDIATRIC, DECONAMINE, DORCOL CHILDREN'S COLD FORMULA, DURA-TAP PD, FEDAHIST, KRONOFED-A JR., PEDIACARE COLD FORMULA, RYNA, SUDAFED PLUS, T-DRY JUNIOR): Rx, OTC

- Capsules (CO-PYRONIL 2 PEDIATRIC):

Children to 6 years: Dose has not been established.

Children 6–12 years: By mouth, 1 capsule every 6 hours as needed.

Children 12 years and older: By mouth, 2 capsules every 6 hours as needed.

- Oral solution and syrup:

Children to 2 years: Dose must be individualized for patient.

Children 2–6 years: By mouth, 2.5 milliliters (½ teaspoonful) every 4–6 hours as needed, not to exceed 10 milliliters (2 teaspoonsful) daily.

Children 6–12 years: By mouth, 2.5–5 milliliters (½ to 1 teaspoonful) every 4–6 hours as needed, not to exceed 20 milliliters daily.

Children 12 years and older: By mouth, 10 milliliters (2 teaspoonsful) every 4–6 hours as needed.

- Tablets:

Children to 2 years: Use is not recommended.

Children 2–6 years: By mouth, ¼ tablet every 4 hours as needed, not to exceed 1 tablet daily.

Children 6–12 years: By mouth, ½ tablet every 4–6 hours as needed.

Children 12 years and older: By mouth, 1 tablet every 4–6 hours as needed.

5. **Diphenhydramine/Pseudoephedrine** (BENYLIN DECONGESTANT): Rx

- Elixir:

Children to 6 years: Dose must be individualized for patient.

Children 6–12 years: By mouth, 5 milliliters (1 teaspoonful) every 4 hours as needed, not to exceed 20 milliliters daily.

Children 12 years and older: By mouth, 10 milliliters (2 teaspoonsful) every 4 hours as needed, not to exceed 40 milliliters daily.

6. **Phenylephrine/Brompheniramine** (DIMETANE DECONGESTANT): Rx
   - Elixir:
   Premature infants and newborns: Use is not recommended.
   Children to 2 years: Dose must be individualized for patient.
   Children 2–6 years: By mouth, 2.5 milliliters (½ teaspoonful) every 4 hours as needed, not to exceed 15 milliliters daily.
   Children 6–12 years: By mouth, 5 milliliters (1 teaspoonful) every 4 hours as needed, not to exceed 30 milliliters daily.
   Children 12 years and older: By mouth, 10 milliliters (2 teaspoonsful) every 4 hours as needed, not to exceed 60 milliliters daily.
   - Tablets:
   Children to 6 years: Dose has not been established.
   Children 6–12 years: By mouth, ½ tablet every 4 hours as needed, not to exceed 3 tablets daily.
   Children 12 years and older: By mouth, 1 tablet every 4 hours as needed, not to exceed 6 tablets daily.

7. **Phenylephrine/Chlorpheniramine** (COLTAB CHILDREN'S, NOVAHISTINE): Rx, OTC
   - Chewable tablets:
   Children to 3 years: Dose must be individualized for patient.
   Children 3 years and older: By mouth, 1–2 tablets every 4 hours as needed.
   - Elixir and syrup:
   Children to 3 years: Dose must be individualized for patient.
   Children 3–6 years: By mouth, 2.5 milliliters (½ teaspoonful) every 4 hours as needed.
   Children 6–12 years: By mouth, 5 milliliters (1 teaspoonful) every 4 hours as needed.
   Children 12 years and older: By mouth, 10 milliliters (2 teaspoonsful) every 4 hours as needed.

8. **Phenylephrine/Chlorpheniramine with Pyrilamine** (R-TANNATE, RYNATAN): Rx, OTC

- Oral suspension:
  Premature infants and newborns: Use is not recommended.
  Children to 2 years: Dose must be individualized for patient.
  Children 2–6 years: By mouth, 2.5–5 milliliters (½ to 1 teaspoonful) every 12 hours as needed.
  Children 6 years and older: By mouth, 5–10 milliliters (1–2 teaspoonsful) every 12 hours as needed.
- Tablets (nontannate forms):
  Children to 6 years: Dose must be individualized for patient.
  Children 6–12 years: By mouth, ½ tablet 3 times a day as needed.
  Children 12 years and older: By mouth, 1 tablet 3–4 times a day as needed.

9. **Phenylephrine/Phenylpropanolamine with Pyrilamine/ Chlorpheniramine** (HISTALET FORTE): Rx
   - Extended-release tablets:
     Children to 6 years: Dose has not been established.
     Children 6–12 years: By mouth, ½ tablet 2–3 times daily as needed.
     Children 12 years and older: By mouth, 1 tablet 2–3 times daily as needed.

10. **Phenylpropanolamine/Chlorpheniramine** (ALLEREST, A.R.M. MAXIMUM STRENGTH, CORSYM, DEMAZIN, GENAMIN, MYMINIC, NORAMINIC, SNAPLETS-D, TRIAMINIC ALLERGY, TRIAMINIC CHEWABLES, TRIAMINIC COLD, TRIND): Rx, OTC
    - Chewable tablets:
      Children to 2 years: Dose must be individualized for patient.
      Children 2–6 years: By mouth, 1 tablet every 6 hours as needed.
      Children 6–12 years: By mouth, 2 tablets every 4–6 hours as needed.
    - Extended-release oral suspension:
      Children to 6 years: Dose must be individualized for patient.
      Children 6–12 years: By mouth, 5 milliliters (1 teaspoonful) every 12 hours as needed.
      Children 12 years and older: By mouth, 10 milliliters (2 teaspoonsful) every 12 hours as needed.
    - Oral solution and syrup:
      Children to 3 months: Use is not recommended.
      Children 3–10 months: By mouth, 0.62 milliliter every 4 hours as needed.

Children 10 months to 2 years: By mouth, 1.25 milliliters every 4 hours as needed.

Children 2–6 years: By mouth, 2.5 milliliters (½ teaspoonful) every 4 hours as needed.

Children 6–12 years: By mouth, 5 milliliters (1 teaspoonful) every 4 hours as needed.

Children 12 years and older: By mouth, 10 milliliters (2 teaspoonsful) every 4 hours as needed.

- Tablets:

Children to 6 years: Dose has not been established.

Children 6–12 years: By mouth, ½ to 1 tablet every 4 hours as needed, depending on strength.

11. **Phenylpropanolamine/Pheniramine with Pyrilamine** (TRIAMINIC ORAL INFANT DROPS): Rx
    - Oral solution: By mouth, 1 drop for each 2.2 pounds of body weight 4 times daily as needed.

12. **Phenylpropanolamine/Phenylephrine with Phenyltoloxamine/ Chlorpheniramine** (AMARIL D, NALDECON, NEW-DECON-GEST, TRI-PHEN-CHLOR): Rx
    - Extended-release tablets:

    Children to 6 years: Use is not recommended.

    Children 6–12 years: By mouth, ½ tablet every 8–12 hours as needed.

    Children 12 years and older: By mouth, 1 tablet every 8–12 hours as needed.

    - Pediatric drops and pediatric syrup:

    Children to 3 months: Use is not recommended.

    Children 3–6 months: By mouth, 0.25 milliliter of the pediatric drops every 3–4 hours as needed, not to exceed 4 doses daily.

    Children 6–12 months: By mouth, 0.5 milliliter of the pediatric drops, or 2.5 milliliters (½ teaspoonful) of the pediatric syrup, every 3–4 hours as needed, not to exceed 4 doses daily.

    Children 1–6 years: By mouth, 1 milliliter of the pediatric drops, or 5 milliliters (1 teaspoonful) of the pediatric syrup, every 3–4 hours as needed, not to exceed 4 doses daily.

    Children 6–12 years: By mouth, 10 milliliters (2 teaspoonsful) of the pediatric syrup, or 2.5 milliliters (½ teaspoonful) of the adult syrup, every 3–4 hours as needed, not to exceed 4 doses daily.

Children 12 years and older: By mouth, 5 milliliters (1 tea-spoonful) every 3–4 hours as needed.

13. **Phenylpropanolamine/Phenyltoloxamine with Pyrilamine/ Pheniramine** (POLY-HISTINE-D PED): Rx
    - Pediatric extended-release capsules:
    Children to 6 years: Use is not recommended.
    Children 6–12 years: By mouth, 1 tablet every 8–12 hours as needed.

14. **Promethazine/Phenylephrine** (PHENERGAN VC, PROMETH VC PLAIN): Rx
    - Syrup:
    Premature infants and neonates: Use is not recommended.
    Children to 2 years: Dose must be individualized for patient.
    Children 2–6 years: By mouth, 1.25–2.5 milliliters every 4–6 hours as needed.
    Children 6 years and older: By mouth, 2.5–5 milliliters (½ to 1 teaspoonful) every 4–6 hours as needed.

15. **Triprolidine/Pseudoephedrine** (ACTIFED): Rx
    - Syrup:
    Children to 2 years: By mouth, 1.25 milliliters every 4–6 hours as needed.
    Children 2–4 years: By mouth, 2.5 milliliters (½ teaspoonful) every 4–6 hours as needed.
    Children 4–6 years: By mouth, 3.75 milliliters every 4–6 hours as needed.
    Children 6–12 years: By mouth, 5 milliliters (1 teaspoonful) every 4–6 hours as needed.
    Children 12 years and older: By mouth, 10 milliliters (2 tea-spoonsful) every 4–6 hours as needed.

GROUP NAME
ANTITHYROID AGENTS

1. METHIMAZOLE (TAPAZOLE). 2. PROPYLTHIOURACIL.

USES AND INDICATIONS

The antithyroid medications are used in the treatment of hyperthyroidism and in clinical situations associated with unexpected increases in thyroid hormone being released by the thyroid gland.

ADVERSE EFFECTS

The incidence of adverse effects is usually dose-related and includes the following:

- Blood: abnormal bleeding and sore throat.
- Liver: jaundice and inflammation of the liver (which can be fatal).
- Dermatological: rash, itching, scaling, skin eruptions, and skin discoloration.
- Gastrointestinal: nausea, vomiting, loss of taste, and upset stomach.
- Central nervous system: motion sickness, headache, and numbing or tingling sensation in the hands and feet.
- Other: fever, joint or muscle pains, loss of hair, water retention, and goiter.

WARNINGS AND PRECAUTIONS

- Children on long-term therapy should receive periodic blood counts.
- Antithyroid medication should be used with caution in children with blood or liver disorders.

MEDICATION AND FOOD INTERACTIONS

- Antithyroid agents may increase the toxicity of corticosteroids (see Appendix II).
- Iodine-containing preparations may increase the effects of antithyroid agents.

- Antithyroid agents may interfere with various diagnostic laboratory tests for blood, thyroid function, and liver function.

BRAND NAME(S)
1. TAPAZOLE   Rx
See also general information on antithyroid agents on page 113.

GENERIC NAME
METHIMAZOLE

USES AND INDICATIONS
TAPAZOLE is used in treating hyperthyroidism.

DOSAGE GUIDELINES
- Tablets: By mouth, 400 micrograms (0.4 milligrams) daily for each 2.2 pounds of body weight in 1–2 divided doses. As a maintenance dose, 200 micrograms (0.2 milligrams) daily by mouth for each 2.2 pounds of body weight in 1–2 divided doses.

GENERIC NAME
2. PROPYLTHIOURACIL   Rx
See also general information on antithyroid agents on page 113.

USES AND INDICATIONS
Propylthiouracil is used in treating hyperthyroidism, and in thyrotoxicosis or thyroid storm (Propylthiouracil is preferred over TAPAZOLE for this use.

ADVERSE EFFECTS
Swelling of the feet and lower legs, as well as shortness of breath, may occur more frequently with Propylthiouracil than with TAPAZOLE.

DOSAGE GUIDELINES
- Tablets
  Children to 6 years: Use is not recommended.
  Children 6–10 years: By mouth, 50–150 milligrams daily in 1–4 divided doses.
  Children 10 years and older: By mouth, 50–300 milligrams daily in 1–4 divided doses.

GROUP NAME
BENZODIAZEPINES

1. CHLORDIAZEPOXIDE (LIBRIUM). 2. CLONAZEPAM (KLONOPIN).
3. CLORAZEPATE (TRANXENE). 4. DIAZEPAM (VALIUM).

USES AND INDICATIONS
The benzodiazepines are central nervous system depressant medications that are useful in treating seizures, convulsions, and muscle spasm disorders in children.

ADVERSE EFFECTS
In general, the adverse effects of benzodiazepines are related to the dose of the medication used, with the possibility for side effects increasing as the dose is increased. Generally, adverse effects are usually mild and disappear when the medication is stopped. They include nausea, vomiting, hiccups, swollen tongue, metallic taste, dry mouth, anxiety, euphoria, hyperactivity and aggressiveness in children, difficulty sleeping, nightmares, loss or gain in appetite, skin rash, itching, difficulty urinating, visual disturbances, joint pains, and muscle cramps. Children may be especially sensitive to the depressant effects of these medications.

WARNINGS AND PRECAUTIONS

- Liver and kidney function tests should be performed regularly in long-term treatment.
- Benzodiazepines are contraindicated in glaucoma.
- Benzodiazepines should be used cautiously in children with breathing, liver, or kidney disorders, or in children who are hyperkinetic or who have myasthenia gravis.

MEDICATION AND FOOD INTERACTIONS

- The use of benzodiazepines with the following may increase the central nervous system toxicity of both medications: alcohol, antidepressants (see Appendix II), and anticonvulsants (see Appendix II).
- TAGAMET may increase the toxicity of benzodiazepines.

- VALIUM may increase the toxicity of LANOXIN by slowing its elimination from the body.
- Aluminum- and magnesium-containing antacids (see Appendix II) may decrease the effectiveness of benzodiazepines (see Appendix II).

DOSAGE GUIDELINES

The following products are listed by brand or proprietary name.

1. **LIBRIUM** (Chlordiazepoxide): Rx
   - Capsules and tablets:
   Children to 6 years: Dosage has not been established.
   Children 6 years and older: By mouth, 5 milligrams 2 to 4 times daily, then increase as necessary to 10 milligrams 2 to 3 times daily.

2. **KLONOPIN** (Clonazepam): Rx
   For dosage information, see *Anticonvulsants, Benzodiazepines* (page 65).

3. **TRANXENE** (Clorazepate): Rx
   - Capsules and tablets:
   Children to 9 years: Dosage has not been established.
   Children 9–12 years: By mouth, up to 7.5 milligrams twice daily initially, then may be increased as necessary up to 7.5 milligrams per week, not to exceed 60 milligrams daily.
   Children 12 years and older: By mouth, up to 7.5 milligrams 3 times daily initially, then may be increased by no more than 7.5 milligrams per week as necessary to control the seizures, not to exceed 90 milligrams daily.

4. **VALIUM** (Diazepam): Rx
   - Oral solution:
   Children to 6 months: Use is not recommended.
   Children 6 months and older: By mouth, 40–200 micrograms for each 2.2 pounds of body weight 3–4 times daily, then may gradually be increased; or 1–2.5 milligrams 3–4 times daily, then may gradually be increased.
   - Tablets:
   Children to 6 months: Use is not recommended.
   Children 6 months and older: By mouth, 1–2.5 milligrams 3–4 times daily, then may gradually be increased.

GROUP NAME
BRONCHODILATORS, ADRENERGIC

1. ALBUTEROL (PROVENTIL, VENTOLIN). 2. EPHEDRINE. 3. EPINEPHRINE (ADRENALIN, ASTHMAHALER, ASTHMANEFRIN, BRONITIN, BRONKAID, MEDIHALER-EPI, PRIMATENE, VAPONEFRIN). 4. ISOPROTERENOL (AEROLONE, ISUPREL, MEDIHALER-ISO, VAPO-ISO). 5. METAPROTERENOL (ALUPENT, METAPREL).

USES AND INDICATIONS
Asthma and related breathing disorders constitute the most significant group of chronic diseases in children. In fact, the number of child deaths related to these diseases is on the increase, in contrast to mortality from other chronic diseases.

Adrenergic bronchodilators, which work by increasing the airway openings, are used in treating various breathing disorders, including asthma, emphysema, bronchitis, and other lung disorders.

ADVERSE EFFECTS
The adverse effects of the adrenergic bronchodilators are related to both the medication and dosage.

- Cardiovascular: rapid heartbeats and palpitations, increase or decrease in blood pressure, sweating, headache, chills and fever, and chest pain.
- Gastrointestinal: nausea, vomiting, heartburn, increased appetite, dry mouth or throat, and unusual taste.
- Central nervous system: tremors, nervousness, hyperexcitement, difficulty sleeping, weakness, ringing in the ears, hallucinations, and mood changes.
- Other: blurred vision, muscle cramps, conjunctivitis, rash, dilated pupils, bluish or pale skin color, difficulty breathing, painful urination, flushing, and hives.

Medical attention should be obtained if the above symptoms continue or become more severe.

WARNINGS AND PRECAUTIONS

- Children allergic to sulfites, a preservative found in many food products, may also be sensitive to adrenergic bronchodilators.
- Epinephrine-containing products should be used cautiously in infants and children with asthma, due to the possibility of the products' causing temporary loss of consciousness.
- High doses of adrenergic bronchodilators may result in excessive potassium loss.
- Children taking inhalation medication should avoid spraying the medication in their eyes.
- Adrenergic bronchodilators may increase blood sugar in diabetic children.
- Inhalation therapy may cause dry mouth and throat, which may be alleviated by rinsing the mouth with water after each dose.
- Children receiving adrenergic bronchodilator medication should not receive corticosteroid (see Appendix II) therapy by inhalation at the same time.
- Children may become tolerant to some adrenergic bronchodilators, requiring adjustments in treatment.
- Parents whose child is being treated for asthma should not utilize over-the-counter asthma medication unless it is approved by their child's doctor.

MEDICATION AND FOOD INTERACTIONS

- Adrenergic bronchodilators may decrease the effectiveness of loop diuretics (see Appendix II).
- The use of adrenergic bronchodilators with LANOXIN may increase the risk of toxicity to the heart.
- The use of adrenergic bronchodilators and thyroid hormones (see Appendix II) may increase the toxicity of both medications.

COMMENTS

Adrenergic bronchodilators are available in devices that are used for oral inhalation. Patients using these devices should receive instructions in their use and care (including proper cleaning) from their pharmacist or physician. The abbreviated monographs below will highlight the major differences among the adrenergic bronchodilators, as well as give respective dosages.

BRAND NAME(S)

1. VENTOLIN (and PROVENTIL) Rx

See also general information on adrenergic bronchodilators on page 117.

GENERIC NAME

ALBUTEROL

USES AND INDICATIONS

VENTOLIN is used to relieve the wheezing and shortness of breath associated with asthma, bronchitis, emphysema, and other respiratory disorders caused by a narrowing of the bronchial vessels of the lungs, including bronchospasms brought about by too much exercise.

ADVERSE EFFECTS

The most common adverse effects of VENTOLIN are dryness of the mouth and throat (which may be relieved by gargling with water), nervousness, flushing, nausea, vomiting, hyperactivity, restlessness, rapid heartbeats, sweating, headache, and difficulty sleeping. Some of these effects may occur more often in children 2–5 years old than in older children or adults. If the symptoms persist or are severe, the medication should be stopped, and your child's doctor consulted.

WARNINGS AND PRECAUTIONS

- The use of VENTOLIN with other drugs that have similar effects is not recommended.
- VENTOLIN should be used with caution in children who have a history of heart disease, high blood pressure, diabetes, hyperthyroidism, or pheochromocytoma.

DOSAGE GUIDELINES

- Syrup:
  Children to 2 years: Dosage has not been established.
  Children 2–6 years: By mouth, 100 micrograms (0.1 milligram) for each 2.2 pounds of body weight 3 times daily initially, then may be increased as needed up to 200 micrograms (0.2 milligrams) for each 2.2 pounds of body weight, not to exceed 4 milligrams 3 times daily.
  Children 6–14 years: By mouth, 2 milligrams (1 teaspoonful) 3–4

times daily initially, then may be increased as needed up to 24 milligrams daily in divided doses, as prescribed by a physician.

Children 14 years and older: By mouth, 2–6 milligrams (1–3 teaspoonsful) 3–4 times daily initially, then may be increased as needed up to 8 milligrams 4 times daily.

- Tablets:
Children to 6 years: Dosage has not been established.
Children 6–12 years: By mouth, 2 milligrams 3–4 times daily initially, then may be increased as needed up to 24 milligrams daily in divided doses, as prescribed by a physician.
Children 12 years and older: By mouth, 2–6 milligrams 3–4 times daily initially, then may be increased as needed up to 8 milligrams 4 times daily.

COMMENTS

If the dose of VENTOLIN prescribed is not producing the desired effect in your child, do not give a greater dose; instead, call your child's doctor, who may want to adjust the dose or prescribe another medication. The aerosol cap and plastic case should be cleaned at least daily in warm water, rinsed well in warm running water, and dried thoroughly.

Because VENTOLIN interacts with many other medications to produce undesirable side effects, you should tell your child's doctor what other medication your child is taking, including nonprescription medications. VENTOLIN inhalation aerosol should be shaken well before using, and the inhalation solution should be refrigerated.

GENERIC NAME
2. EPHEDRINE   Rx, OTC

See also general information on adrenergic bronchodilators on page 117.

USES AND INDICATIONS

Ephedrine is used as a bronchodilator, and it also has nasal decongestant properties. It is used in treating asthma, emphysema, bronchitis, and other bronchospasm disorders. Ephedrine is also used in combination with other medications as a nasal decongestant.

ADVERSE EFFECTS

In addition to the adverse effects discussed above under the monograph for adrenergic bronchodilators, Ephedrine produces more central nervous system side effects at higher doses, which are often required as children on long-term Ephedrine therapy develop tolerance to the medication. Also, Ephedrine may cause more heart side effects, such as high blood pressure, abnormal heartbeats, and other heart irregularities.

WARNINGS AND PRECAUTIONS

- The chronic or long-term use of Ephedrine may result in the development of patient tolerance, requiring a higher dose to achieve the same therapeutic response.
- In order to minimize the possibility of insomnia, the last dose of Ephedrine should be administered a few hours before bedtime if possible.
- Ephedrine should be used cautiously in children with high blood pressure or heart disorders.
- Children using adrenergic bronchodilators on a long-term basis should be tested periodically for heart function.

MEDICATION AND FOOD INTERACTIONS

- Ephedrine may decrease the effectiveness of corticosteroids (see Appendix II) by speeding their elimination from the body.
- Sodium Bicarbonate may increase the potential toxicity of Ephedrine by slowing its elimination from the body.
- RITALIN may produce increased central nervous system stimulation and increased blood pressure when used with Ephedrine.

DOSAGE GUIDELINES
- Capsules, syrup, and tablets: By mouth, 3 milligrams daily for each 2.2 pounds of body weight, divided into 4–6 doses.

COMMENTS
Ephedrine is available as a nasal jelly and as a solution that may be used as a nasal decongestant in room humidifiers. Ephedrine is also combined with other medications in antitussive, antihistamine expectorant, and sedative products; many are available over the counter. Ephedrine should not be used in infants and young children unless directed by a physician.

GENERIC NAME
3. EPINEPHRINE   Rx, OTC
See also general information on adrenergic bronchodilators on page 117.

BRAND NAME(S)
ADRENALIN, ASTHMAHALER, ASTHMANEFRIN, BRONITIN, BKONKAID, MEDIHALER-EPI, PRIMATENE, VAPONEFRIN

USES AND INDICATIONS
In addition to its bronchodilator properties, Epinephrine is also used as a heart stimulant and to increase blood pressure. Because of the potential adverse effects on the heart, the use of Epinephrine in relieving breathing disorders has declined.

ADVERSE EFFECTS
The major adverse effects of Epinephrine are associated with its effects upon the heart and blood vessels and upon the central nervous system. Due to its rapid absorption as an inhalant, the side effects of Epinephrine may be similar to those of injectable Epinephrine, and parents should be aware of the signs of toxicity. Those symptoms that may require medical attention include tremors, headache, hyperexcitability and restlessness, difficulty sleeping, muscle rigidity and weakness, disorientation, hallucinations, nightmares, and abnormal heartbeats.

WARNINGS AND PRECAUTIONS

- The last dose of Epinephrine should be administered a few hours before bedtime, if possible, to avoid hyperexcitation and insomnia.
- Epinephrine should be used cautiously, if at all, in children with impaired heart function, Parkinson's disease, diabetes, hyperthyroidism, high blood pressure, convulsive disorders, pheochromocytoma, or glaucoma.
- Some patients may be allergic to sulfites found in some Epinephrine inhalation products.
- Solutions of Epinephrine intended for inhalation may be more concentrated than the parenteral forms are, and should *not* be used for injection.

- Some patients may experience severe, prolonged asthma attacks from Epinephrine.
- Tolerance to Epinephrine may develop and may require an adjustment in dosage to get the same beneficial effects. If the medication does not produce the desired results, parents should not increase the dosage or frequency without consulting their child's doctor first.

MEDICATION AND FOOD INTERACTIONS

- Epinephrine may decrease the effectiveness of insulin.

DOSAGE GUIDELINES
- Inhalation aerosol:
  Children to 6 years: Dosage must be individualized for patient.
  Children 6 years and older: By mouth, 1 spray, which may be repeated in 1–2 minutes if necessary. If an additional dose is required, it should not be given for at least 4 hours after the second dose.

COMMENTS
Epinephrine inhalation aerosol should be shaken well before use. Epinephrine should not be used in infants and young children unless directed by a physician.

GENERIC NAME
4. ISOPROTERENOL   Rx
See also general information on adrenergic bronchodilators on page 117.

BRAND NAME(S)
AEROLONE, ISUPREL, MEDIHALER-ISO, VAPO-ISO

DOSAGE GUIDELINES
- Inhalation aerosol:
  Acute bronchial asthma: By mouth, 1 spray, repeated in 1–5 minutes as necessary, 4–6 times daily.
  Other bronchospasm disorders: By mouth, 1 spray every 3–4 hours as necessary.

GENERIC NAME
5. METAPROTERENOL   Rx
See also general information on adrenergic bronchodilators on page 117.

BRAND NAME(S)
ALUPENT, METAPREL

DOSAGE GUIDELINES
- Syrup and tablets:
  Children to 6 years: By mouth, 0.325 mg–0.65 milligram for each 2.2 pounds of body weight, 4 times daily.
  Children over 6 years, or weighing 60 pounds or more: By mouth, 10 milligrams (1 teaspoonful or 1 10-milligram tablet) 3–4 times daily.

GROUP NAME
BRONCHODILATORS, XANTHINE

1. AMINOPHYLLINE (PHYLOCONTIN, SOMOPHYLLIN, TRUPHYLLINE).
2. OXTRIPHYLLINE (CHOLEDYL). 3. THEOPHYLLINE (AEROLATE, ASMALIX, BRONKODYL, ELIXOMIN, ELIXOPHYLLIN, LANOPHYLLIN, LIXOLIN, SLO-BID, SLO-PHYLLIN, SOMOPHYLLIN-CRT, SOMOPHYLLIN-T, THEOBID JR., THEOCLEAR L.A., THEO-DUR, THEOLAIR, THEOSPAN-SR, THEOVENT LONG-ACTING, THEO-24, TRUXOPHYLLIN).

USES AND INDICATIONS
The xanthine bronchodilators are used in treating breathing disorders, including asthma, bronchitis, and emphysema. Their ability to relax the smooth muscles of the lungs results in the opening of air passages to improve breathing, and allows the removal of mucous from the lungs.

ADVERSE EFFECTS
The major adverse effects of Theophylline medications are upset stomach and central nervous system stimulation (the latter often being more severe in children). Close monitoring is necessary due to the narrow

range between the therapeutic and toxic levels (low therapeutic index) for Theophylline products. If the gastrointestinal and central nervous system effects persist or are severe, parents should contact their doctor to determine whether the dosage should be reduced.

The major adverse effects include:

- Gastrointestinal: nausea, vomiting (in rare instances, bloody), loss of appetite, stomach cramps or pain, and diarrhea. (Stomach irritation may be minimized by adjusting the dosage or by taking the medication with liquid or after meals.)
- Central nervous system: restlessness, headache, nervousness, irritability, inability to sleep, dizziness, and seizures. These symptoms usually occur with higher doses of Theophylline and may be more severe in children than in adults.
- Cardiovascular: flushing, rapid heartbeats, rapid pulse, and decrease in blood pressure. These symptoms occur more often at higher doses.
- Other: redness of the skin, itching, and increased urination.

WARNINGS AND PRECAUTIONS

- Theophylline medications should be used with extreme caution in children with liver, kidney, or heart disease.
- Theophylline medications should be used cautiously in children who are receiving flu vaccine or who have peptic ulcer, glaucoma, angina, diabetes, hyperthyroidism, high blood pressure, or abnormal heartbeats.
- Some Theophylline preparations contain sulfites, which some children may be allergic to.
- Children on Theophylline therapy should be monitored periodically for pulmonary function and should have serum Theophylline levels performed.
- Children being treated for asthma should not receive other over-the-counter asthma medication unless prescribed by their doctors.

MEDICATION AND FOOD INTERACTIONS

- The effects of Theophylline may be affected by diets too high, or too low, in sugars (carbohydrates) and proteins.
- The use of Theophylline with tetracyclines (see Appendix II) may result in stomach distress.
- Theophylline may decrease the effectiveness of DILANTIN.

- Aluminum- and magnesium-containing antacids (see the general monograph for antacids) may reduce the effectiveness of Theophylline medications.
- The following medications may increase the toxicity of Theophylline: ZYLOPRIM, TAGAMET, flu vaccine, Erythromycin, CLEOCIN, LINCOCIN, MINTEZOL, and corticosteroids (see Appendix II).
- The use of Theophylline with adrenergic bronchodilators (see Appendix II) may result in increased toxicity, particularly stomach irritation.
- Theophylline may increase the effects of COUMADIN and may result in increased bleeding.
- Theophylline may increase the toxicity of LANOXIN.

COMMENTS

Dosing with Theophylline products does not follow the "normal" pattern of most medications in infants under 1 year of age. During the first year of life, Theophylline is eliminated from the body more rapidly than in older children and adults, and may require a higher dose in order to achieve the desired effect. Because no two children are alike, the dosage for each child receiving Theophylline must be titrated to determine the "right" dose and the "right" frequency. The successful use of Theophylline, particularly, in children on long-term therapy, is dependent upon close monitoring of blood levels and breathing function. In order to avoid toxicity from overuse or from overdosing, good cooperation between the child, the parents, and the doctor is required.

There are numerous products containing Theophylline combined with other medications. Most physicians feel that these are less effective than Theophylline alone, however, because the Theophylline concentration is usually not high enough to produce the desired effect.

Theophylline medications should be used only as directed by a physician.

GENERIC NAME
1 . AMINOPHYLLINE   Rx
See also general information on xanthine bronchodilators on page 124.

BRAND NAME(S)
PHYLOCONTIN, SOMOPHYLLIN,
TRUPHYLLINE

Uses and Indications

Aminophylline Dihydrate contains approximately 79% anhydrous Theophylline and is used as a bronchodilator and respiratory stimulant. Aminophylline is used in treating asthma, bronchitis, emphysema, and other disorders in which there is breathing obstruction or breathing difficulty.

Adverse Effects

The most common adverse effects of Aminophylline are nausea, vomiting, diarrhea, stomach pain, loss of appetite, nervousness, hyperexcitability, severe depression, muscle twitching, behavior changes, rapid breathing, convulsions, fast irregular heartbeats, headache, insomnia, dizziness, and seizures.

Warnings and Precautions

- Theophylline serum levels should be performed regularly, particularly in newborns.
- Theophylline should be used with caution in children with heart disease, kidney or liver disorders, high blood pressure, or hyperthyroidism, as well as in newborns.

Medication and Food Interactions

- The following medications may increase the toxic effects of Aminophylline: TAGAMET, Erythromycin, oral flu vaccine, CLEOCIN, LINCOCIN, ZYLOPRIM, MINTEZOL, and RIMACTANE.
- Aminophylline increases the effects of Ephedrine and LANOXIN.
- Aminophylline decreases the effectiveness of DILANTIN.
- The use of Aminophylline with SERPASIL may cause abnormal rapid heartbeats.
- Charcoal-broiled foods may decrease the effectiveness of Aminophylline.

Dosage Guidelines

Because Aminophylline is approximately 80% Theophylline, an equivalent Aminophylline-to-Theophylline dose may be obtained by giving 1.25 times the amount of Theophylline needed. For example, if 100 milligrams of Theophylline is needed, 125 milligrams of Aminophylline is required.

- Oral solution (105 milligrams equivalent to 90 milligrams anhydrous Theophylline) and tablets (100 milligrams equivalent to 79 milligrams anhydrous Theophylline): See under dosage guidelines for Theophylline elixir (page 128).
- Rectal solution (60 milligrams equivalent to 51 milligrams anhydrous Theophylline per milliliter):
  - Acute attack: For children currently on Theophylline therapy, insert rectally 2.5 milligrams of anhydrous Theophylline equivalent for each 2.2 pounds of body weight as a single dose.
  - Maintenance:
    Children to 1 year: Only as directed by a physician.
    Children 1–9 years: By rectum, the dose of anhydrous Theophylline equivalent in milligrams for each 2.2 pounds every 6 hours.
    Children 9–12 years: By rectum, the dose of anhydrous Theophylline equivalent in milligrams for each 2.2 pounds every 6 hours.
    Children 12–16 years: By rectum, 3 milligrams of anhydrous Theophylline equivalent for each 2.2 pounds every 6 hours.

COMMENTS

Solutions of Aminophylline that have crystallized should be shaken well or warmed under warm-to-hot water until the crystals have dissolved.

BRAND NAME(S)
2. CHOLEDYL   Rx

See also general information on xanthine bronchodilators on page 124.

GENERIC NAME
OXTRIPHYLLINE

USES AND INDICATIONS

CHOLEDYL, the choline salt of Theophylline, is used in treating asthma, bronchitis, and emphysema.

DOSAGE GUIDELINES

- Elixir, syrup, and tablets: See dosage guidelines for under Theophylline elixir (page 129).

GENERIC NAME
3. THEOPHYLLINE   Rx
See also general information on xanthine bronchodilators on page 124.

BRAND NAME(S)
AEROLATE, ASMALIX, BRONKODYL,
ELIXOMIN, ELIXOPHYLLIN,
LANOPHYLLIN, LIXOLIN, SLO-BID, SLO-
PHYLLIN, SOMOPHYLLIN-CRT,
SOMOPHYLLIN-T, THEOBID JR.,
THEOCLEAR L.A., THEO-DUR,
THEOLAIR, THEOLAIR-SR, THEON,
THEOPHYL, THEOPHYL-SR, THEOSPAN
SR, THEOVENT LONG-ACTING, THEO-24,
TRUXOPHYLLIN.

USES AND INDICATIONS
Theophylline, the most prevalent of all the oral bronchodilators, is often used with other medications in treating chronic asthma, bronchitis, and emphysema.

DOSAGE GUIDELINES
- Capsules, elixir, oral solution, oral suspension, Sodium Glycinate elixir (110 milligrams equivalent to 55 milligrams anhydrous Theophylline), syrup, and tablets:
  - Acute attacks: For children currently on Theophylline therapy, give 2.5 milligrams of anhydrous Theophylline equivalent by mouth for each 2.2 pounds of body weight as a single dose.
  - Maintenance (for acute attacks):
    Children to 1 year: Only as directed by a physician.
    Children 1–9 years: By mouth, 5 milligrams of anhydrous Theophylline equivalent for each 2.2 pounds of body weight given every 6 hours.
    Children 9–12 years: By mouth, 4 milligrams of anhydrous Theophylline equivalent for each 2.2 pounds of body weight given every 6 hours.
    Children 12–16 years: By mouth, 3 milligrams of anhydrous Theophylline equivalent for each 2.2 pounds of body weight given 6 hours.
  - Chronic use: By mouth, 16 milligrams of anhydrous Theophylline equivalent for each 2.2 pounds of body weight, up to a

maximum of 400 milligrams daily in 3–4 divided doses at 6–8 hour intervals, initially. The dose may be increased in increments of 25% (approximately) at 2–3 day intervals, up to the following maximum doses:

Children 1–9 years: By mouth, 24 milligrams daily for each 2.2 pounds of body weight.

Children 9–12 years: By mouth, 20 milligrams daily for each 2.2 pounds of body weight.

Children 12–16 years: By mouth, 18 milligrams daily for each 2.2 pounds of body weight.

Children 16 years and older: By mouth, 13 milligrams daily for each 2.2 pounds of body weight, or 900 milligrams daily, whichever is less.

COMMENTS

Because of the close relationship between the therapeutic and toxic dose for Theophylline medications, close supervision and monitoring are necessary in order to prevent toxicity from occurring. For more information regarding adverse effects, warnings and precautions, and medication and food interactions, see the general monograph for xanthine bronchodilators (page 124).

Theophylline products are available as salts of Theophylline, with each salt containing different amounts of Theophylline. Using anhydrous Theophylline as the standard, the following table shows the anhydrous Theophylline equivalent for each Theophylline salt.

THEOPHYLLINE SALT	THEOPHYLLINE EQUIVALENT (MILLIGRAMS)
Aminophylline (Anhydrous)	116
Aminophylline (Dihydrate)	127
Oxtriphylline	156
Theophylline (Anhydrous)	100
Theophylline (Monohydrate)	110
Theophylline (Sodium Glycinate)	217

GROUP NAME
Cephalosporins

1. Cefaclor (CECLOR). 2. Cefadroxil (DURICEF, ULTRACEF). 3. Cefixime (SUPRAX). 4. Cefuroxime (CEFTIN). 5. Cephalexin (KEFLEX). 6. Cephradine (ANSPOR, VELOSEF)

Uses and Indications
Cephalosporins are broad-spectrum antibiotics used in treating a variety of infections, including those of the bones, skin and soft tissues, lungs, urinary tract, and middle ear. Like the penicillins, cephalosporins are widely used in infants and children.

Adverse Effects
In general, cephalosporins are relatively safe and have few major adverse effects, which are usually associated with the injectable forms. The major adverse effects of oral cephalosporins include nausea, vomiting, diarrhea, skin rash, sore mouth or tongue, and stomach pains. Medical attention should be obtained as soon as possible if your child experiences stomach cramps or bloating, nausea, vomiting, watery or bloody diarrhea, fever, thirst, and unusual weakness or tiredness.

Warnings and Precautions

- Use cephalosporins with caution in children who have kidney or liver disorders.
- Use with caution in children with seizure disorders; discontinue the cephalosporin if seizures occur.
- Use cautiously in children who may be allergic to penicillin-type antibiotics.
- Cephalosporins may be administered on an empty stomach or with food.
- Pseudomembranous colitis has occurred with cephalosporins; the symptoms are as follows: severe diarrhea, severe abdominal cramps, and unusual weakness (stop medication, give fluids, and obtain medical attention).

Medication and Food Interactions

Most of the clinically significant interactions occur with the injectable forms of cephalosporins.

Comments

Oral suspensions and liquid drop solutions should be shaken well before use and should be stored in the refrigerator. Discard any unused portion at the end of the treatment period or after the expiration date noted on the label.

BRAND NAME(S)
1. CECLOR   Rx

See also general information on cephalosporins on page 131.

GENERIC NAME
CEFACLOR

Uses and Indications

CECLOR is used in treating infections of the lungs, middle ear, skin and soft tissues, and urinary tract.

Dosage Guidelines

- Capsules and oral suspension:
  Infants to 1 month: Dosage has not been established.
  Infants 1 month and older: By mouth, 6.7–13.4 milligrams for each 2.2 pounds of body weight every 8 hours. The maximum daily dose should not exceed 1 gram.

Comments

CECLOR oral suspension should be shaken well before use and should be stored in the refrigerator.

BRAND NAME(S)
2. DURICEF (and ULTRACEF)   Rx

See also general information on cephalosporins on page 131.

GENERIC NAME
CEFADROXIL

USES AND INDICATIONS
DURICEF is an antibiotic used in treating urinary tract infections, skin and soft tissue infections, pharyngitis, and tonsilitis.

ADVERSE EFFECTS
The adverse effects of DURICEF include nausea, vomiting, diarrhea, and skin rash. The potential for pseudomembranous colitis exists, and parents should be alert to the signs (see *Warnings and Precautions* in general monograph for cephalosporins, page 131). For children with kidney impairment, your child's doctor may have to decrease the dosage.

DOSAGE GUIDELINES
- Capsules, oral suspension, and tablets:
  Pharyngitis and tonsilitis: By mouth, 15 milligrams for each 2.2 pounds of body weight every 12 hours, or 30 milligrams for each 2.2 pounds of body weight once daily for 10 days.
  Other infections: By mouth, 15 milligrams for each 2.2 pounds of body weight every 12 hours.

COMMENTS
DURICEF oral suspensions should be shaken well before use and should be stored in the refrigerator.

BRAND NAME(S)
3. SUPRAX   Rx
See also general information on cephalosporins on page 131.

GENERIC NAME
CEFIXIME

USES AND INDICATIONS
SUPRAX is an oral cephalosporin used in urinary tract infections, middle ear infections, pharyngitis, tonsilitis, and acute and chronic bronchitis. SUPRAX is effective against many organisms when used on a once-a-day basis.

DOSAGE GUIDELINES
- Oral suspension and tablets: By mouth, 8 milligrams daily for each 2.2 pounds of body weight, given as a single dose, or in 2 divided doses every 12 hours.

Or:

Children weighing 6 pounds: By mouth, 48 milligrams (½ teaspoonful) daily, administered as a single dose, or in 2 divided doses every 12 hours.

Children weighing 12.5 pounds: By mouth, 100 milligrams (1 teaspoonful) daily, administered as a single dose, or in 2 divided doses every 12 hours.

Children weighing 19 pounds: By mouth, 152 milligrams (1½ teaspoonsful) daily, administered as a single dose, or in 2 divided doses every 12 hours.

Children weighing 25 pounds: By mouth, 200 milligrams (2 teaspoonsful) daily, administered as a single dose, or in 2 divided doses every 12 hours.

Children weighing 35 pounds: By mouth, 280 milligrams (3 teaspoonsful) daily, administered as a single dose, or in 2 divided doses every 12 hours.

COMMENTS

SUPRAX oral suspension should be shaken well before use and should be stored in the refrigerator after reconstitution.

BRAND NAME(S)
4. CEFTIN   Rx
See also general information on cephalosporins on page 131.

GENERIC NAME
CEFUROXIME

USES AND INDICATIONS

CEFTIN is used in treating skin and soft tissue infections, middle ear infections, pharyngitis, tonsilitis, and urinary tract and lung infections.

WARNINGS AND PRECAUTIONS

The possibility of pseudomembranous colitis exists with the use of CEFTIN, and parents should be alert to the symptoms (see *Warnings and Precautions* in general monograph for cephalosporins, page 131).

DOSAGE GUIDELINES

- Tablets:
  - Middle ear infections (otitis media):
    Children to 2 years: By mouth, 125 milligrams every 12 hours.

Children 2 years and older: By mouth, 250 milligrams every 12 hours.
- Other infections:
  Infants and children to 12 years: By mouth, 125 milligrams every 12 hours.
  Children 12 years and older: See usual adult dose.

BRAND NAME(S)
5. KEFLEX   Rx
See also general information on cephalosporins on page 131.

GENERIC NAME
CEPHALEXIN

USES AND INDICATIONS
KEFLEX is an antibiotic used in treating infections of the bones, lungs, skin and soft tissues, and urinary tract.

WARNINGS AND PRECAUTIONS
- For more information regarding adverse effects, warnings and precautions, and medication and food interactions, see the general monograph for cephalosporins (page 131).
- Parents should also be alert for the symptoms of pseudomembranous colitis (see *Warnings and Precautions* under general monograph for cephalosporins, page 131).
- A reduction in dosage may be required in children with kidney disorders.

DOSAGE GUIDELINES
- Capsules, oral suspension, and tablets:
  Skin, soft tissue, and pharyngitis infections: By mouth, 12.5–50 milligrams for each 2.2 pounds of body weight every 12 hours.

COMMENTS
KEFLEX oral suspension should be shaken well before use and should be stored in the refrigerator.

BRAND NAME(S)
6. VELOSEF (and ANSPOR)   Rx
See also general information on cephalosporins on page 131.

GENERIC NAME
CEPHRADINE

USES AND INDICATIONS

VELOSEF is used in treating infections of the lungs, skin and soft tissues, and urinary tract.

WARNINGS AND PRECAUTIONS

For more information regarding adverse effects, warnings and precautions, and medication and food interactions, see the general monograph for cephalosporins (page 131). Parents should be alert for the symptoms of pseudomembranous colitis. A reduction in dosage may be required in children who have impaired kidney function.

DOSAGE GUIDELINES

- Capsules and oral suspension: By mouth, 6.25–25 milligrams for each 2.2 pounds of body weight every 6 hours. Children over 9 months of age may receive the total daily dose in equally divided doses every 12 hours.

COMMENTS

VELOSEF oral suspensions should be shaken well before use and should be stored in the refrigerator. Unused portions should be discarded at the end of the treatment period or on the expiration date noted on the label.

BRAND NAME(S)
CLEOCIN   Rx

GENERIC NAME
CLINDAMYCIN

USES AND INDICATIONS

CLEOCIN is an antibiotic used in treating bone infections, urinary tract infections, pneumonias, skin and soft tissue infections, and middle ear infections. CLEOCIN acts by suppressing protein synthesis in bacteria.

ADVERSE EFFECTS

The adverse effects of CLEOCIN may be serious, and they include potentially fatal pseudomembranous colitis, particularly with oral CLEOCIN use. Other adverse effects include the following:

- Gastrointestinal: nausea, vomiting, abdominal pain, loss of appetite, severe diarrhea, and colitis.
- Allergic: skin rash, itching, and anaphylactic reactions.
- Kidney: decreased urination.
- Liver: jaundice and decreased liver function.
- Bone and muscle: inflammation of the joints (polyarthritis).

WARNINGS AND PRECAUTIONS

- CLEOCIN may cause severe and potentially fatal colitis characterized by severe and persistent diarrhea, severe abdominal cramps, and, possibly, the passage of blood in the stools. Discontinue CLEOCIN and call your physician immediately should any of these symptoms occur. Do not administer opiates, such as LOMOTIL, as these may aggravate or prolong the condition.
- Use CLEOCIN only for serious infections when other, less toxic medications are not indicated.
- Use cautiously in children who are asthmatic, who have a history of allergies, or who have liver or kidney disorders.
- Closely monitor the use of CLEOCIN in newborns and infants due to immature organ development, as well as the possible accumulation of the medication, leading to toxicity.
- Do not use in children who are allergic to LINCOCIN.
- Some children may be sensitive to tartrazine (a dye used in the capsules), which may cause an allergic response, including bronchial asthma.

MEDICATION AND FOOD INTERACTIONS

- Erythromycin and CHLOROMYCETIN may decrease the effectiveness of CLEOCIN.
- KAOPECTATE and other kaolin-containing preparations may decrease the absorption of CLEOCIN from the stomach.

DOSAGE GUIDELINES
- Capsules and oral solutions:
  Infants 1 month and older: By mouth, 2–6.3 milligrams for each 2.2 pounds of body weight every 6 hours; or 2.7–8.3 milligrams for each 2.2 pounds of body weight every 8 hours. For children up to 22 pounds, give at least 37.5 milligrams every 8 hours.

COMMENTS

CLEOCIN oral solution should be shaken well before use.

GROUP NAME

CORTICOSTEROIDS

1. ORAL INHALATION CORTICOSTEROIDS (BECLOMETHASONE [BECLOVENT, VANCERIL], DEXAMETHASONE [DECADRON RESPIHALER], FLUNISOLIDE [AEROBID], TRIAMCINOLONE [AZMACORT]). 2. NASAL CORTICOSTEROIDS (BECLOMETHASONE [BECONASE, BECONASE AQ, VANCENASE, VANCENASE AQ], DEXAMETHASONE [DECADRON TURBINAIRE], FLUNISOLIDE [NASALIDE]). 3. TOPICAL CORTICOSTEROIDS (AMCINONIDE [CYLCOCORT], BETAMETHASONE [DIPROSONE, UTICORT, VALISONE, AND OTHERS], DESONIDE [DESOWEN, TRIDESILON], DESOXIMETASONE [TOPICORT], DEXAMETHASONE [AEROSEB-DEX, DECADERM, DECADRON, DECASPRAY], DIFLORASONE [FLORONE, MAXIFLOR, PSORCON], FLUOCINOLONE [FLUROSYN, SYNALAR, AND OTHERS], FLUOCINONIDE [FLUOCIN, LIDEX, AND OTHERS], FLURANDRENOLIDE [CORDRAN, CORDRAN SP], HALCINONIDE [HALOG, HALOG-E], HYDROCORTISONE [AEROSEB-HC, ALLERCORT, BACTINE, CETACORT, CORTAID, CORT-DOME, CORTICAINE, CORTRIL, DERMICORT, HYTONE, LANACORT, LOCOID, NUTRACORT, TEXACORT, WESTCORT, AND OTHERS], METHYLPREDNISOLONE [MEDROL], TRIAMCINOLONE [ARISTOCORT, FLUTEX, KENALOG, TRIACET, AND OTHERS]).

USES AND INDICATIONS

Corticosteroids are synthetically produced steroids that mirror the hormones produced by the body's adrenal cortex gland. As therapeutic agents, the corticosteroids represent an important pharmacological group of medications used in treating a variety of disorders. They may be used as single-ingredient products or in combination with other medications, particularly in products intended for use on the skin or in the eyes or ears.

Although corticosteroids have wide application in the treatment of numerous disorders, their major use in children is in treating chronic bronchial asthma; allergic disorders of the eyes, ears, and nose; and skin disorders associated with inflammation. The following information regarding corticosteroids, therefore, will be limited to the use of oral inhalation dosage forms, nasal inhalation dosage forms, and topical dosage forms, excluding those used in the eyes and ears.

MEDICATION	DOSE (MILLI-GRAMS)	ANTI-INFLAM-MATORY PROPERTY	SALT-SPARING PROPERTY
Short-Acting			
Hydrocortisone	20	1	2
Intermediate-Acting			
Methylprednisolone	4	5	0
Triamcinolone	4	5	0
Long-Acting			
Betamethasone	0.6–0.75	25	0
Dexamethasone	0.75	25–30	0

The above table compares the approximate dose equivalents; the relative anti-inflammatory properties; and the relative (sodium-retaining or salt-sparing) properties for the corticosteroids listed.

ADVERSE EFFECTS

The prolonged use of corticosteroids may result in significant adverse effects. The following list of potential adverse effects, though by no means complete, does include the more clinically significant side effects that have been observed. Additional side effects that are related to the use of specific corticosteroid dosage forms are discussed under the individual dosage form sections below.

- Fluid and electrolyte imbalances: water retention, high blood pressure, and serious imbalance in body salts.
- Cardiovascular effects: abnormal heartbeats, high blood pressure, inflammation of veins due to blood clots, and episodes of fainting.
- Neurological effects: convulsions; vertigo; headache; feeling of burning, tingling, or numbness; and inability to sleep.
- Endocrine effects: growth suppression in children, obesity and moonface or fatty growth on body, increased sweating, and increased blood sugar.

- Muscle and skeletal effects: muscle weakness, loss of muscle mass, spontaneous fractures of the long bones and spinal cord, calcium deficiency due to osteoporosis, and tendon ruptures. Long-term use of these drugs in children may retard bone growth, and such use may cause a general suppression of body growth.
- Gastrointestinal effects: nausea, vomiting, gas, ulcers with bleeding, weight gain, and constipation or diarrhea.
- Skin effects: fragile skin, slower wound healing, abnormal hair growth, redness of skin and skin eruptions, allergic dermatitis, itching, black and blue spots on the skin, or purplish-red spots due to hemorrhage.
- Ophthalmic effects: cataracts, increased pressure in the eye, and protruding eyeballs.
- Corticosteroid toxicity: There are two general types of toxicity that result from the long-term use of corticosteroids. The first may be identified by the side effects described above. The second type of toxicity is called "acute adrenal insufficiency," which may occur if long-term corticosteroid treatment is stopped abruptly or withdrawn too rapidly, or if a systemic corticosteroid is discontinued and the child placed on oral inhalation therapy. The symptoms of adrenal insufficiency include fever, loss of appetite, nausea, dizziness, fainting, joint or muscle pain, peeling of the skin, and a general feeling of illness. Acute adrenal insufficiency may also result in death if therapy is withdrawn too rapidly.

WARNINGS AND PRECAUTIONS

- Corticosteroids should be used with caution in children with hypothyroidism, peptic ulcer, liver or kidney disease, myasthenia gravis, seizure disorders, herpes eye infections, osteoporosis, and high blood pressure.
- The use of corticosteroids over a prolonged period may result in a decreased function of the adrenal gland, as well as a loss of body protein.
- Additional warnings and precautions associated with specific corticosteroid dosage forms are discussed in related dosage-form sections below.

MEDICATION AND FOOD INTERACTIONS

- Corticosteroids may increase the liver toxic effects of TYLENOL.
- Alcohol-containing products and NSAIDs (see Appendix II) may

cause stomach irritation and bleeding when used with corticosteroids.

- Antacids (see Appendix II) may decrease the absorption of Prednisone and DECADRON.
- COUMADIN used with corticosteroids may result in increased bleeding.
- The use of TAPAZOLE, Propylthiouracil, or thyroid hormones (see Appendix II) may require an adjustment in the corticosteroid dose.
- Corticosteroids may increase the toxicity of LANOXIN.
- Loop diuretics (see Appendix II) used with corticosteroids may result in reduced effects of both medications.
- DILANTIN, RIMACTANE, Ephedrine, and Phenobarbital may decrease the effects of corticosteroids.
- Corticosteroids may decrease the effects of FOLVITE, NYDRAZID, salicylates, and potassium supplements (see Appendix II).
- Corticosteroids taken with sodium-containing foods or medications may result in water retention and high blood pressure.
- The administration of vaccines to children taking corticosteroids may result in the child's developing the disease or in a decreased response to the vaccine.

The following discussion of corticosteroids is divided into the following dosage form categories: oral inhalants, nasal inhalants, ophthalmic agents, otic agents, and topical agents.

GROUP NAME AND GENERIC NAMES
1. ORAL INHALATION CORTICOSTEROIDS (BECLOMETHASONE, DEXAMETHASONE, FLUNISOLIDE, TRIAMCINOLONE)
See general information on corticosteroids on page 138.

BRAND NAME(S)
BECLOVENT, VANCERIL (BECLOMETHASONE); DECADRON RESPIHALER (DEXAMETHASONE); AEROBID (FLUNISOLIDE); AZMACORT (TRIAMCINOLONE)

USES AND INDICATIONS
The inhalation corticosteroids are used in children to treat chronic bronchial asthma. Although the exact action mechanism for these medi-

cations is unknown, they are thought to inhibit the inflammatory response of the body, preventing the accumulation of inflammatory cells in the lungs.

ADVERSE EFFECTS

Adverse effects of inhalation corticosteroids include cough, dryness of the mouth and throat, throat irritation, fungal infections of the mouth and throat, and rash. Systemic absorption does occur, and systemic adverse effects can occur. Chronic long-term use of corticosteroids may suppress growth in children and adolescents, particularly with DECADRON RESPIHALER. Death has occurred in patients who have been transferred from systemic to inhalation therapy.

WARNINGS AND PRECAUTIONS

Inhalation corticosteroids should be used with caution in children who may be allergic to fluorocarbons used in aerosol propellants, and they should not be used to treat acute asthmatic attacks.

DOSAGE GUIDELINES

Following are the dosage guidelines for oral inhalation corticosteroids.

- **Beclomethasone** (BECLOVENT, VANCERIL): Rx
  - Aerosol (1 metered spray = 42 micrograms):
    Children to 6 years: Dosage guidelines have not been established.
    Children 6–12 years: By oral inhalation, 1–2 metered sprays 3–4 times daily. Do not exceed 10 sprays per day.

- **Dexamethasone** (DECADRON RESPIHALER): Rx
  - Aerosol (1 metered spray = 84 micrograms):
    Children: By oral inhalation, 2 metered sprays 3–4 times daily initially, then decrease number of doses according to the child's response. Do not exceed 8 metered sprays per day.

- **Flunisolide** (AEROBID): Rx
  - Aerosol (1 metered spray = 250 micrograms):
    Children to 6 years: Dosage guidelines have not been established.
    Children 6–15 years: By oral inhalation, 4 metered sprays (1 milligram) daily.

- **Triamcinolone** (AZMACORT): Rx
  - Aerosol (1 metered spray = 100 micrograms):
    Children to 6 years: Dosage guidelines have not been estab-lished.
    Children 6–12 years: By oral inhalation, 1–2 metered sprays 3–4 times daily. Do not exceed 12 metered sprays per day.

COMMENTS

Parents whose children are on oral inhalation therapy should receive instructions from their pharmacist or physician regarding the use of aerosol devices when receiving these medications. Inhalant corticoste-roids should be used only as directed by a physician.

GROUP NAME AND GENERIC NAMES
2. NASAL CORTICOSTEROIDS (BECLOMETHASONE, DEXAMETHASONE, FLUNISOLIDE)

See general information on corticosteroids on page 138.

BRAND NAME(S)
BECONASE, BECONASE AQ, VANCENASE, VANCENASE AQ (BECLOMETHASONE); DECADRON TURBINAIRE (DEXAMETHASONE); NASALIDE (FLUNISOLIDE)

USES AND INDICATIONS

The nasal corticosteroids are used in children to treat nasal disorders associated with inflammation, including runny nose; allergic disorders; nasal polyps; and inflammatory nasal disorders not associated with in-fection.

ADVERSE EFFECTS

While nasal corticosteroids may exhibit the usual problems associated with all corticosteroids, the more common adverse effects are nose-bleeds, sore throat, and crusting inside the nose. Other adverse effects include headache, nausea and vomiting, stuffy nose or watery eyes, loss of taste or smell (with DECADRON TURBINAIRE and NASALIDE), hives (with DECADRON TURBINAIRE), shortness of breath or diffi-culty breathing (with DECADRON TURBINAIRE), and sneezing or throat irritation (with BECONASE, VANCENASE, and NASALIDE). Some symptoms of chronic overdose with nasal corticosteroids are moonface (Cushing's syndrome) and acne. If these symptoms occur, contact your physician immediately.

WARNINGS AND PRECAUTIONS

Children who are allergic to fluorocarbon propellants or to propylene or polyethylene glycols may not be able to use BECONASE, VANCENASE, and NASALIDE aerosols. For more information, see the general monograph for corticosteroids (page 138).

MEDICATION AND FOOD INTERACTIONS

See under the general monograph for corticosteroids (page 138).

DOSAGE GUIDELINES

Following are the dosage guidelines for nasal corticosteroids.

- **Beclomethasone** (BECONASE, BECONASE AQ, VANCENASE, VANCENASE AQ): Rx
  – Nasal aerosol [BECONASE, VANCENASE] (1 metered spray = 42 micrograms):
    Children to 6 years: Not recommended for use.
    Children 6–12 years: 1 metered spray in each nostril 3–4 times a day.
    Children over 12 years: 1 metered spray in each nostril 2–4 times a day.
  – Nasal spray [BECONASE AQ, VANCENASE AQ] (1 metered spray = 42 micrograms):
    Children to 6 years: Use is not recommended.
    Children 6 years and older: 1–2 metered sprays in each nostril twice a day.

- **Dexamethasone** (DECADRON TURBINAIRE): Rx
  – Aerosol (1 metered spray = 100 micrograms):
    Children to 6 years: Use is not recommended.
    Children 6–12 years: By nasal administration, 1–2 metered sprays in each nostril twice daily, not to exceed 8 metered sprays per day.

- **Flunisolide** (NASALIDE): Rx
  – Nasal spray (1 metered spray = 25 micrograms):
    Children to 6 years: Dosage guideline has not been established.
    Children 6–14 years: 1 metered spray in each nostril 3 times a

day. The maintenance dose is 1 metered spray in each nostril daily.

COMMENTS
All of the nasal corticosteroids should be used only as directed by a physician.

GROUP NAME AND GENERIC NAMES
3. TOPICAL CORTICOSTEROIDS (AMCINONIDE, BETAMETHASONE, DESONIDE, DESOXIMETASONE, DEXAMETHASONE, DIFLORASONE, FLUOCINOLONE, FLUOCINONIDE, FLURANDRENOLIDE, HALCINONIDE, HYDROCORTISONE, METHYLPREDNISONE, TRIAMCINOLONE)

See also general information on corticosteroids on page 138.

BRAND NAME(S)
AEROSEB-DEX, DECADERM, DECARON, DECASPRAY (DEXAMETHASONE); AEROSEB-HC, ALLERCORT, BACTINE, CETACORT, CORTAID, CORT-DOME, CORTICAINE, CORTRIL, DERMICORT, HYTONE, LANACORT, LOCOID, NUTRACORT, TEXACORT, WESTCORT, AND OTHERS (HYDROCORTISONE); ARISTOCORT, FLUTEX, KENALOG, TRIACET, AND OTHERS (TRIAMCINOLONE); CORDRAN, CORDRAN SP (FLURANDRENOLIDE); CYCLOCORT (AMCINONIDE); DESOWEN, TRIDESILON (DESONIDE); DIPROSONE, UTICORT, VALISONE, AND OTHERS (BETAMETHASONE); FLORONE, MAXIFLOR, PSORCON (DIFLORASONE); FLUOCIN, LIDEX, AND OTHERS (FLUOCINONIDE); FLUROSYN, SYNALAR, AND OTHERS (FLUOCINOLONE); HALOG, HALOG-E (HALCINONIDE); MEDROL (METHYLPREDNISOLONE); TOPICORT (DESOXIMETASONE)

USES AND INDICATIONS

Topical corticosteroids are generally used for their local anti-inflammatory properties, as well as in a variety of skin and mucous membrane disorders, including burns, insect bites, poison ivy, poison oak, poison sumac, various forms of dermatitis, dermatoses, eczema, psoriasis, diaper rash, itching of the skin and rectum, lupus, pemphigus, blistering, and other inflammatory skin disorders.

ADVERSE EFFECTS

Adverse effects are similar to those of other corticosteroids and are discussed in the general monograph (see page 138).

WARNINGS AND PRECAUTIONS

Corticosteroids should be used sparingly, especially in newborns and infants because of the increased risk of greater, and more rapid, absorption due to the immature development of skin tissues. Disorders that are more severe may require the use of topical corticosteroids with greater anti-inflammatory properties, in conjunction with nonabsorbent dressings, in order to maintain maximum exposure of the affected area to the medication. In general, the following guide is suggested if a topical corticosteroid is to be applied to more than 10% of the child's body, or if a nonabsorbent dressing is to be used. (Remember, tight-fitting clothing, such as a diaper, is considered an occlusive dressing.)

- Topical corticosteroids other than TRIDESILON and Hydrocortisone should not be used more than once daily for more than 2 weeks.
- TRIDESILON and Hydrocortisone should not be used more than twice daily for more than 2 weeks.
- Topical corticosteroids should be applied in a thin coat and rubbed in gently. Do not get in eyes.
- Prewashing of the affected area may increase absorption of the medication.
- Lotions should be shaken well before using.
- Unless instructed otherwise by a physician, topical corticosteroids should not be used for more than 2 weeks.

DOSAGE GUIDELINES

Following are the dosage guidelines for topical corticosteroids.

- **Amcinonide** (CYCLOCORT): Rx
  - Cream, lotion, and ointment: Apply to the skin once a day.

- **Betamethasone** (DIPROSONE, UTICORT, VALISONE, and others): Rx
  - Aerosol, cream, gel, lotion, and ointment: Apply to the skin once a day. (Note: **Betamethasone** Valerate cream (VALISONE), 0.01%, may be applied to the skin 1–2 times a day.)

- **Desonide** (DESOWEN, TRIDESILON): Rx
  - Cream and ointment: Apply to the skin once a day.

- **Desoximetasone** (TOPICORT): Rx
  - Cream, gel, and ointment: Apply to the skin once a day.

- **Dexamethasone** (AEROSEB-DEX, DECADERM, DECADRON, DECASPRAY): Rx
  - Aerosol and gel: Spray or apply to the skin 1–2 times a day.
  - Cream: Apply to the skin once a day.

- **Diflorasone** (FLORONE, MAXIFLOR, PSORCON): Rx
  - Cream and ointment: Apply to the skin once a day. (Note: PSORCON should not be used in children up to 12 years.)

- **Fluocinolone** (FLUROSYN, SYNALAR, and others): Rx
  - Cream (0.01%) and solution: Apply to the skin once a day.
  - Ointment: Apply to the skin 1–2 times a day.

- **Fluocinonide** (FLUOCIN, LIDEX, and others): Rx
  - Cream, gel, ointment, and topical solution: Apply to the skin once a day.

- **Flurandrenolide** (CORDRAN, CORDRAN SP): Rx
  - Cream (0.025%) and ointment: Apply to the skin 1–2 times a day.
  - Cream (0.05%), lotion, and ointment (0.05%): Apply to the skin once a day.

- **Halcinonide** (HALOG, HALOG-E): Rx
  - Cream, ointment, and solution: Apply to the skin once a day.

- **Hydrocortisone** (AEROSEB-HC, ALLERCORT, BACTINE, CETACORT, CORTAID, CORT-DOME, CORTICAINE, CORTRIL, DERMICORT, HYTONE, LANACORT, LOCOID, NUTRACORT, TEXACORT, WESTCORT, and others): Rx, OTC

- Hydrocortisone Base and Hydrocortisone Acetate:
Products containing 0.25% or 0.5%: Apply to the skin 1–4 times a day.
Products containing 1.0%: Apply to the skin 1–2 times a day.
Products containing 2.5%: Apply to the skin once a day.
- Hydrocortisone Butyrate cream and ointment: Apply to the skin 1–2 times a day.
- Hydrocortisone Valerate cream and ointment: Apply to the skin once a day.

- **Methylprednisolone** (MEDROL): Rx
Cream and ointment: Apply to the skin 1–2 times a day.

- **Triamcinolone** (ARISTOCORT, FLUTEX, KENALOG, TRIACET, and others): Rx
  - Cream and ointment: Products containing 0.015% or 0.025%: Apply to the skin 1–2 times a day.
Products containing 0.1% or 0.5%: Apply to the skin once a day.

GROUP NAME
COUGH AND COLD PREPARATIONS

USES AND INDICATIONS
The family of products that comprises the cough and cold preparations is huge and contains numerous combinations of medications, most of which may be broken down into the following therapeutic ingredient classifications: analgesics, antihistamines, decongestants, cough preparations (including opiates), expectorants, antimuscarinics, and bronchodilators. Cough and cold preparations may consist of single-ingredient products, such as Guaifenesin (e.g., ROBITUSSIN), to products containing five ingredients. These products may be purchased both with or without a doctor's prescription and are among the most widely used medicines in children.

COMMENTS
Because coughs often result from the body's response to different stimuli, such as allergens (air-borne contaminants), infection, lung congestion, and dry or irritated throat, these products are often formulated to

be effective against a specific "type" of cough. Parents should remember that it is difficult enough to treat children, especially infants and small children, when using products containing a single ingredient. This becomes a greater problem when the product is a "shotgun" medication—one that contains multiple ingredients. That's why the old adage "the fewer, the better" is especially true when dealing with medications in children. Before using over-the-counter medication in infants and small children, parents should first check with their physician or pharmacist to determine the need and appropriate dosage. At the least, parents should read all of the manufacturer's label information before administering any medication to a child. Remember, many cough and cold products contain significant amounts of alcohol, which should be limited in small infants and children. Again, be safe and read all the labeling before using.

The ingredients found in cough and cold preparations are discussed more fully in other sections of this book. For more information regarding uses and indications (for coughs only), adverse effects, warnings and precautions, and medication and food interactions, see the general monographs for antihistamines (page 96) and antihistamine/decongestant combinations (page 105). Also, see under the monograph for ROBITUSSIN (page 233).

DOSAGE GUIDELINES

Following is a partial list of cough and cold preparations in alphabetical order, by brand name, showing only the dosage forms that have suggested pediatric dosage guidelines. The information is taken from *USP DI, Drug Information for the Health Care Professional* (1991 edition), published by the United States Pharmacopeial Convention, Inc. Products designated "Rx" are by prescription only, and those designated "OTC" may be purchased over the counter. Some products containing narcotics are classified as Schedule V Controlled Substances, which may be limited to a prescription-only basis in some states. The information shown within parenthesis identifies whether the specific product contains alcohol, dyes, or sugar, as well as its therapeutic or active ingredients. For most products listed below, the maximum number of doses for infants and small children should not exceed 4 in a 24-hour period, and the medication should be stopped as soon as the cough ceases. If the cough persists for more than 48 hours, your child should be seen by a physician. Use of the following products is not recommended for age groups that are not specified.

1. **ACTAGEN-C** Cough Syrup (alcohol 4.3%; Codeine, Pseudoephedrine, Triprolidine): OTC

Children 2–6 years: By mouth, 2.5 milliliters (½ teaspoonful) every 4–6 hours as needed.

Children 6–12 years: By mouth, 5 milliliters (1 teaspoonful) every 4–6 hours as needed.

2. **ACTIFED WITH CODEINE** Cough Syrup (alcohol 4.3%; Codeine, Pseudoephedrine, Triprolidine): OTC

Children 2–6 years: By mouth, 2.5 milliliters (½ teaspoonful) every 4–6 hours as needed.

Children 6–12 years: By mouth, 5 milliliters (1 teaspoonful) every 4–6 hours as needed.

3. **ADATUSS D.C.** Oral Solution (alcohol 5%; Guaifenesin, Hydrocodone): Rx

Children 2–6 years: By mouth, 1.25 milliliters every 4–6 hours as needed.

Children 6–12 years: By mouth, 2.5 milliliters (½ teaspoonful) every 4–6 hours as needed.

4. **ALAMINE-C** Liquid (alcohol 5%; Codeine, Chlorpheniramine, Pseudoephedrine): OTC

Children 2–6 years: By mouth, 1.25–2.5 milliliters every 6 hours as needed.

Children 6–12 years: By mouth, 2.5–5 milliliters (½–1 teaspoonful) every 6 hours as needed.

5. **ALAMINE** Expectorant (alcohol 5%; Codeine, Guaifenesin, Pseudoephedrine): OTC. See 4. *ALAMINE-C Liquid* (above).

6. **ALLERFRIN WITH CODEINE** (alcohol 4.3%; Codeine, Pseudoephedrine, Triprolidine): OTC

Children 2–6 years: By mouth, 2.5 milliliters (½ teaspoonful) every 4–6 hours as needed.

Children 6–12 years: By mouth, 5 milliliters (1 teaspoonful) every 4–6 hours as needed.

7. **AMBAY** Cough Syrup (alcohol 5%; Bromdiphenhydramine, Codeine): OTC

Children 2–6 years: By mouth, 1.25–2.5 milliliters every 6 hours as needed.

Children 6–12 years: By mouth, 2.5–5 milliliters (½–1 teaspoonful) every 6 hours as needed.

8. **AMBENYL** Cough Syrup (alcohol 5%; Codeine, Brom-diphenhydramine): OTC
   Children 6–12 years: By mouth, 2.5–5 milliliters (½–1 teaspoon-ful) every 6 hours as needed.

9. **AMBENYL-D** Decongestant Cough Formula (alcohol 9.5%; Dex-tromethorphan, Guaifenesin, Pseudoephedrine): OTC
   Children 2–6 years: By mouth, 2.5 milliliters (½ teaspoonful) every 6 hours as needed.
   Children 6–12 years: By mouth, 5 milliliters (1 teaspoonful) ev-ery 6 hours as needed.

10. **AMBOPHEN** Expectorant (alcohol 5%; Ammonium Chloride, Bromdiphenhydramine, Codeine, Diphenhydramine, Potassium Guaiacolsulfonate): OTC
    Children 2–6 years: By mouth, 1.25–2.5 milliliters every 6 hours as needed.
    Children 6–12 years: By mouth, 2.5–5 milliliters (½–1 teaspoon-ful) every 6 hours as needed.

11. **ANAMINE HD** Syrup (Chlorpheniramine, Hydrocodone, Phenylephrine): Rx
    Children 6–12 years: By mouth, 5 milliliters (1 teaspoonful) ev-ery 6–8 hours as needed.

12. **ANATUSS** Tablets (alcohol 12%; Acetaminophen, Chlor-pheniramine, Dextromethorphan, Guaifenesin, Phenylephrine, Phenylpropanolamine): Rx
    Children 6–12 years: By mouth, 1–2 tablets every 4 hours as needed.

13. **ANATUSS WITH CODEINE** Tablets (Acetaminophen, Chlorpheniramine, Codeine, Guaifenesin, Phenylpropanol-amine): OTC
    Children 6–12 years: By mouth, ½–1 tablet every 6 hours as needed.

14. **ANI-TUSS DM** Expectorant (alcohol 1.4%; Dextromethorphan, Guaifenesin): OTC
    Children 2–6 years: By mouth, 2.5 milliliters (½ teaspoonful) every 6–8 hours as needed.

Children 6–12 years: By mouth, 5 milliliters (1 teaspoonful) every 6–8 hours as needed.

15. **BANEX** Liquid (alcohol 5%; Guaifenesin, Phenylephrine, Phenylpropanolamine): Rx
   Children 2–4 years: By mouth, 2.5 milliliters (½ teaspoonful) every 6 hours as needed.
   Children 4–6 years: By mouth, 5 milliliters (1 teaspoonful) every 6 hours as needed.
   Children 6–12 years: By mouth, 7.5 milliliters (1½ teaspoonsful) every 6 hours as needed.

16. **BAYAMINIC** Expectorant (alcohol 5%; dye-free; Guaifenesin, Phenylpropanolamine): OTC
   Children 2–6 years: By mouth, 2.5 milliliters (½ teaspoonful) every 4 hours as needed.
   Children 6–12 years: By mouth, 5 milliliters (1 teaspoonful) every 4 hours as needed.

17. **BAYAMINICOL** Oral Solution (Chlorpheniramine, Dextromethorphan, Phenylpropanolamine): OTC
   Children 2–6 years: By mouth, 2.5 milliliters (½ teaspoonful) every 4 hours as needed.
   Children 6–12 years: By mouth, 5 milliliters (1 teaspoonful) every 4 hours as needed.

18. **BAYCODAN** Syrup (Homatropine, Hydrocodone): Rx
   Children to 2 years: By mouth, 1.25 milliliters every 4–6 hours as needed.
   Children 2–12 years: By mouth, 2.5 milliliters (½ teaspoonful) every 4–6 hours as needed.

19. **BAYCOMINE PEDIATRIC** Syrup (Hydrocodone, Phenylpropanolamine): Rx
   Children 2–6 years: By mouth, 2.5 milliliters (½ teaspoonful) every 4–6 hours as needed.
   Children 6–12 years: By mouth, 5 milliliters (1 teaspoonful) every 4–6 hours as needed.

20. **BAYCOMINE** Syrup (Hydrocodone, Phenylpropanolamine): Rx
   Children 6–12 years: By mouth, 2.5 milliliters (½ teaspoonful) every 4–6 hours as needed.

21. **BAYCOTUSSEND** Liquid (alcohol 5%; Hydrocodone, Pseudoephedrine): Rx

Children 2–6 years: By mouth, 1.25 milliliters every 4–6 hours as needed.

Children 6–12 years: By mouth, 2.5 milliliters (½ teaspoonful) every 4–6 hours as needed.

22. **BAYDEC DM** Drops (alcohol less than 0.6%; Carbinoxamine, Dextromethorphan, Pseudoephedrine): Rx

Children 1–3 months: By mouth, 0.25 milliliter every 4–6 hours as needed.

Children 3–6 months: By mouth, 0.5 milliliter every 4–6 hours as needed.

Children 6–9 months: By mouth, 0.75 milliliter every 4–6 hours as needed.

Children 9–18 months: By mouth, 1 milliliter every 4–6 hours as needed.

23. **BAYHISTINE DH** Oral Solution (alcohol 5%; Chlorpheniramine, Codeine, Pseudoephedrine): OTC

Children 2–6 years: By mouth, 2.5 milliliters (½ teaspoonful) every 4 hours as needed.

Children 6–12 years: By mouth, 5 milliliters (1 teaspoonful) every 4 hours as needed.

24. **BAYHISTINE** Expectorant (alcohol 7.5%; Codeine, Guaifenesin, Pseudoephedrine): OTC. See 23. *BAYHISTINE DH Oral Solution* (above).

25. **BAYTUSSIN AC** Oral Solution (alcohol 3.5%; Codeine, Guaifenesin): OTC. See 23. *BAYHISTINE DH* (above).

26. **BAYTUSSIN DM** Syrup (alcohol 1.4%; Dextromethorphan, Guaifenesin): OTC

Children 2–6 years: By mouth, 2.5 milliliters (½ teaspoonful) every 6–8 hours as needed.

Children 6–12 years: By mouth, 5 milliliters (1 teaspoonful) every 6–8 hours as needed.

27. **BENYLIN** Expectorant Cough Formula (alcohol 5%; Dextromethorphan, Guaifenesin): OTC

Children 2–6 years: By mouth, 2.5–5 milliliters (½–1 teaspoonful) every 4 hours as needed.

Children 6–12 years: By mouth, 5–10 milliliters (1–2 teaspoonsful) every 4 hours as needed.

28. **BIPHETANE DC** Syrup (alcohol 0.95%; Brompheniramine, Codeine, Phenylpropanolamine): OTC
Children 2–6 years: By mouth, 2.5 milliliters (½ teaspoonful) every 4 hours as needed.
Children 6–12 years: By mouth, 5 milliliters (1 teaspoonful) every 4 hours as needed.

29. **BREXSIN** Oral Solution (Carbinoxamine, Guaifenesin, Pseudoephedrine): Rx
Children 2–6 years: By mouth, 1.25–2.5 milliliters every 4 hours as needed.
Children 6–12 years: By mouth, 2.5–5 milliliters (½–1 teaspoonful) every 4 hours as needed.

30. **BROMANATE DC** Cough Syrup (alcohol 0.95%; Brompheniramine, Codeine, Phenylpropanolamine): OTC
Children 2–6 years: By mouth, 2.5 milliliters (½ teaspoonful) every 4 hours as needed.
Children 6–12 years: By mouth, 5 milliliters (1 teaspoonful) every 4 hours as needed.

31. **BROMFED-AT** Syrup (Brompheniramine, Dextromethorphan, Pseudoephedrine): OTC
Children 2–6 years: By mouth, 2.5 milliliters (½ teaspoonful) every 4 hours as needed.
Children 6–12 years: By mouth, 5 milliliters (1 teaspoonful) every 4 hours as needed.

32. **BROMFED-DM** Syrup (Brompheniramine, Dextromethorphan, Pseudoephedrine): OTC
Children 2–6 years: By mouth, 2.5 milliliters (½ teaspoonful) every 4 hours as needed.
Children 6–12 years: By mouth, 5 milliliters (1 teaspoonful) every 4 hours as needed.

33. **BROMPHEN DC WITH CODEINE** Cough Syrup (alcohol 0.95%; Brompheniramine, Codeine, Phenylpropanolamine): OTC. See 29. *BREXSIN Oral Solution* (above).

34. BRONCHOLATE Syrup (Ephedrine, Guaifenesin): Rx
Children 2–6 years: By mouth, 2.5–5 milliliters (½–1 teaspoon-ful) every 4 hours as needed.
Children 6–12 years: By mouth, 5–10 milliliters (1–2 teaspoons-ful) every 4 hours as needed.

35. BRONKOTUSS Expectorant (alcohol 5%; Chlorpheniramine, Ephedrine, Guaifenesin): Rx
Children 6–12 years: By mouth, 2.5 milliliters (½ teaspoonful) every 3–4 hours as needed.

36. CALCIDRINE Syrup (alcohol 6%; Calcium Iodide, Codeine): OTC
Children 2–6 years: By mouth, 2.5 milliliters (½ teaspoonful) every 4 hours as needed.
Children 6–10 years: By mouth, 2.5–5 milliliters (½–1 teaspoon-ful) every 4 hours as needed.

37. CARBODEC DM Drops (alcohol less than 0.6%; Carbinox-amine, Dextromethorphan, Pseudoephedrine): Rx
Children 1–3 months: By mouth, 0.25 milliliter every 4 hours as needed.
Children 3–6 months: By mouth, 0.5 milliliter every 4 hours as needed.
Children 6–9 months: By mouth, 0.75 milliliter every 4 hours as needed.
Children 9–18 months: By mouth, 1 milliliter every 4 hours as needed.

38. CARBODEC Syrup (alcohol less than 0.6%; Carbinoxamine, Dextromethorphan, Pseudoephedrine): Rx
Children 18 months–6 years: By mouth, 2.5 milliliters (½ tea-spoonful) every 4–6 hours as needed.
Children over 6 years: By mouth, 5 milliliters (1 teaspoonful) every 4–6 hours as needed.

39. CEROSE-DM Oral Solution (alcohol 2.4%; sugar-free; Chlorpheniramine, Dextromethorphan, Phenylephrine): OTC
Children 6–12 years: By mouth, 5 milliliters (1 teaspoonful) 4 times daily as needed.

40. CHERACOL D Cough Syrup (alcohol 4.75%; Dextromethorphan, Guaifenesin): OTC
Children 2–6 years: By mouth, 2.5 milliliters (½ teaspoonful) every 4 hours as needed.
Children 6–12 years: By mouth, 5 milliliters (1 teaspoonful) every 4 hours as needed.

41. CHERACOL PLUS Oral Solution (alcohol 8%; Chlorpheniramine, Dextromethorphan, Phenylpropanolamine): OTC
Children 6–12 years: By mouth, 7.5 milliliters (1½ teaspoonsful) every 4 hours as needed.

42. CHERACOL Syrup (alcohol 4.75%; Codeine, Guaifenesin): OTC
Children 2–6 years: By mouth, 1.25–2.5 milliliters every 4–6 hours as needed.
Children 6–12 years: By mouth, 2.5–5 milliliters (½–1 teaspoonful) every 4–6 hours as needed.

43. CITRA FORTE Syrup (alcohol 2%; Ascorbic Acid; Hydrocodone, Pheniramine, Potassium Citrate, Pyrilamine): Rx
Children 6–12 years: By mouth, 2.5–5 milliliters (½–1 teaspoonful) every 3–4 hours as needed.

44. CO-APAP Tablets (Acetaminophen, Chlorpheniramine, Dextromethorphan, Pseudoephedrine): OTC
Children 6–12 years: By mouth, 1 tablet every 6 hours as needed.

45. CODAMINE Syrup (Hydrocodone, Phenylpropanolamine): Rx
Children 6–12 years: By mouth, 2.5 milliliters (½ teaspoonful) every 4–6 hours as needed.

46. CODAN Syrup (Homatropine, Hydrocodone): Rx
Children to 2 years: By mouth, 1.25 milliliters every 4–6 hours as needed.
Children 2–12 years: By mouth, 2.5 milliliters (½ teaspoonful) every 4–6 hours as needed.

47. CODEHIST DH Elixir (alcohol 5%; Chlorpheniramine, Codeine, Pseudoephedrine): OTC

Children 2–6 years: By mouth, 1.25–2.5 milliliters every 4 hours as needed.

Children 6–12 years: By mouth, 2.5–5 milliliters (½–1 teaspoonful) every 4 hours as needed.

48. **Codeine and Terpin Hydrate Elixir** (alcohol 40%): OTC
Children 6–12 years: By mouth, 2.5–5 milliliters (½–1 teaspoonful) every 4–6 hours as needed.

49. **CODICLEAR DH** Syrup (contains no alcohol, dye, or sugar; Guaifenesin, Hydrocodone): Rx
Children 3–6 years: By mouth, 1.25–2.5 milliliters every 4–6 hours as needed.
Children 6–12 years: By mouth, 2.5–5 milliliters (½–1 teaspoonful) every 4–6 hours as needed.

50. **CODIMAL DH** Syrup (Hydrocodone, Phenylephrine, Pyrilamine): Rx
Children 6 months–2 years: By mouth, 1.25 milliliters every 6 hours as needed.
Children 2–6 years: By mouth, 2.5 milliliters (½ teaspoonful) every 4 hours as needed.
Children 6–12 years: By mouth, 5 milliliters (1 teaspoonful) every 4 hours as needed.

51. **CODIMAL DM** Oral Solution (alcohol 4%; sugar-free; Dextromethorphan, Phenylephrine, Pyrilamine): OTC
Children 6–12 years: By mouth, 5 milliliters (1 teaspoonful) every 4 hours as needed.

52. **CODIMAL** Expectorant (Guaifenesin, Phenylpropanolamine): OTC
Children 2–6 years: By mouth, 1.25 milliliters every 4 hours as needed.
Children 6–12 years: By mouth, 2.5 milliliters (½ teaspoonful) every 4 hours as needed.

53. **CODIMAL PH** Syrup (Codeine, Phenylephrine, Pyrilamine): OTC
Children 6–12 years: By mouth, 5 milliliters (1 teaspoonful) every 4 hours as needed.

54. CODISTAN NO. 1 Syrup (alcohol 1.4%; Dextromethorphan, Guaifenesin): OTC
   Children 2–6 years: By mouth, 2.5 milliliters (½ teaspoonful) every 6–8 hours as needed.
   Children 6–12 years: By mouth, 5 milliliters (1 teaspoonful) every 6–8 hours as needed.

55. COMTREX MULTI-SYMPTOM COLD RELIEVER Capsules (Acetaminophen, Chlorpheniramine, Dextromethorphan, Phenylpropanolamine): OTC
   Children 6–12 years: By mouth, 1 tablet every 4 hours as needed.

56. COMTREX MULTI-SYMPTOM COLD RELIEVER Oral Solution (alcohol 20%; Acetaminophen, Chlorpheniramine, Dextromethorphan, Phenylpropanolamine): OTC
   Children 6–12 years: By mouth, 15 milliliters (1 tablespoonful) every 4 hours as needed.

57. COMTREX MULTI-SYMPTOM COLD RELIEVER Tablets (Acetaminophen, Chlorpheniramine, Dextromethorphan, Phenylpropanolamine): OTC
   Children 6–12 years: 1 tablet every 4 hours as needed.

58. CONAR Oral Suspension (sugar-free; Dextromethorphan, Phenylephrine): OTC
   Children 2–6 years: By mouth, 1.25–2.5 milliliters every 3–4 hours as needed.
   Children 6–12 years: By mouth, 2.5–5 milliliters (½–1 teaspoonful) every 3–4 hours as needed.

59. CONAR Expectorant (Dextromethorphan, Guaifenesin, Phenylephrine): OTC. See *58. CONAR Oral Suspension* (above).

60. CONCENTRIN Capsules (Dextromethorphan, Guaifenesin, Pseudoephedrine): OTC
   Children 6–12 years: By mouth, 1 capsule every 6 hours as needed.

61. CONEX Syrup (Guaifenesin, Phenylpropanolamine): OTC
   Children 2–6 years: By mouth, 2.5 milliliters (½ teaspoonful) every 4–6 hours as needed.

Children 6–12 years: By mouth, 5 milliliters (1 teaspoonful) every 4–6 hours as needed.

62. CONEX WITH CODEINE Liquid (Codeine, Guaifenesin, Phenylpropanolamine): OTC
Children 2–6 years: By mouth, 1.25–2.5 milliliters every 4–6 hours as needed.
Children 6–12 years: By mouth, 2.5–5 milliliters (½–1 teaspoonful) every 4–6 hours as needed.

63. CONGESS JR Extended-release Capsules (Guaifenesin, Pseudoephedrine): Rx
Children 6–12 years: By mouth, 1 capsule every 12 hours as needed.

64. CONTAC JR. CHILDREN'S COLD MEDICINE Oral Solution (alcohol 10%; Acetaminophen, Dextromethorphan, Phenylpropanolamine): OTC
Children 31–47 pounds: By mouth, 2.5 milliliters (½ teaspoonful) every 4 hours as needed.
Children 47–65 pounds: By mouth, 5 milliliters (1 teaspoonful) every 4 hours as needed.
Children 65–85 pounds: By mouth, 7.5 milliliters (1½ teaspoonsful) every 4 hours.

65. COPHENE-S Syrup (Chlorpheniramine, Dihydrocodone, Phenylephrine, Phenylpropanolamine): Rx
Children 2–6 years: By mouth, 0.625–1.25 milliliters every 4–6 hours as needed.
Children 6–12 years: By mouth, 1.25–2.5 milliliters every 4–6 hours as needed.

66. COPHENE-XP Syrup (Carbetapentane, Chlorpheniramine, Phenylephrine, Phenylpropanolamine, Potassium Guaicolsulfonate): Rx
Children 2–6 years: By mouth, 1.25–2.5 milliliters every 6 hours as needed.
Children 6–12 years: By mouth, 2.5–5 milliliters (½–1 teaspoonful) every 6 hours as needed.

67. CORICIDIN Cough Syrup (alcohol less than 0.5%; Dextromethorphan, Guaifenesin, Phenylpropanolamine): OTC

Children 2–6 years: By mouth, 2.5 milliliters (½ teaspoonful) every 4 hours as needed.

Children 6–12 years: By mouth, 5 milliliters (1 teaspoonful) every 4 hours as needed.

68. COTYLENOL COLD MEDICATION (Acetaminophen, Chlorpheniramine, Dextromethorphan, Pseudoephedrine): OTC
- Capsules:
  Children 6–12 years: By mouth, 1 capsule every 6 hours as needed.
- Oral solution (also contains alcohol 7.5%):
  Children 6–12 years: By mouth, 15 milliliters (1 tablespoonful) every 4–6 hours as needed.
- Tablets:
  Children 6–12 years: By mouth, 1 tablet every 6 hours as needed.

69. C-TUSSIN Expectorant (alcohol 7.5%; Codeine, Guaifenesin, Pseudoephedrine): Rx
Children 2–6 years: By mouth, 2.5 milliliters (½ teaspoonful) every 4 hours as needed.
Children 6–12 years: By mouth, 5 milliliters (1 teaspoonful) every 4 hours as needed.

70. DAYCARE Oral Solution (alcohol 10%; Acetaminophen, Dextromethorphan, Guaifenesin, Pseudoephedrine) and Tablets: OTC
Children 6–12 years: By mouth, 15 milliliters (1 tablespoonful) or 1 tablet every 4 hours as needed.

71. DEPROSIT EXPECTORANT W/CODEINE (alcohol 7.5%; Codeine, Guaifenesin, Pseudoephedrine): Rx
Children 2–6 years: By mouth, 2.5 milliliters (½ teaspoonful) every 4 hours as needed.
Children 6–12 years: By mouth, 5 milliliters (1 teaspoonful) every 4 hours as needed.

72. DE-TUSS Syrup (alcohol 5%; Hydrocodone, Pseudoephedrine): Rx
Children 2–6 years: By mouth, 1.25 milliliters every 4–6 hours as needed.

Children 6–12 years: By mouth, 2.5 milliliters (½ teaspoonful) every 4–6 hours as needed.

73. DETUSSIN Liquid (alcohol 5%; Hydrocodone, Pseudoephedrine): Rx
Children 2–6 years: By mouth, 1.25 milliliters every 4–6 hours as needed.
Children 6–12 years: By mouth, 2.5 milliliters (½ teaspoonful) every 4–6 hours as needed.

74. DIHISTINE DH (alcohol 5%; Chlorpheniramine, Codeine, Pseudoephedrine): Rx
Children 2–6 years: By mouth, 1.25–2.5 milliliters every 6 hours as needed.
Children 6–12 years: By mouth, 2.5–5 milliliters (½–1 teaspoonful) every 6 hours as needed.

75. DIMETANE-DC Cough Syrup (alcohol 0.95%; Brompheniramine, Codeine, Phenylpropanolamine): Rx
Children 2–6 years: By mouth, 2.5 milliliters (½ teaspoonful) every 4 hours as needed.
Children 6–12 years: By mouth, 5 milliliters (1 teaspoonful) every 4 hours as needed.

76. DIMETANE-DX Cough Syrup (alcohol 0.95%; Brompheniramine, Dextromethorphan, Pseudoephedrine): Rx. See *75. DIMETANE-DC Cough Syrup* (above).

77. DIMETAPP DM COUGH AND COLD Syrup (alcohol 2.3%; Brompheniramine, Dextromethorphan, Phenylpropanolamine): OTC
Children 2–6 years: By mouth, 1.25–2.5 milliliters every 4 hours as needed.
Children 6–12 years: By mouth, 2.5–5 milliliters (½–1 teaspoonful) every 4 hours as needed.

78. DONATUSSIN DC Syrup (Guaifenesin, Hydrocodone, Phenylephrine): Rx
Children 2–6 years: By mouth, 2.5 milliliters (½ teaspoonful) every 6 hours as needed.
Children 6–12 years: By mouth, 5 milliliters (1 teaspoonful) every 6 hours as needed.

79. DONATUSSIN Drops (Chlorpheniramine, Guaifenesin, Phenylephrine): Rx
Children to 3 months: By mouth, 2–3 drops per month of age every 4–6 hours as needed.
Children 3–6 months: By mouth, 0.3–0.6 milliliter every 4–6 hours as needed.
Children 6 months–1 year: By mouth, 0.6–1 milliliter every 4–6 hours as needed.
Children 1–2 years: By mouth, 1–2 milliliters every 4–6 hours as needed.

80. DONATUSSIN Syrup (Chlorpheniramine, Dextromethorphan, Guaifenesin, Phenylephrine): Rx
Children 2–4 years: By mouth, 1.5 milliliters every 4–6 hours as needed.
Children 4–12 years: By mouth, 2.5–5 milliliters ($\frac{1}{2}$–1 teaspoonful) every 4–6 hours as needed.

81. DONDRIL Tablets (Chlorpheniramine, Dextromethorphan, Phenylephrine): OTC
Children 6–12 years: By mouth, 1 tablet every 4 hours as needed.

82. DORCOL CHILDREN'S Cough Syrup (Dextromethorphan, Guaifenesin, Pseudoephedrine): OTC
Children 3–12 months: By mouth, 3 drops for each 2.2 pounds of body weight every 4 hours as needed.
Children 1–2 years: By mouth, 7 drops for each 2.2 pounds of body weight every 4 hours as needed.
Children 2–6 years: By mouth, 5 milliliters (1 teaspoonful) every 4 hours as needed.
Children 6–12 years: By mouth, 10 milliliters (2 teaspoonsful) every 4 hours as needed.

83. DURA-VENT Extended-release Tablets (dye-free; Guaifenesin, Phenylpropanolamine): Rx
Children 6–12 years: By mouth, $\frac{1}{2}$ tablet every 12 hours as needed.

84. EFFICOL COUGH WHIP (COUGH SUPPRESSANT/DECON-GESTANT/ANTIHISTAMINE) Oral Gel (Dextromethorphan, Phenylpropanolamine): OTC

Children 6–12 years: By mouth, 10 milliliters (2 teaspoonsful) every 4 hours as needed.

85. **EFFICOL COUGH WHIP (COUGH SUPPRESSANT/EXPEC- TORANT)** Oral Gel (Chlorpheniramine, Dextromethorphan, Phenylpropanolamine): OTC
Children 2–6 years: By mouth, 5 milliliters (1 teaspoonful) every 4 hours as needed.
Children 6–12 years: By mouth, 10 milliliters (2 teaspoonsful) every 4 hours as needed.

86. **EFRICON** Expectorant (Ammonium Chloride, Chlor- pheniramine, Codeine, Phenylephrine, Potassium Guaiacol- sulfonate, sodium citrate): Rx
Children 2–6 years: By mouth, 1.25–2.5 milliliters every 4–6 hours as needed.
Children 6–12 years: By mouth, 2.5–5 milliliters (½–1 teaspoon- ful) every 4–6 hours as needed.

87. **ENDAL-HD** Oral Solution (Chlorpheniramine, Hydrocodone, Phenylephrine): Rx
Children 6–12 years: By mouth, 5 milliliters (1 teaspoonful) ev- ery 6–8 hours as needed.

88. **ENTEX LA** Extended-release Tablets (Guaifenesin, Phenylprop- anolamine): Rx
Children 6–12 years: By mouth, ½ tablet every 12 hours as needed.

89. **ENTEX** Liquid (alcohol 5%; Guaifenesin, Phenylephrine, Phenylpropanolamine): Rx
Children 2–4 years: By mouth, 2.5 milliliters (½ teaspoonful) every 6 hours as needed.
Children 4–6 years: By mouth, 5 milliliters (1 teaspoonful) every 6 hours as needed.
Children 6–12 years: By mouth, 7.5 milliliters (1½ teaspoonsful) every 6 hours as needed.

90. **ENTUSS-D** (Hydrocodone, Pseudoephedrine): Rx
• Oral Solution (dye-free; sugar-free):
   Children 3–6 years: By mouth, 1.25–2.5 milliliters every 4–6 hours as needed.

Children 6–12 years: By mouth, 2.5–5 milliliters (½–1 tea-spoonful) every 4–6 hours as needed.
- Tablets:
Children 6–12 years: By mouth, ½–1 tablet every 4–6 hours as needed.

91. ENTUSS Expectorant (sugar-free; Hydrocodone, Potassium Guaiacolsulfonate): Rx
Children 3–6 years: By mouth, 1.25–2.5 milliliters every 4–6 hours as needed.
Children 6–12 years: By mouth, 2.5–5 milliliters (½–1 teaspoon-ful) every 4–6 hours as needed.
- Pediatric Expectorant (Guaifenesin, Hydrocodone, Pseudo-ephedrine): Rx
Children 6–12 years: By mouth, 5 milliliters (1 teaspoonful) every 4–6 hours as needed.

92. EXTRA ACTION Cough Syrup (alcohol 1.4%; Dex-tromethorphan, Guaifenesin): OTC
Children 2–6 years: By mouth, 2.5 milliliters (½ teaspoonful) every 6–8 hours as needed.
Children 6–12 years: By mouth, 5 milliliters (1 teaspoonful) every 6–8 hours as needed.

93. FATHER JOHN'S MEDICINE PLUS (Ammonium Chloride, Chlorpheniramine, Dextromethorphan, Guaifenesin, Phenyl-ephrine): OTC
Children 2–6 years: By mouth, 5 milliliters (1 teaspoonful) every 6–8 hours as needed.
Children 6–12 years: By mouth, 5–10 milliliters (1–2 teaspoons-ful) every 6–8 hours as needed.

94. FEDAHIST Expectorant (Guaifenesin, Pseudoephedrine): OTC
Children 2–6 years: By mouth, 2.5 milliliters (½ teaspoonful) every 6 hours as needed.
Children 6–12 years: By mouth, 5 milliliters (1 teaspoonful) every 6 hours as needed.
- Pediatric Drops: OTC
Children 2–6 years: By mouth, 2 milliliters every 4–6 hours as needed.
Children 6–12 years: By mouth, 4 milliliters every 4–6 hours as needed.

95. 2/G-DM Cough Syrup (alcohol 5%; Dextromethorphan, Guaifenesin): OTC
Children 2–6 years: By mouth, 2.5 milliliters (½ teaspoonful) every 6–8 hours as needed.
Children 6–12 years: By mouth, 5 milliliters (1 teaspoonful) every 6–8 hours as needed.

96. GLYCOTUSS-DM Tablets (Dextromethorphan, Guaifenesin): OTC
Children 6–12 years: By mouth, 1 tablet every 4 hours as needed.

97. GLYDEINE Cough Syrup (alcohol 3.5%; Codeine, Guaifenesin): Rx
Children 2–6 years: By mouth, 2.5 milliliters (½ teaspoonful) every 4 hours as needed.
Children 6–12 years: By mouth, 5 milliliters (1 teaspoonful) every 4 hours as needed.

98. GUAIFED-PD Extended-release Capsules (Guaifenesin, Pseudoephedrine): Rx
Children 6–12 years: By mouth, 1 capsule every 12 hours as needed.

99. GUAIPAX Extended-release Tablets (Guaifenesin, Phenylpropanolamine): Rx
Children 6–12 years: By mouth, ½ tablet every 12 hours as needed.

100. GUIAMID D.M. Liquid (alcohol 1.4%; Dextromethorphan, Guaifenesin): OTC
Children 2–6 years: By mouth, 2.5 milliliters (½ teaspoonful) every 6–8 hours as needed.
Children 6–12 years: By mouth, 5 milliliters (1 teaspoonful) every 6–8 hours as needed.

101. GUIATUSS A.C. Syrup (alcohol 3.5%; Codeine, Guaifenesin): Rx
Children 2–6 years: By mouth, 1.25–2.5 milliliters every 4–6 hours as needed.
Children 6–12 years: By mouth, 2.5–5 milliliters (½–1 teaspoonful) every 4–6 hours as needed.

102. **GUIATUSS-DM** Syrup (alcohol 1.4%; Dextromethorphan, Guaifenesin): OTC
Children 2–6 years: By mouth, 2.5 milliliters (½ teaspoonful) every 6–8 hours as needed.
Children 6–12 years: By mouth, 5 milliliters (1 teaspoonful) every 6–8 hours as needed.

103. **GUIATUSSIN W/CODEINE** Liquid (alcohol 3.5%; Codeine, Guaifenesin): Rx
Children 2–6 years: By mouth, 1.25–2.5 milliliters every 4–6 hours as needed.
Children 6–12 years: By mouth, 2.5–5 milliliters (½–1 teaspoonful) every 4–6 hours as needed.

104. **HALOTUSSIN-DM** Expectorant (alcohol 1.4%; Dextromethorphan, Guaifenesin): OTC
Children 2–6 years: By mouth, 2.5 milliliters (½ teaspoonful) every 6–8 hours as needed.
Children 6–12 years: By mouth, 5 milliliters (1 teaspoonful) every 6–8 hours as needed.

105. **HISTAFED C** Syrup (Codeine, Pseudoephedrine, Triprolidine): Rx
Children 2–6 years: By mouth, 2.5 milliliters (½ teaspoonful) every 4–6 hours as needed.
Children 6–12 years: By mouth, 5 milliliters (1 teaspoonful) every 4–6 hours as needed.

106. **HISTALET X** Syrup (alcohol 1.5%; Guaifenesin, Pseudoephedrine): Rx
Children 2–6 years: By mouth, 2.5 milliliters (½ teaspoonful) every 6 hours as needed.
Children 6–12 years: By mouth, 5 milliliters (1 teaspoonful) every 6 hours as needed.

107. **HISTALET X** Tablets (Guaifenesin, Pseudoephedrine): Rx
Children 6–12 years: By mouth, ½ tablet every 12 hours as needed.

108. **HISTATUSS PEDIATRIC** Suspension (Carbetapentane, Chlorpheniramine, Ephedrine, Phenylephrine): Rx

Children 2–6 years: By mouth, 2.5–5 milliliters ($\frac{1}{2}$–1 teaspoon-ful) every 12 hours as needed.

Children 6–12 years: By mouth, 5–10 milliliters (1–2 teaspoons-ful) every 12 hours as needed.

109. HOLD (Children's Formula) Lozenges (Dextromethorphan, Phenylpropanolamine): OTC

Children 3–6 years: By mouth, 1 lozenge every 4 hours as needed.

Children over 6 years: By mouth, 2 lozenges every 4 hours as needed.

110. HYCODAN (Homatropine, Hydrocodone): Rx
- Syrup
  Children to 2 years: By mouth, 1.25 milliliters every 4–6 hours as needed.
  Children 2–12 years: By mouth, 2.5 milliliters ($\frac{1}{2}$ teaspoonful) every 4–6 hours as needed.
- Tablets:
  Children to 2 years: By mouth, $\frac{1}{4}$ tablet every 4–6 hours as needed.
  Children 2–12 years: By mouth, $\frac{1}{2}$ tablet every 4–6 hours as needed.

111. HYCOMINE COMPOUND Tablets (Acetaminophen, Caffeine, Chlorpheniramine, Hydrocodone, Phenylephrine): Rx

Children 2–6 years: By mouth, $\frac{1}{2}$ tablet every 12 hours as needed.

Children 6–12 years: By mouth, $\frac{1}{2}$ tablet every 6 hours as needed.

112. HYCOMINE PEDIATRIC Syrup (sugar-free; Hydrocodone, Phenylpropanolamine): Rx

Children 2–6 years: By mouth, 2.5 milliliters ($\frac{1}{2}$ teaspoonful) every 4–6 hours as needed.

Children 6–12 years: By mouth, 5 milliliters (1 teaspoonful) every 4–6 hours as needed.

113. HYCOMINE Syrup (sugar-free; Hydrocodone, Phenylpropanol-amine): Rx

Children 6–12 years: By mouth, 2.5 milliliters ($\frac{1}{2}$ teaspoonful) every 4–6 hours as needed.

114. HYCOTUSS Expectorant (alcohol 10%; Guaifenesin, Hydrocodone): Rx
Children 2–12 years: By mouth, 2.5 milliliters (½ teaspoonful) every 4–6 hours as needed.

115. HYDROMINE PEDIATRIC Syrup (Hydrocodone, Phenylpropanolamine): Rx
Children 6–12 years: By mouth, 5 milliliters (1 teaspoonful) every 4 hours as needed.

116. HYDROPANE Syrup (Homatropine, Hydrocodone): Rx
Children to 2 years: By mouth, 1.25 milliliters every 4–6 hours as needed.
Children 2–12 years: By mouth, 2.5 milliliters (½ teaspoonful) every 4–6 hours as needed.

117. HYDROPHEN Oral Solution (Hydrocodone, Phenylpropanolamine): Rx
Children 6–12 years: By mouth, 2.5 milliliters (½ teaspoonful) every 4–6 hours as needed.

118. IOPHEN-C Liquid (Codeine, Iodinated Glycerol): Rx
Children 2–6 years: By mouth, 1.25–2.5 milliliters every 4–6 hours as needed.
Children 6–12 years: By mouth, 2.5–5 milliliters (½–1 teaspoonful) every 4–6 hours as needed.

119. IOTUSS-DM Oral Solution (Dextromethorphan, Iodinated Glycerol): Rx. See *120. IOTUSS Oral Solution* (below).

120. IOTUSS Oral Solution (Codeine, Iodinated Glycerol): Rx
Children 6–12 years: By mouth, 2.5–5 milliliters (½–1 teaspoonful) every 4 hours as needed.

121. IPSATOL COUGH FORMULA FOR CHILDREN (Dextromethorphan, Guaifenesin, Phenylpropanolamine): OTC
Children 2–6 years: By mouth, 2.5–5 milliliters (½–1 teaspoonful) every 4–6 hours as needed.
Children over 6 years: By mouth, 5–10 milliliters (1–2 teaspoonful) every 4–6 hours as needed.

122. **ISOCLOR** Expectorant (alcohol 5%; Codeine, Guaifenesin, Pseudoephedrine): Rx
Children 2–6 years: By mouth, 1.25–2.5 milliliters every 4–6 hours as needed.
Children 6–12 years: By mouth, 2.5–5 milliliters (½–1 teaspoonful) every 4–6 hours as needed.

123. **KIDDY KOFF** (alcohol 5%; Dextromethorphan, Guaifenesin, Phenylpropanolamine): OTC
Children 2–6 years: By mouth, 5 milliliters (1 teaspoonful) every 4 hours as needed.
Children 6–12 years: By mouth, 10 milliliters (2 teaspoonsful) every 4 hours as needed.

124. **KIE** Syrup (Ephedrine, Potassium Iodide): Rx
Children 2–6 years: By mouth, 2.5–5 milliliters (½–1 teaspoonful) every 4–6 hours as needed.
Children 6–12 years: By mouth, 5–10 milliliters (1–2 teaspoonsful) every 4–6 hours as needed.

125. **KOLEPHRIN GG/DM** Oral Solution (Dextromethorphan, Guaifenesin): OTC
Children 2–6 years: By mouth, 2.5 milliliters (½ teaspoonful) every 6–8 hours as needed.
Children 6–12 years: By mouth, 5 milliliters (1 teaspoonful) every 6–8 hours as needed.

126. **KOLEPHRIN NN** Liquid (Dextromethorphan, Phenylpropanolamine, Pyrilamine, Sodium Salicylate): OTC
Children 2–6 years: By mouth, 2.5–5 milliliters (½–1 teaspoonful) every 6–8 hours as needed.
Children 6–12 years: By mouth, 5–10 milliliters (1–2 teaspoonsful) every 6–8 hours as needed.

127. **KOPHANE COUGH AND COLD FORMULA** (Chlorpheniramine, Dextromethorphan, Phenylpropanolamine): OTC
Children 3–12 months: By mouth, 1 drop for each 2.2 pounds of body weight every 4 hours as needed.
Children 1–2 years: By mouth, 3 drops for each 2.2 pounds of body weight every 4 hours as needed.
Children 2–6 years: By mouth, 2.5 milliliters (½ teaspoonful) every 4 hours as needed.

Children 6–12 years: By mouth, 5 milliliters (1 teaspoonful) every 4 hours as needed.

128. KOPHANE Syrup (sucrose; Ammonium Chloride, Chlorpheniramine, Dextromethorphan, Phenylpropanolamine): OTC
Children 2–6 years: By mouth, 1.25–2.5 milliliters every 4 hours as needed.
Children 6–12 years: By mouth, 2.5–5 milliliters (½–1 teaspoonful) every 4 hours as needed.

129. LANATUSS Expectorant (Chlorpheniramine, Citric Acid, Guaifenesin, Phenylpropanolamine, Sodium Citrate): OTC
Children 2–6 years: By mouth, 1.25–2.5 milliliters every 6–8 hours as needed.
Children 6–12 years: By mouth, 2.5–5 milliliters (½–1 teaspoonful) every 6–8 hours as needed.

130. MALLERGAN-VC W/CODEINE Syrup (alcohol 7%; Codeine, Phenylephrine, Promethazine): Rx
Children 2–6 years: By mouth, 1.25–2.5 milliliters every 4–6 hours as needed.
Children 6–12 years: By mouth, 2.5–5 milliliters (½–1 teaspoonful) every 4–6 hours as needed.

131. MEDA Syrup Forte (Chlorpheniramine, Dextromethorphan, Guaifenesin, Phenylephrine): OTC
Children 6–12 years: By mouth, 2.5–5 milliliters (½–1 teaspoonful) every 4–6 hours as needed.

132. MEDATUSSIN Syrup (sugar-free; Citric Acid, Dextromethorphan, Guaifenesin, Potassium Citrate): OTC
Children 6–12 years: By mouth, 5 milliliters (1 teaspoonful) every 6–8 hours as needed.

133. MEDIQUELL DECONGESTANT FORMULA Chewable Tablets (Dextromethorphan, Pseudoephedrine): OTC
Children 2–6 years: By mouth, ½ tablet every 6 hours as needed.
Children 6–12 years: By mouth, 1 tablet every 6 hours as needed.

134. MIDAHIST DH Elixir (alcohol 5%; Chlorpheniramine, Codeine, Pseudoephedrine): Rx

Children 2–6 years: By mouth, 1.25–2.5 milliliters every 6 hours as needed.
Children 6–12 years: By mouth, 2.5–5 milliliters (½–1 teaspoonful) every 6 hours as needed.

135. MYCOTUSSIN Oral Solution (alcohol 5%; Hydrocodone, Pseudoephedrine): Rx
Children 2–6 years: By mouth, 1.25 milliliters every 4–6 hours as needed.
Children 6–12 years: By mouth, 2.5 milliliters (½ teaspoonful) every 4–6 hours as needed.

136. MYHISTINE DH Elixir (alcohol 5%; Chlorpheniramine, Codeine, Pseudoephedrine): Rx
Children 2–6 years: By mouth, 1.25–2.5 milliliters every 6 hours as needed.
Children 6–12 years: By mouth, 2.5–5 milliliters (½–1 teaspoonful) every 6 hours as needed.

137. MYHISTINE Expectorant (alcohol 7.5%; Codeine, Guaifenesin, Pseudoephedrine): Rx
Children 2–6 years: By mouth, 2.5 milliliters (½ teaspoonful) every 4 hours as needed.
Children 6–12 years: By mouth, 5 milliliters (1 teaspoonful) every 4 hours as needed.

138. MYHYDROMINE PEDIATRIC Syrup (Hydrocodone, Phenylpropanolamine): Rx
Children 6–12 years: By mouth, 5 milliliters (1 teaspoonful) every 4 hours as needed.

139. MYHYDROMINE Syrup (Hydrocodone, Phenylpropanolamine): Rx
Children 6–12 years: By mouth, 2.5 milliliters (½ teaspoonful) every 4–6 hours as needed.

140. MYPHETANE DC Cough Syrup (alcohol 0.95%; Brompheniramine, Codeine, Phenylpropanolamine): Rx
Children 2–6 years: By mouth, 2.5 milliliters (½ teaspoonful) every 4 hours as needed.
Children 6–12 years: By mouth, 5 milliliters (1 teaspoonful) every 4 hours as needed.

141. MYTUSSIN AC Oral Solution (alcohol 3.5%; Codeine, Guaifenesin): Rx

Children 2–6 years: By mouth, 2.5 milliliters (½ teaspoonful) every 4 hours as needed.

Children 6–12 years: By mouth, 5 milliliters (1 teaspoonful) every 4 hours as needed.

142. MYTUSSIN DAC Oral Solution (alcohol 1.4%; Codeine, Guaifenesin, Pseudoephedrine): Rx. See *141. MYTUSSIN AC Oral Solution* (above).

143. MYTUSSIN DM Oral Solution (alcohol 1.4%; Dextromethorphan, Guaifenesin): OTC

Children 2–6 years: By mouth, 2.5 milliliters (½ teaspoonful) every 6–8 hours as needed.

Children 6–12 years: By mouth, 5 milliliters (1 teaspoonful) every 6–8 hours as needed.

144. NALDECON-CX ADULT Liquid (sugar-free; Codeine, Guaifenesin, Phenylpropanolamine): Rx

Children 2–6 years: By mouth, 1.25–2.5 milliliters every 4–6 hours as needed.

Children 6–12 years: By mouth, 2.5–5 milliliters (½–1 teaspoonful) every 4–6 hours as needed.

145. NALDECON-DX CHILDREN'S Syrup (alcohol 0.6%; Dextromethorphan, Guaifenesin, Phenylpropanolamine): OTC

Children 2–6 years: By mouth, 5 milliliters (1 teaspoonful) every 4–6 hours as needed.

Children over 6 years: By mouth, 10 milliliters (2 teaspoonsful) every 4–6 hours as needed.

146. NALDECON-DX PEDIATRIC Drops (alcohol 0.6%; Dextromethorphan, Guaifenesin, Phenylpropanolamine): OTC

Children over 2 years: By mouth, 1 milliliter every 4 hours as needed.

147. NALDECON-EX Oral Solution (alcohol 0.6%; Guaifenesin, Phenylpropanolamine): OTC

Children 1–3 months: By mouth, 0.25 milliliter every 4–6 hours as needed.

Children 4–6 months: By mouth, 0.5 milliliter every 4–6 hours as needed.

Children 7–9 months: By mouth, 0.75 milliliter every 4–6 hours as needed.

Children over 10 months: By mouth, 1 milliliter every 4–6 hours as needed.

148. NALDECON-EX Syrup (alcohol 5%; Guaifenesin, Phenylpropanolamine): OTC

Children 2–6 years: By mouth, 5 milliliters (1 teaspoonful) every 4 hours as needed.

Children 6–12 years: By mouth, 10 milliliters (2 teaspoonsful) every 4 hours as needed.

149. NALDECON SENIOR DX Oral Solution (Dextromethorphan, Guaifenesin): OTC

Children 2–6 years: By mouth, 1.25–2.5 milliliters every 6–8 hours as needed.

Children 6–12 years: By mouth, 2.5–5 milliliters (½–1 teaspoonful) every 6–8 hours as needed.

150. NORATUSS II Liquid (sodium and sugar-free; Dextromethorphan, Guaifenesin, Pseudoephedrine): OTC

Children 2–6 years: By mouth, 5 milliliters (1 teaspoonful) every 4 hours as needed.

Children 6–12 years: By mouth, 10 milliliters (2 teaspoonsful) every 4 hours as needed.

151. NORMATANE DC Syrup (alcohol 0.95%; Brompheniramine, Codeine, Phenylpropanolamine): Rx

Children 2–6 years: By mouth, 2.5 milliliters (½ teaspoonful) every 4 hours as needed.

Children 6–12 years: By mouth, 5 milliliters (1 teaspoonful) every 4 hours as needed.

152. NORTUSSIN W/CODEINE Oral Solution (alcohol 3.5%; Codeine, Guaifenesin): Rx

Children 2–6 years: By mouth, 1.25–2.5 milliliters every 4–6 hours as needed.

Children 6–12 years: By mouth, 2.5–5 milliliters (½–1 teaspoonful) every 4–6 hours as needed.

153. NOVAHISTINE DH Liquid (alcohol 5%; Chlorpheniramine, Codeine, Pseudoephedrine): Rx
Children 2–6 years: By mouth, 1.25–2.5 milliliters every 4–6 hours as needed.
Children 6–12 years: By mouth, 2.5–5 milliliters (½–1 teaspoonful) every 4–6 hours as needed.

154. NOVAHISTINE DMX Liquid (alcohol 10%; Dextromethorphan, Guaifenesin, Pseudoephedrine): OTC
Children 2–6 years: By mouth, 2.5 milliliters (½ teaspoonful) every 4–6 hours as needed.
Children 6–12 years: By mouth, 5 milliliters (1 teaspoonful) every 4–6 hours as needed.

155. NOVAHISTINE Expectorant (alcohol 7.5%; Codeine, Guaifenesin, Pseudoephedrine): Rx
Children 2–6 years: By mouth, 2.5 milliliters (½ teaspoonful) every 4–6 hours as needed.
Children 6–12 years: By mouth, 5 milliliters (1 teaspoonful) every 4–6 hours as needed.

156. NUCOCHEM Expectorant (alcohol 1.25%; Codeine, Guaifenesin, Pseudoephedrine): Rx. See 158. *NUCOCHEM Syrup* (below).

157. NUCOCHEM PEDIATRIC Expectorant (alcohol 6%; Codeine, Guaifenesin, Pseudoephedrine): Rx
Children 2–6 years: By mouth, 2.5 milliliters (½ teaspoonful) every 6 hours as needed.
Children 6–12 years: By mouth, 5 milliliters (1 teaspoonful) every 6 hours as needed.

158. NUCOCHEM Syrup (Codeine, Pseudoephedrine): Rx
Children 2–6 years: By mouth, 1.25 milliliters every 6 hours as needed.
Children 6–12 years: By mouth, 2.5 milliliters (½ teaspoonful) every 6 hours as needed.

159. NUCOFED Expectorant (alcohol 12.5%; Codeine, Guaifenesin, Pseudoephedrine): Rx. See 161. *NUCOFED Syrup* (below).

160. **NUCOFED PEDIATRIC** Expectorant (alcohol 6%; Codeine, Guaifenesin, Pseudoephedrine): Rx
Children 2–6 years: By mouth, 1.25–2.5 milliliters every 4–6 hours as needed.
Children 6–12 years: By mouth, 2.5–5 milliliters (½–1 teaspoonful) every 4–6 hours as needed.

161. **NUCOFED** Syrup (sucrose; Codeine, Pseudoephedrine): Rx
Children 2–6 years: By mouth, 0.62–1.25 milliliters every 6 hours as needed.
Children 6–12 years: By mouth, 1.25–2.5 milliliters every 6 hours as needed.

162. **PEDIACARE CHILDREN'S COLD RELIEF NIGHT REST COUGH-COLD FORMULA** (Chlorpheniramine, Dextromethorphan, Pseudoephedrine): OTC
Children 6–11 years: By mouth, 10 milliliters (2 teaspoonsful) every 6–8 hours as needed.

163. **PEDIACARE CHILDREN'S COUGH-COLD FORMULA** Chewable Tablets (Chlorpheniramine, Dextromethorphan, Pseudoephedrine): OTC
Children 6–11 years: By mouth, 4 every 4–6 hours as needed.

164. **PEDIACOF** Cough Syrup (alcohol 5%; Chlorpheniramine, Codeine, Phenylephrine, Potassium Iodide): Rx
Children 6 months–1 year: By mouth, 1.25 milliliters every 4–6 hours as needed.
Children 1–3 years: By mouth, 2.5–5 milliliters (½–1 teaspoonful) every 4–6 hours as needed.
Children 3–6 years: By mouth, 5–10 milliliters (1–2 teaspoonsful) every 4–6 hours as needed.
Children 6–12 years: By mouth, 10 milliliters (2 teaspoonsful) every 4–6 hours as needed.

165. **PERTUSSIN AM** Oral Solution (alcohol 10%; Dextromethorphan, Guaifenesin, Pseudoephedrine): OTC
Children 6–12 years: By mouth, 5 milliliters (1 teaspoonful) every 4 hours as needed.

166. **PERTUSSIN CS** Oral Solution (alcohol 8.5%; Dextromethorphan, Guaifenesin): OTC

Children 2–5 years: By mouth, 5 milliliters (1 teaspoonful) every 3 hours as needed.

Children 6–12 years: By mouth, 10 milliliters (2 teaspoonsful) every 3 hours as needed.

167. PHANADEX Syrup (sodium-free; Citric Acid, Dextromethorphan, Guaifenesin, Phenylpropanolamine, Potassium Citrate, Pyrilamine): OTC

Children 2–6 years: By mouth, 2.5 milliliters (½ teaspoonful) every 4–6 hours as needed.

Children 6–12 years: By mouth, 5 milliliters (1 teaspoonful) every 4–6 hours as needed.

168. PHANATUSS Syrup (sugar-free; Citric Acid, Dextromethorphan, Guaifenesin, Potassium Citrate): OTC

Children 6–12 years: By mouth, 5 milliliters (1 teaspoonful) every 6–8 hours as needed.

169. PHENAMETH VC W/CODEINE Syrup (alcohol 7%; Codeine, Phenylephrine, Promethazine): Rx

Children 2–6 years: By mouth, 1.25–2.5 milliliters every 4–6 hours as needed.

Children 6–12 years: By mouth, 2.5–5 milliliters (½–1 teaspoonful) every 4–6 hours as needed.

170. PHENERGAN VC W/CODEINE Syrup (alcohol 7%; Codeine, Phenylephrine, Promethazine): Rx. See *169. PHENAMETH VC W/CODEINE Syrup* (above).

171. PHENERGAN W/CODEINE Syrup (alcohol 7%; Codeine, Promethazine): Rx. See *169. PHENAMETH VC W/CODEINE Syrup* (above).

172. PHENERGAN W/DEXTROMETHORPHAN Syrup (alcohol 7%; Dextromethorphan, Promethazine): Rx. See *169. PHENAMETH VC W/CODEINE Syrup* (above).

173. PHENHIST Expectorant (alcohol 7.5%; Codeine, Guaifenesin, Pseudoephedrine): Rx. See *169. PHENAMETH VC W/CODEINE Syrup* (above).

174. PHENYLFENESIN L.A. Extended-release Tablets (Guaifenesin, Phenylpropanolamine): Rx
Children 6–12 years: By mouth, ½ tablet every 12 hours as needed.

175. PHERAZINE VC W/CODEINE Syrup (alcohol 7%; Codeine, Phenylephrine, Promethaine): Rx. See *169. PHENAMETH VC W/ CODEINE Syrup* (above).

176. POLARAMINE Expectorant (alcohol 7.2%; Dexchlorpheniramine, Guaifenesin, Pseudoephedrine): Rx
Children 2–6 years: By mouth, 1.25–2.5 milliliters every 6–8 hours as needed.
Children 6–12 years: By mouth, 2.5–5 milliliters (½–1 teaspoonful) every 6–8 hours as needed.

177. POLY-HISTINE-CS Syrup (Brompheniramine, Codeine, Phenylpropanolamine): Rx. See *169. PHENAMETH VC W/CODEINE Syrup* (above).

178. POLY-HISTINE-DM Syrup (Brompheniramine, Dextromethorphan, Phenylpropanolamine): Rx. See *169. PHENAMETH VC W/CODEINE Syrup* (above).

179. PROMETHAZINE AND CODEINE Syrup: Rx. See *169. PHENAMETH VC W/CODEINE Syrup* (above).

180. PROMETH VC W/CODEINE Syrup (alcohol 7%; Codeine, Phenylephrine, Promethazine): Rx. See *169. PHENAMETH VC W/CODEINE Syrup* (above).

181. PROMINIC Expectorant (alcohol 5%; Guaifenesin, Phenylpropanolamine): OTC
Children 2–6 years: By mouth, 2.5 milliliters (½ teaspoonful) every 4 hours as needed.
Children 6–12 years: By mouth, 5 milliliters (1 teaspoonful) every 4 hours as needed.

182. PROMINICOL Cough Syrup (Ammonium Chloride, Dextromethorphan, Pheniramine, Phenylpropanolamine, Pyrilamine): OTC

Children 2–6 years: By mouth, 2.5 milliliters (½ teaspoonful) every 6–8 hours as needed.
Children 6–12 years: By mouth, 5 milliliters (1 teaspoonful) every 6–8 hours as needed.

183. PROMIST HD Liquid (alcohol 5%; Chlorpheniramine, Hydrocodone, Pseudoephedrine): Rx
Children 2–6 years: By mouth, 2.5 milliliters (½ teaspoonful) every 6–8 hours as needed.
Children 6–12 years: By mouth, 5 milliliters (1 teaspoonful) every 6–8 hours as needed.

184. PRUNICODEINE Oral Solution (alcohol 25%; sugar-free; Codeine, Terpin Hydrate): Rx
Children 6–12 years: 2.5–5 milliliters (½–1 teaspoonful) every 4–6 hours as needed.

185. PSEUDO-CAR DM Syrup (alcohol less than 0.6%; Carbinoxamine, Dextromethorphan, Pseudoephedrine): Rx
Children 18 months–6 years: By mouth, 2.5 milliliters (½ teaspoonful) every 4–6 hours as needed.
Children over 6 years: By mouth, 5 milliliters (1 teaspoonful) every 4–6 hours as needed.

186. PSEUDODINE C Cough Syrup (alcohol 4.3%; Codeine, Pseudoephedrine, Triprolidine): Rx
Children 2–6 years: By mouth, 2.5 milliliters (½ teaspoonful) every 4–6 hours as needed.
Children 6–12 years: By mouth, 5 milliliters (1 teaspoonful) every 4–6 hours as needed.

187. P-V-TUSSIN Syrup (alcohol; Ammonium Chloride, Chlorpheniramine, Hydrocodone, Phenindamine, Phenylephrine, Pyrilamine): Rx
Children 1–3 years: By mouth, 2.5 milliliters (½ teaspoonful) every 4–6 hours as needed.
Children 3–6 years: By mouth, 2.5–5 milliliters (½–1 teaspoonful) every 4–6 hours as needed.
Children 6–12 years: By mouth, 5 milliliters (1 teaspoonful) every 4–6 hours as needed.

- Tablets (Guaifenesin, Hydrocodone, Phenindamine): Rx
  Children 6–12 years: By mouth, ½ tablet every 6 hours as needed.

188. QUELIDRINE Cough Syrup (alcohol 2%; Ammonium Chloride, Chlorpheniramine, Dextromethorphan, Ephedrine, Ipecac Fluid-extract, Phenylephrine): OTC
Children 2–6 years: By mouth, 1.25 milliliters every 4–6 hours as needed.
Children 6–12 years: By mouth, 2.5 milliliters (½ teaspoonful) every 4–6 hours as needed.

189. QUELTUSS Tablets (Dextromethorphan, Guaifenesin): OTC
Children 2–6 years: By mouth, ¼–½ tablet every 6–8 hours as needed.
Children 6–12 years: By mouth, ½–1 tablet every 6–8 hours as needed.

190. REMCOL-C Capsules (Acetaminophen, Chlorpheniramine, Dextromethorphan): OTC
Children 6–12 years: By mouth, 1 capsule every 6–8 hours as needed.

191. RESPAIRE-60 SR Extended-release Capsules (Guaifenesin, Pseudoephedrine): Rx
Children 6–12 years: By mouth, 1 capsule every 12 hours as needed.

192. RHINOSYN-DM Syrup (alcohol 1.4%; dye-free; Chlorpheniramine, Dextromethorphan, Pseudoephedrine): OTC
Children 2–6 years: By mouth, 2.5 milliliters (½ teaspoonful) every 6 hours as needed.
Children 6–12 years: By mouth, 5 milliliters (1 teaspoonful) every 6 hours as needed.

193. RHINOSYN-DMX Expectorant (alcohol 6%; dye-free; Dextromethorphan; Guaifenesin): OTC
Children 2–6 years: By mouth, 2.5 milliliters (½ teaspoonful) every 6 hours as needed.
Children 6–12 years: By mouth, 5 milliliters (1 teaspoonful) every 6 hours as needed.

194. RHINOSYN-X Syrup (alcohol 7.5%; dye-free; Dextromethorphan, Guaifenesin, Pseudoephedrine): OTC
Children 2–6 years: By mouth, 2.5 milliliters (½ teaspoonful) every 4 hours as needed.
Children 6–12 years: By mouth, 5 milliliters (1 teaspoonful) every 4 hours as needed.

195. ROBITUSSIN A-C Syrup (alcohol 3.5%; sugar-free; Codeine, Guaifenesin): Rx
Children 2–6 years: By mouth, 2.5 milliliters (½ teaspoonful) every 4–6 hours as needed.
Children 6–12 years: By mouth, 5 milliliters (1 teaspoonful) every 4–6 hours as needed.

196. ROBITUSSIN-CF Syrup (alcohol 4.75%; Dextromethorphan, Guaifenesin, Phenylpropanolamine): OTC
Children 2–6 years: By mouth, 2.5 milliliters (½ teaspoonful) every 4 hours as needed.
Children 6–12 years: By mouth, 5 milliliters (1 teaspoonful) every 4 hours as needed.

197. ROBITUSSIN-DAC Syrup (alcohol 1.9%; sugar-free; Codeine, Guaifenesin, Pseudoephedrine): Rx. See *195. ROBITUSSIN A-C Syrup* (above).

198. ROBITUSSIN NIGHT RELIEF Oral Solution (Acetaminophen, Dextromethorphan, Phenylephrine, Pyrilamine): OTC
Children 6–12 years: By mouth, 15 milliliters (1 tablespoonful) at bedtime, or every 6–8 hours as needed.

199. ROBITUSSIN NIGHT RELIEF COLDS FORMULA Liquid (alcohol 25%; Acetaminophen, Dextromethorphan, Phenylephrine, Pyrilamine): OTC
Children 6–12 years: By mouth, 15 milliliters (1 tablespoonful) every 6–8 hours as needed.

200. ROBITUSSIN-PE Syrup (alcohol 1.4%; Guaifenesin, Pseudoephedrine): OTC. See *196. ROBITUSSIN-CF Syrup* (above).

201. RONDEC-DM Drops (alcohol less than 0.6%; Carbinoxamine, Dextromethorphan, Pseudoephedrine): Rx

Children 1–3 months: By mouth, 0.25 milliliter every 4–6 hours as needed.

Children 3–6 months: By mouth, 0.5 milliliter every 4–6 hours as needed.

Children 6–9 months: By mouth, 0.75 milliliter every 4–6 hours as needed.

Children 9–18 months: By mouth, 1 milliliter every 4–6 hours as needed.

202. RONDEC-DM Syrup (alcohol less than 0.6%; Carbinoxamine, Dextromethorphan, Pseudoephedrine): Rx

Children 18 months–6 years: By mouth, 2.5 milliliters (½ teaspoonful) every 4–6 hours as needed.

Children over 6 years: By mouth, 5 milliliters (1 teaspoonful) every 4–6 hours as needed.

203. RU-TUSS Expectorant (alcohol 10%; Dextromethorphan, Guaifenesin, Pseudoephedrine): OTC

Children 2–6 years: By mouth, 2.5 milliliters (½ teaspoonful) every 4–6 hours as needed.

6–12 years: By mouth, 5 milliliters (1 teaspoonful) every 4–6 hours as needed.

204. RU-TUSS W/HYDROCODONE Liquid (alcohol 5%; Hydrocodone, Pheniramine, Phenylephrine, Phenylpropanolamine, Pyrilamine): Rx

Children 2–6 years: By mouth, 2.5–5 milliliters (½–1 teaspoonful) every 4–6 hours as needed.

Children 6–12 years: By mouth, 5 milliliters (1 teaspoonful) every 4–6 hours as needed.

205. RYMED Liquid (alcohol 5%; sugar-free; Guaifenesin, Phenylephrine, Phenylpropanolamine): Rx

Children 2–4 years: By mouth, 2.5 milliliters (½ teaspoonful) every 4–6 hours as needed.

Children 4–6 years: By mouth, 5 milliliters (1 teaspoonful) every 4–6 hours as needed.

Children 6–12 years: By mouth, 7.5 milliliters (1½ teaspoonsful) every 4–6 hours as needed.

206. RYNA-C Liquid (dye-free; sugar-free; Chlorpheniramine, Codeine, Pseudoephedrine): Rx

Children 2–6 years: By mouth, 2.5 milliliters (½ teaspoonful) every 6 hours as needed.

Children 6–12 years: By mouth, 5 milliliters (1 teaspoonful) every 6 hours as needed.

207. RYNA-CX Liquid (dye-free; sugar-free; Codeine, Guaifenesin, Pseudoephedrine): Rx

Children 2–6 years: By mouth, 1.25–2.5 milliliters every 6 hours as needed.

Children 6–12 years: By mouth, 2.5–5 milliliters (½–1 teaspoonful) every 6 hours as needed.

208. RYNATUSS PEDIATRIC Suspension (Carbetapentane, Chlorpheniramine, Ephedrine, Phenylephrine): Rx

Children 2–6 years: By mouth, 2.5–5 milliliters (½–1 teaspoonful) every 12 hours as needed.

Children 6–12 years: By mouth, 5–10 milliliters (1–2 teaspoonsful) every 12 hours as needed.

209. RYNATUSS Tablets (Carbetapentane, Chlorpheniramine, Ephedrine, Phenylephrine): Rx

Children 6–12 years: By mouth, ½–1 tablet every 12 hours as needed.

210. SALETO-CF Tablets (Acetaminophen, Dextromethorphan, Phenylpropanolamine): OTC

Children 6–12 years: By mouth, 1 tablet every 4 hours as needed.

211. SILEXIN Cough Syrup (sugar-free; Dextromethorphan, Guaifenesin): OTC

Children 2–6 years: By mouth, 2.5–5 milliliters (½–1 teaspoonful) every 4 hours as needed.

Children 6–12 years: By mouth, 5–10 milliliters (1–2 teaspoonsful) every 4 hours as needed.

212. SINUFED TIMECELLES Extended-release Capsules (Guaifenesin, Pseudoephedrine): Rx

Children 6–12 years: By mouth, 1 capsule every 12 hours as needed.

213. SNAPLETS-DM Granules (Dextromethorphan, Phenylpropanolamine): OTC

Children 2–6 years: By mouth, 1 pack sprinkled on soft food every 4 hours as needed.

Children 6–12 years: By mouth, 2 packs sprinkled on soft food every 4 hours as needed.

214. SNAPLETS-EX Granules (Guaifenesin, Phenylpropanolamine): OTC. See *213. SNAPLETS-DM Granules* (above).

215. SNAPLETS-MULTI Granules (Chlorpheniramine, Dextromethorphan, Phenylpropanolamine): OTC. See *213. SNAPLETS-DM Granules* (above).

216. SUDAFED COUGH Syrup (alcohol 2.4%; Dextromethorphan, Guaifenesin, Pseudoephedrine): OTC

Children 2–6 years: By mouth, 5 milliliters (1 teaspoonful) every 4–6 hours as needed.

Children 6–12 years: By mouth, 10 milliliters (2 teaspoonsful) every 4–6 hours as needed.

217. SUDAFED DM Oral Solution (Dextromethorphan, Pseudoephedrine): OTC

Children 2–6 years: By mouth, 2.5 milliliters (½ teaspoonful) every 6–8 hours as needed.

Children 6–12 years: By mouth, 5 milliliters (1 teaspoonful) every 6–8 hours as needed.

218. SUDAFED Expectorant (alcohol 4.8%; Guaifenesin, Pseudoephedrine): OTC

Children to 4 months: By mouth, 2.5 milliliters (½ teaspoonful) every 6–8 hours as needed.

Children 4 months–6 years: By mouth, 5 milliliters (1 teaspoonful) every 6–8 hours as needed.

Children over 6 years: By mouth, 10 milliliters (2 teaspoonsful) every 6–8 hours as needed.

219. SYRACOL Liquid (Dextromethorphan, Phenylpropanolamine): OTC

Children 2–6 years: By mouth, 2.5 milliliters (½ teaspoonful) every 4 hours as needed.

Children 6–12 years: By mouth, 5 milliliters (1 teaspoonful) every 4 hours as needed.

220. T-KOFF Syrup (Chlorpheniramine, Codeine, Phenylephrine, Phenylpropanolamine): Rx
Children 2–6 years: By mouth, 1.25–2.5 milliliters every 4–6 hours as needed.
Children 6–12 years: By mouth, 2.5–5 milliliters (½–1 teaspoonful) every 4–6 hours as needed.

221. TOLU-SED Cough Syrup (alcohol 10%; sugar-free; Codeine, Guaifenesin): Rx
Children 1–6 years: By mouth, 1.25–2.5 milliliters every 4–6 hours as needed.
Children 6–12 years: By mouth, 2.5–5 milliliters (½–1 teaspoonful) every 4–6 hours as needed.

222. TOLU-SED DM Cough Syrup (alcohol 10%; sugar-free; Dextromethorphan, Guaifenesin): OTC
Children 1–6 years: By mouth, 1.25–2.5 milliliters every 4 hours as needed.
Children 6–12 years: By mouth, 2.5–5 milliliters (½–1 teaspoonful) every 4 hours as needed.

223. TRIACIN C Cough Syrup (alcohol 4.3%; Codeine, Pseudoephedrine, Triprolidine): Rx
Children 2–6 years: By mouth, 2.5 milliliters (½ teaspoonful) every 4–6 hours as needed.
Children 6–12 years: By mouth, 5 milliliters (1 teaspoonful) every 4–6 hours as needed.

224. TRIAMINIC-DM Cough Formula (Dextromethorphan, Phenylpropanolamine): OTC
Children 3 months–1 year: By mouth, 1 drop for each 2.2 pounds of body weight every 4 hours as needed.
Children 1–2 years: By mouth, 3 drops for each 2.2 pounds of body weight every 4 hours as needed.
Children 2–6 years: By mouth, 2.5 milliliters (½ teaspoonful) every 4 hours as needed.
Children 6–12 years: By mouth, 5 milliliters (1 teaspoonful) every 4 hours as needed.

225. TRIAMINIC Expectorant (alcohol 5%; Guaifenesin, Phenylpropanolamine): OTC
Children 3 months–1 year: By mouth, 2 drops for each 2.2 pounds of body weight every 4 hours as needed.

Children 1–2 years: By mouth, 3 drops for each 2.2 pounds of body weight every 4 hours as needed.

Children 2–6 years: By mouth, 2.5 milliliters (½ teaspoonful) every 4 hours as needed.

Children 6–12 years: By mouth, 5 milliliters (1 teaspoonful) every 4 hours as needed.

226. TRIAMINIC EXPECTORANT W/CODEINE (alcohol 5%; Codeine, Guaifenesin, Phenylpropanolamine): Rx

Children 3 months–2 years: By mouth, 2 drops for each 2.2 pounds of body weight every 4 hours as needed.

Children 2–6 years: By mouth, 2.5 milliliters (½ teaspoonful) every 4 hours as needed.

Children 6–12 years: By mouth, 5 milliliters (1 teaspoonful) every 4 hours as needed.

227. TRIAMINIC NIGHT LIGHT Oral Solution (Chlorpheniramine, Dextromethorphan, Pseudoephedrine): OTC

Children 2–6 years: By mouth, 5 milliliters (1 teaspoonful) every 6 hours as needed.

Children 6–12 years: By mouth, 10 milliliters (2 teaspoonsful) every 6 hours as needed.

Children over 12 years: By mouth, 20 milliliters (4 teaspoonsful) every 6 hours as needed.

228. TRIAMINICOL   MULTI-SYMPTOM   RELIEF   (Chlorpheniramine, Dextromethorphan, Phenylpropanolamine): OTC
• Syrup: See 224. *TRIAMINIC-DM Cough Formula* (above).
• Tablets:
  Children 6–12 years: By mouth, 1 tablet every 4 hours as needed.

229. TRICODENE   FORTE   Syrup   (Chlorpheniramine, Dextromethorphan, Phenylpropanolamine): OTC

Children 2–6 years: By mouth, 1.25–2.5 milliliters every 4 hours as needed.

Children 6–12 years: By mouth, 2.5–5 milliliters (½–1 teaspoonful) every 4 hours as needed.

230. TRICODENE   NN   Syrup   (Chlorpheniramine, Dextromethorphan, Phenylpropanolamine): OTC. See *229. TRICODENE FORTE Syrup* (above).

231. TRICODENE #1 Syrup (Codeine, Menthol, Pyrilamine, Terpin Hydrate): Rx
Children 2–6 years: By mouth, 2.5 milliliters (½ teaspoonful) every 4–6 hours as needed.
Children 6–12 years: By mouth, 5 milliliters (1 teaspoonful) every 4–6 hours as needed.

232. TRICODENE PEDIATRIC Syrup (Dextromethorphan, Phenylpropanolamine): OTC. See *229. TRICODENE FORTE Syrup* (above).

233. TRIFED-C Cough Syrup (alcohol 4.3%; Codeine, Pseudoephedrine, Triprolidine): Rx
Children 2–6 years: By mouth, 2.5 milliliters (½ teaspoonful) every 4–6 hours as needed.
Children 6–12 years: By mouth, 5 milliliters (1 teaspoonful) every 4–6 hours as needed.

234. TRIMEDINE Liquid (sugar-free; Chlorpheniramine, Dextromethorphan, Phenylephrine): OTC
Children 2–6 years: 2.5 milliliters (½ teaspoonful) every 6–8 hours as needed.
Children 6–12 years: By mouth, 5 milliliters (1 teaspoonful) every 6–8 hours as needed.

235. TRIND DM Liquid (alcohol 5%; sugar-free; Chlorpheniramine, Dextromethorphan, Phenylpropanolamine): OTC
Children 3–10 months: By mouth, 0.62 milliliter every 4 hours as needed.
Children 10 months–2 years: By mouth, 1.25 milliliters every 4 hours as needed.
Children 2–6 years: By mouth, 2.5 milliliters (½ teaspoonful) every 4 hours as needed.
Children 6–12 years: By mouth, 5 milliliters (1 teaspoonful) every 4 hours as needed.

236. TRIPHENYL Expectorant (alcohol 5%; Guaifenesin, Phenylpropanolamine): OTC
Children 2–6 years: By mouth, 2.5 milliliters (½ teaspoonful) every 4 hours as needed.
Children 6–12 years: By mouth, 5 milliliters (1 teaspoonful) every 4 hours as needed.

237. TUSQUELIN Syrup (alcohol 5%; Chlorpheniramine, Dextromethorphan, Phenylephrine, Phenylpropanolamine): Rx
Children 2–6 years: By mouth, 1.25–2.5 milliliters every 6 hours as needed.
Children 6–12 years: By mouth, 2.5–5 milliliters (½–1 teaspoonful) every 6 hours as needed.

238. TUSSAFED Syrup (alcohol less than 0.6%; Carbinoxamine, Dextromethorphan, Pseudoephedrine): Rx
Children 18 months–6 years: By mouth, 2.5 milliliters (½ teaspoonful) every 4–6 hours as needed.
Children over 6 years: By mouth, 5 milliliters (1 teaspoonful) every 4–6 hours as needed.

239. TUSSANIL DH Syrup (alcohol 5%; Chlorpheniramine, Hydrocodone, Phenylephrine): Rx
Children 2–6 years: By mouth, 1.25 milliliters every 4–6 hours as needed.
Children 6–12 years: By mouth, 2.5 milliliters (½ teaspoonful) every 4–6 hours as needed.

240. TUSSAR DM Syrup (Chlorpheniramine, Dextromethorphan, Pseudoephedrine): OTC
Children 2–6 years: By mouth, 2.5 milliliters (½ teaspoonful) every 6–8 hours as needed.
Children 6–12 years: By mouth, 5 milliliters (1 teaspoonful) every 6–8 hours as needed.

241. TUSSAR-2 Syrup (alcohol 6%; Chlorpheniramine, Codeine, Guaifenesin): Rx
Children 2–6 years: By mouth, 1.25–2.5 milliliters every 4–6 hours as needed.
Children 6–12 years: By mouth, 2.5–5 milliliters (½–1 teaspoonful) every 4–6 hours as needed.

242. TUSS-DM Tablets (Dextromethorphan, Guaifenesin): OTC
Children 6–12 years: By mouth, ½–1 tablet every 4 hours as needed.

243. TUSSIGON Tablets (Homatropine, Hydrocodone): Rx. See *242. TUSS-DM Tablets* (above).

244. **TUSSI-ORGANIDIN DM** Liquid (Dextromethorphan, Iodinated Glycerol): Rx
Children 2–6 years: By mouth, 1.25–2.5 milliliters every 4 hours as needed.
Children 6–12 years: By mouth, 2.5–5 milliliters (½–1 teaspoonful) every 4 hours as needed.

245. **TUSSI-ORGANIDIN** Liquid (Codeine, Iodinated Glycerol): Rx
Children 2–6 years: By mouth, 1.25–2.5 milliliters every 4–6 hours as needed.
Children 6–12 years: By mouth, 2.5–5 milliliters (½–1 teaspoonful) every 4–6 hours as needed.

246. **TUSSIREX W/CODEINE** Liquid (with and without sugar; Caffeine, Codeine, Pheniramine, Phenylephrine, Sodium Citrate, Sodium Salicylate): Rx
Children 2–6 years: By mouth, 1.25–2.5 milliliters every 6–8 hours as needed.
Children 6–12 years: By mouth, 2.5–5 milliliters (½–1 teaspoonful) every 6–8 hours as needed.

247. **TUSS-LA** Extended-release Tablets (Guaifenesin, Pseudoephedrine): Rx
Children 6–12 years: By mouth, ½ tablet every 12 hours as needed.

248. **TUSSO-DM** Oral Solution (sugar-free; Dextromethorphan, Iodinated Glycerol): Rx. See 244. *TUSSI-ORGANIDIN DM Liquid* (above).

249. **TUSS-ORNADE** Liquid (alcohol 5%; Caramiphen Edisylate, Phenylpropanolamine): Rx. See 244. *TUSSI-ORGANIDIN DM Liquid* (above).

250. **TY-COLD COLD FORMULA** Tablets (Acetaminophen, Chlorpheniramine, Dextromethorphan, Pseudoephedrine): OTC
Children 6–12 years: By mouth, 1 every 6 hours as needed.

251. **TYLENOL COLD MEDICATION, NON-DROWSY** Tablets (Acetaminophen, Dextromethorphan, Pseudoephedrine): OTC. See 250. *TY-COLD COLD FORMULA Tablets* (above).

252. TYLENOL COLD MEDICATION Tablets (Acetaminophen, Chlorpheniramine; Dextromethorphan, Pseudoephedrine): OTC. See 250. *TY-COLD COLD FORMULA Tablets* (above).

253. VANEX Expectorant (alcohol 5%; Guaifenesin, Hydrocodone, Pseudoephedrine): Rx
Children 2–6 years: By mouth, 2.5 milliliters (½ teaspoonful) every 6 hours as needed.
Children 6–12 years: By mouth, 5 milliliters (1 teaspoonful) every 6 hours as needed.

254. VANEX-HD Syrup (Chlorpheniramine; Hydrocodone, Phenylephrine): Rx
Children 6–12 years: By mouth, 5 milliliters (1 teaspoonful) every 6–8 hours as needed.

255. VICKS CHILDREN'S Cough Syrup (alcohol 5%; Dextromethorphan, Guaifenesin): OTC
Children 2–6 years: By mouth, 5 milliliters (1 teaspoonful) every 4 hours as needed.
Children 6–12 years: By mouth, 10 milliliters (2 teaspoonsful) every 4 hours as needed.

256. VICKS FORMULA 44 Cough Mixture (alcohol 10%; Chlorpheniramine, Dextromethorphan): OTC
Children 6–12 years: By mouth, 5 milliliters (1 teaspoonful) every 6–8 hours as needed.

257. VICKS FORMULA 44D DECONGESTANT Cough Mixture (alcohol 10%; Dextromethorphan, Guaifenesin, Pseudoephedrine): OTC
Children 2–6 years: By mouth, 3.75 milliliters (¾ teaspoonful) every 6 hours as needed.
Children 6–12 years: By mouth, 7.5 milliliters (1½ teaspoonsful) every 6 hours as needed.

258. VICKS FORMULA 44M MULTI-SYMPTOM Cough Mixture (alcohol 20%; Acetaminophen, Dextromethorphan, Guaifenesin, Pseudoephedrine): OTC
Children 6–12 years: By mouth, 10 milliliters (2 teaspoonsful) every 6 hours as needed.

259. **VIRO-MED** Tablets (Aspirin, Chlorpheniramine, Dextromethorphan, Guaifenesin, Pseudoephedrine): OTC
Children 6–12 years: By mouth, 1 tablet every 4 hours as needed.

BRAND NAME(S)
CYLERT   Rx

GENERIC NAME
PEMOLINE

USES AND INDICATIONS
CYLERT is a central nervous system stimulant used in treating attention deficit disorder with hyperactivity. Although not related chemically to amphetamines and RITALIN, CYLERT produces similar effects.

ADVERSE EFFECTS
The following adverse effects may occur with CYLERT use:

- Gastrointestinal: loss of appetite, weight loss, nausea, and stomach pain.
- Central nervous system: seizures with convulsions; hallucinations; uncontrolled, repetitive movements of the lips, tongue, face, and hands and feet; abnormal eye movements; headache; increased irritability; nervousness; difficulty sleeping; depression; and dizziness.
- Other: liver toxicity with yellow eyes or skin (fatalities are rare), suppression of growth in children, skin rash, and itching.

WARNINGS AND PRECAUTIONS

- CYLERT is contraindicated in children with liver disorders.
- Children on long-term therapy should be closely monitored for body development, weight, and bone growth.
- CYLERT should be used with caution in children with kidney disorders.
- Children on long-term therapy should be allowed medication-free periods and should receive periodic determinations regarding the need to continue treatment with CYLERT.
- Periodic laboratory testing of liver and kidney functions should be performed.

MEDICATION AND FOOD INTERACTIONS

- CYLERT may increase the potential for seizures when used with anticonvulsants (see Appendix II).
- The use of CYLERT with other central nervous system stimulants may result in increased toxicity of both: SYMMETREL, RITALIN, amphetamines (see Appendix II), and xanthine bronchodilators (see Appendix II).

DOSAGE GUIDELINES
- Chewable tablets (must be chewed before swallowing) and tablets: Children to 6 years: Dosage has not been established.
  Children 6 years and older: By mouth, 37.5 milligrams as a single dose each morning, then may be increased as necessary in increments of 18.75 milligrams daily at 1-week intervals until desired response is achieved, up to a maximum total daily dose of 112.5 milligrams.

GROUP NAME
DECONGESTANT/ ANALGESIC COMBINATIONS

1. PHENYLEPHRINE/ACETAMINOPHEN (CONGESPIRIN FOR CHILDREN).
2. PHENYLPROPANOLAMINE/ACETAMINOPHEN (CONGESPIRIN FOR CHILDREN SOLUTION).

USES AND INDICATIONS
The decongestant/analgesic combination products are used in treating the nasal and sinus congestion and sinus headaches of colds and allergies.

For more specific information regarding uses and indications, adverse effects, warnings and precautions, and medication and food interactions, see the monographs for TYLENOL (page 253), antihistamines (page 96), and decongestant/antihistamine combinations (page 105). Dosage guidelines only are included.

These products should not be used after the symptoms have subsided.

DOSAGE GUIDELINES

The following products are listed by brand names.

1. **CONGESPIRIN FOR CHILDREN** (Phenylephrine/Acetaminophen): OTC

- Chewable tablets:
  Children to 2 years: Use is not recommended.
  Children 2–3 years: By mouth, 2 tablets chewed every 4 hours as needed.
  Children 4–5 years: By mouth, 3 tablets chewed every 4 hours as needed.
  Children 6–8 years: By mouth, 4 tablets chewed every 4 hours as needed.
  Children 9–11 years: By mouth, 5 tablets chewed every 4 hours as needed.
  Children 11–12 years: By mouth, 6 tablets chewed every 4 hours as needed.

2. **CONGESPIRIN FOR CHILDREN** Solution (Phenylpropanolamine/Acetaminophen): OTC

- Oral Solution:
  Children to 3 years: Use is not recommended.
  Children 3–5 years: By mouth, 5 milliliters (1 teaspoonful) every 3–4 hours as needed.
  Children 6–12 years: By mouth, 10 milliliters (2 teaspoonsful) every 3–4 hours as needed.

GENERIC NAME
ERYTHROMYCIN   Rx

BRAND NAME(S)
AKNE-MYCIN, E.E.S., E-MYCIN, E-MYCIN
E, ERYC, ERYCETTE, ERYDERM, ERYGEL,
ERYMOX, ERYPAR, ERY-TAB,
ERYTHROCIN, ETHRIL, ETS, ILOSONE,
ILOTYCIN, MYTHROMYCIN, PCE
DISPERSATABS, PEDIAMYCIN,
PEDIAZOLE, ROBIMYCIN, STATICIN,
T-STAT, WYAMYCIN E, WYAMYCIN S

USES AND INDICATIONS
Erythromycin is an antibiotic used in treating lung infections, legion-naires' disease, amoebic dysentery, middle ear infections, skin and soft tissue infections, conjunctivitis in the newborn, and infant pneumonia. In addition, Erythromycin is used in patients who are allergic to penicillins.

ADVERSE EFFECTS
The following adverse effects may occur with Erythromycin use:

- Gastrointestinal: nausea, vomiting, stomach cramps, diarrhea, loss of appetite, and pseudomembranous colitis (see under CLEOCIN, page 136).
- Other: liver toxicity, sore mouth or tongue, dark-colored urine, and unusual weakness.

WARNINGS AND PRECAUTIONS

- Use cautiously in children with impaired liver function or in those who are allergic to tartrazine (found in ETHRIL).
- If any of the following symptoms occur, stop the medication and contact your doctor as soon as possible: severe abdominal pain, yellow eyes or skin, darkened urine color, pale-colored stools, or unusual weakness.

MEDICATION AND FOOD INTERACTIONS

- Erythromycin may increase the toxic effects of TEGRETOL, LAN-OXIN, and xanthine bronchodilators (see Appendix II).
- Erythromycin may decrease the effectiveness of CHLOROMYCE-TIN, CLEOCIN, and LINCOCIN.
- Erythromycin may increase the toxic effects of MEDROL and COUMADIN.

DOSAGE GUIDELINES

- Ophthalmic ointment: Apply a thin strip to the conjunctiva of the affected eye once daily, or more frequently, as required.
- Ointment, pledgets, and topical solution: Apply to the affected area of the skin twice daily, morning and evening. Do not use the topical solution in children under 12 years.
- **Erythromycin ethylsuccinate** products only (chewable tablets, oral suspension, and tablets):
  - Antibacterial: By mouth, 7.5–25 milligrams (base) for each 2.2 pounds of body weight every 6 hours, or 15–50 milligrams for each 2.2 pounds of body weight every 12 hours.
  - Pertussis: By mouth, 10–12.5 milligrams (base) for each 2.2 pounds of body weight every 6 hours for 14 days.
- **Erythromycin base,** estolate, and stearate products only (cap-sules, chewable tablets, delayed-release capsules, delayed-release tablets, oral suspension, and tablets):
  - Antibacterial: By mouth, 7.5–25 milligrams (base) for each 2.2 pounds of body weight every 6 hours, or 15–50 milligrams for each 2.2 pounds of body weight every 12 hours.
  - Pertussis: By mouth, 10–12.5 milligrams (base) for each 2.2 pounds of body weight every 6 hours for 14 days.
  - Sore throat (streptococcal pharyngitis): By mouth, 5–12.5 milli-grams (base) for each 2.2 pounds of body weight every 6 hours, or 10–25 milligrams for each 2.2 pounds of body weight every 12 hours.

PEDIAZOLE   (Erythromycin/Sulfisoxazole):

- Infants to 1 month: Should not be used.
- Infants and children 1 month and older: By mouth, 12.5 milli-grams (of Erythromycin) or 37.5 milligrams (of Sulfisoxazole) for

each 2.2 pounds of body weight every 6 hours for 10 days. The dose may be based either on the Erythromycin or Sulfisoxazole portion of the mixture.

COMMENTS
Erythromycin suspensions should be refrigerated, and they should be shaken before use. Discard any unused portion at the end of the treatment period.

BRAND NAME(S)
FLAGYL   Rx
(Other brands: **METIZOLE, METRIC 21, METRYL, PROTOSTAT, SATRIC**)

GENERIC NAME
METRONIDAZOLE

USES AND INDICATIONS
FLAGYL is an anti-infective used in treating infections caused by bacteria and nonbacterial parasites, including worms and protozoal organisms.

ADVERSE EFFECTS
The adverse effects of FLAGYL that may require medical attention are burning or tingling of the hands or feet, vaginal discharge or irritation, skin rash, hives or itching, sore throat and fever, mood changes, and seizures. Other adverse effects include nausea, vomiting, diarrhea, dizziness, headache, stomach cramps, loss of appetite, constipation, dark-colored urine, changes in taste, unusual weakness, and dryness of the mouth.

WARNINGS AND PRECAUTIONS

- FLAGYL should be used with caution in children with heart or liver disorders or with epilepsy or any other diseases of the central nervous system.
- Alcohol-containing products should be avoided when taking FLAGYL.

DOSAGE GUIDELINES
- Capsules and tablets:
  - Amebiasis: By mouth, 11.6–16.7 milligrams for each 2.2 pounds of body weight 3 times daily for 10 days.
  - Giardiasis: By mouth, 5 milligrams for each 2.2 pounds of body weight 3 times daily for 5–7 days.
  - Trichomoniasis: By mouth, 5 milligrams for each 2.2 pounds of body weight 3 times daily for 7 days.
  - Anthelmintic: By mouth, 8.3 milligrams for each 2.2 pounds of body weight, up to a maximum of 250 milligrams, 3 times daily for 10 days.

BRAND NAME(S)
FURADANTIN   Rx
(Other brands: **FURALAN, MACRODANTIN**)

GENERIC NAME
NITROFURANTOIN

USES AND INDICATIONS
FURADANTIN is an anti-infective used in treating urinary infections caused by a variety of microorganisms. It is used both as a treatment drug and as a preventative (prophylaxis) for some urinary infections.

ADVERSE EFFECTS
The adverse effects of FURADANTIN that may require medical attention include chills, chest pain, fever, difficulty breathing, cough, headache, dizziness or drowsiness, yellow eyes or skin, unusual weakness, tingling or numbness of the face or mouth, and pale skin color. Other adverse effects include nausea, vomiting, loss of appetite, diarrhea, stomach pain, and skin rash or itching.

WARNINGS AND PRECAUTIONS

- FURADANTIN should be used with caution in children with kidney or lung disorders or in those who have a specific enzyme deficiency.
- The use of FURADANTIN is contraindicated in infants under 1 month because of the potential for severe toxicity due to the lack of adequate enzyme development.

- The testing of liver and lung functions should be performed in long-term therapy.
- FURADANTIN should be taken with food or milk, and for at least 7 days.

MEDICATION AND FOOD INTERACTIONS
FURADANTIN may interfere with urine glucose determination tests.

DOSAGE GUIDELINES
- Capsules, oral suspension, and tablets:
  Infants to 1 month: Use is contraindicated.
  Infants and children 1 month and over: By mouth, 1.25–1.75 milligrams for each 2.2 pounds of body weight every 6 hours. For prophylaxis use, the dose is 1–2 milligrams for each 2.2 pounds of body weight daily at bedtime, or 0.5–1.0 milligrams for each 2.2 pounds of body weight every 12 hours.

COMMENTS
FURADANTIN oral suspensions should be shaken well before use.

BRAND NAME(S)
INDERAL (and IPRAN) Rx

GENERIC NAME
PROPRANOLOL

USES AND INDICATIONS
INDERAL belongs to the family of drugs known as beta-adrenergic blocking agents. INDERAL has a wide variety of uses, including the treatment of angina, abnormal heartbeats, high blood pressure, and other heart disorders.

ADVERSE EFFECTS
The adverse effects of INDERAL may occur with all or most of the beta-adrenergic blockers, and include:

- Cardiovascular: abnormal rapid or slow heartbeats; chest pain; cold, clammy hands; shortness of breath and worsening of chest pain (angina); fainting; and water retention.
- Central nervous system: dizziness, lethargy, mental depression, difficulty sleeping, weakness, nightmares or other sleep disturbances, slurred speech, ringing in the ears, memory loss, inability

to perform activities requiring mental-physical coordination, paranoia, and other behavioral changes.

- Allergic: skin rash, fever, difficulty breathing, and sore throat.
- Gastrointestinal: nausea, vomiting, diarrhea, dry mouth, gas, loss of appetite, constipation, and abdominal pain.
- Dermatological: skin rash, itching, dry skin, increased skin color (pigmentation), excessive sweating, and other skin irritations.
- Ophthalmic: blurred vision, dry eyes, conjunctivitis, and other eye irritations.
- Other adverse effects: muscle cramps, joint pains, and increase or decrease in blood sugar.

WARNINGS AND PRECAUTIONS

- INDERAL is contraindicated in children with bronchial asthma or other obstructive lung disorders.
- INDERAL should be used cautiously in children with high or low blood pressure, psoriasis, or hyperthyroidism.
- INDERAL should also be used with caution in children with diabetes, myasthenia gravis, or liver or kidney disorders.

MEDICATION AND FOOD INTERACTIONS

- The effects of INDERAL and xanthine bronchodilators (see Appendix II) may be offset when these are used together.
- The use of the following drugs with INDERAL may increase the risk of high blood pressure and heart toxicity: amphetamines (see Appendix II) and adrenergic bronchodilators (see Appendix II).
- NSAIDs (see Appendix II) may decrease the effectiveness of INDERAL.
- TAGAMET may increase the toxic heart effects of INDERAL.

DOSAGE GUIDELINES
- Oral solution and tablets:
  By mouth, 0.5–1 milligram daily for each 2.2 pounds of body weight in 2–4 divided doses initially, then adjusted as required. The maintenance dose is 2–4 milligrams daily for each 2.2 pounds of body weight in 2 divided doses.

BRAND NAME(S)
LANOXIN   Rx

GENERIC NAME
DIGOXIN

USES AND INDICATIONS
LANOXIN, a member of the digitalis family, is the preferred digitalis product for use in children. LANOXIN is used in treating abnormal heartbeats and acts directly on the heart muscle to increase the force of contraction of the muscle; it also increases the "rest period" between heart muscle contractions. The effects of LANOXIN are to make the heart muscle pump more effectively (forcefully) and to alter electrical conduction within the heart itself.

ADVERSE EFFECTS
There are important differences between the early symptoms of LANOXIN toxicity in infants and children and those in adults. Whereas in adults, the early signs may be the gastrointestinal and central nervous system side effects, these are seldom seen in infants and children, making early detection very difficult. Following are some of the major side effects:

- Cardiac: abnormal heartbeats (both rapid and slow), significant decrease in pulse rate, heart block, and even death.
- Central nervous system: visual disturbances, headache, drowsiness, weakness, confusion and disorientation, and seizures.
- Gastrointestinal: nausea, vomiting, diarrhea, loss of appetite, and stomach pains.
- Dermatological: skin rash, hives, itching.

WARNINGS AND PRECAUTIONS

- Because early detection of the signs of LANOXIN toxicity in infants and children is difficult, parents should contact their physician as soon as toxic symptoms are observed.
- LANOXIN should be used with caution in children with kidney disease (may require a dosage reduction).
- Newborn and premature infants may be especially sensitive to the effects of LANOXIN because they lack the kidney development necessary to eliminate LANOXIN from the body.

- Not all brands or dosage forms of Digoxin have the same therapeutic effects in the body, and parents are cautioned against changing brands or dosage forms once the child has achieved an appropriate response to the particular brand and dosage form of Digoxin prescribed by the child's doctor.

MEDICATION AND FOOD INTERACTIONS

- Thyroid hormones (see Appendix II) may decrease the effectiveness of LANOXIN (dosage adjustment may be required).
- The loop diuretics (see Appendix II) may increase LANOXIN toxicity.
- The effectiveness of LANOXIN may be decreased by the following: RIMACTANE and hydantoin anticonvulsants (see Appendix II).
- The toxicity of LANOXIN may be increased by the following: Erythromycin, PLAQUENIL, ADVIL, INDOCIN, Quinidine, Quinine, Tetracycline, and benzodiazepines (see Appendix II).
- The effectiveness of Digoxin may be decreased by the following: KAOPECTATE, AZULFIDINE, and antacids (see Appendix II).
- Children on LANOXIN therapy should be monitored by periodic testing for heart function, serum electrolytes, and LANOXIN serum levels.

DOSAGE GUIDELINES
- Elixir (0.05 milligram per 1 milliliter) and tablets:
  Premature neonates and newborns to 1 month: By mouth, 4–11.7 micrograms for each 2.2 pounds of body weight, given once daily.
  Infants 1 month to 2 years: By mouth, 7–20 micrograms for each 2.2 pounds of body weight, given once daily.
  Children 2–5 years: By mouth, 6–13.3 micrograms for each 2.2 pounds of body weight, given once daily.
  Children 5–10 years: By mouth, 4–11.7 micrograms for each 2.2 pounds of body weight, given once daily.
  Children 10 years and older: 125–500 micrograms (0.125–0.5 milligram) daily.

GROUP NAME
LAXATIVES

1. BISACODYL (CARTER'S LITTLE PILLS, DACODYL, DEFICOL, DULCOLAX, AND OTHERS). 2. CASANTHROL (BLACK DRAUGHT). 3. CASANTHROL/DOCUSATE (DIALOSE PLUS, DISANTHROL, PERI-COLACE, AND OTHERS). 4. CASCARA SAGRADA (AROMATIC CASCARA FLUIDEXTRACT). 5. CASTOR OIL (NEOLOID). 6. DOCUSATE (COLACE, DIALOSE, DIOCTO, DIO-SUL, DISONATE, DOXINATE, MODANE SOFT, REGULAX SS, SURFAK, THERAVAC, AND OTHERS). 7. GLYCERIN (FLEET BABYLAX). 8. MAGNESIUM CITRATE (CITROMA, CITRO-NESIA). 9. MAGNESIUM HYDROXIDE (PHILLIPS' MILK OF MAGNESIA). 10. MAGNESIUM HYDROXIDE/MINERAL OIL (HALEY'S M-O). 11. MALT SOUP EXTRACT (MALTSUPEX). 12. MINERAL OIL (AGORAL PLAIN, FLEET MINERAL OIL, KONDREMUL PLAIN, NEO-CULTOL, PETROGALAR PLAIN, ZYMENOL, AND OTHERS). 13. PHENOLPHTHALEIN (ALOPHEN, CORRECTOL, ESPOTABS, EVAC-U-GEN, EX-LAX, FEEN-A-MINT, MODANE, AND OTHERS). 14. POLYCARBOPHIL (FIBERCON, MITROLAN). 15. SENNA (BLACK DRAUGHT, FLETCHER'S CASTORIA, SENOKOT, X-PREP, AND OTHERS). 16. SODIUM PHOSPHATE (FLEET ENEMA, FLEET PHOSPHO-SODA).

USES AND INDICATIONS
Laxatives are drugs that act to produce bowel emptying in constipation disorders, and they are used in children requiring bowel evacuation. Laxatives are available as bowel lubricants, bowel stimulants, bulk-forming products, and hyperosmotic products. The following is a list of laxatives by their type:

- Lubricants: Mineral Oil.
- Stimulants: Bisacodyl, Casanthrol, Cascara Sagrada, Castor Oil, Phenolphthalein, and Senna.
- Bulk-forming: Malt Soup Extract and Polycarbophil.
- Hyperosmotic: Glycerin, Magnesium Citrate, Magnesium Hydroxide, and Sodium Phosphate.

ADVERSE EFFECTS
The adverse effects of laxatives are usually determined by the type of laxative and include the following:

- Lubricants: irritation of the skin surrounding the anus.
- Stimulants: nausea, vomiting, diarrhea, stomach cramps, gas, and irritation of the skin surrounding the anus.
- Bulk-forming agents: allergic skin rash, itching, asthma, and blockage of the gastrointestinal tract.
- Hyperosmotic (saline) agents: muscle cramps, mental confusion, irregular heartbeats, and unusual weakness.
- Rectal solutions (hyperosmotic): rectal irritation, bleeding, burning, pain or itching.
- Stool softener agents: allergic skin rash.

WARNINGS AND PRECAUTIONS

- Laxatives may mask the symptoms of appendicitis.
- Laxatives should not be used in children who have rectal bleeding, high blood pressure, or intestinal obstruction.
- Hyperosmotic (or saline) laxatives should not be used in children with impaired kidney function, colostomies, or ileostomies.
- Children taking oral laxatives should receive adequate fluids.
- Parents should lubricate the rectum before administering a laxative rectally to a child.
- Laxatives should not be used for prolonged periods unless prescribed by a physician.
- Lubricant-type laxatives (e.g., Mineral Oil) may inhibit absorption of oil-soluble vitamins and food nutrients, including Vitamins A, D, and E.
- The prolonged use of some laxatives may create a "laxative dependency."
- Suppositories may be inserted more easily by moistening the suppository in warm water.

MEDICATION AND FOOD INTERACTIONS

- Hyperosmotic laxatives containing magnesium may reduce the effectiveness of LANOXIN, COUMADIN, and tetracyclines (see Appendix II).
- Bulk-forming laxatives may reduce the effectiveness of LANOXIN, COUMADIN, salicylates (see Appendix II), and tetracyclines (see Appendix II).
- Mineral Oil laxatives may interfere with the absorption of COUMADIN, LANOXIN, and fat-soluble Vitamins A, D, E, and K.
- Children taking laxatives should receive adequate fluids.

DOSAGE GUIDELINES

The following are abbreviated monographs for laxatives, listed by generic name and giving suggested pediatric dosages.

1. **Bisacodyl** (CARTER'S LITTLE PILLS, DACODYL, DEFICOL, DULCOLAX, and others): OTC

   - Tablets (tablets should not be chewed):
     Children 6 years and older: By mouth, 1 tablet as needed.
   - Rectal solution:
     Children to 2 years: Use is not recommended.
     Children 2 years and older: Give the entire dose (30 milliliters) rectally.
   - Rectal suppository:
     Children to 2 years: Insert ½ suppository in rectum as needed.
     Children 2 years and older: Insert 1 suppository rectally as needed.

2. **Casanthrol** (BLACK-DRAUGHT): OTC

   - Syrup
     Children to 2 years: By mouth, 1.25–3.75 milliliters with water or fruit juice as needed.
     Children 2–12 years: By mouth, 2.5–7.5 milliliters (½–1½ teaspoonsful) with water or fruit juice as needed.

3. **Casanthrol/Docusate** (DIALOSE PLUS, DISANTHROL, PERI-COLACE, and others): OTC

   - Capsules and tablets:
     Children to 6 years: Use is not recommended.
     Children 6 years and older: By mouth, 1 capsule or tablet as needed.
   - Syrup:
     Children to 3 years: Use is not recommended.
     Children 3 years and older: By mouth, 5–15 milliliters (1–3 teaspoonsful) as needed.

4. **Cascara Sagrada** (Aromatic Cascara Fluidextract): OTC

- Aromatic Cascara Fluidextract *only* (contains approximately 19% alcohol):
Children to 2 years: Use is not recommended.
Children 2 years and older: By mouth, 1–3 milliliters as needed.

5. **Castor Oil** (NEOLOID): OTC

- Liquid
Children to 2 years: By mouth, 1–5 milliliters as needed.
Children 2 years and older: By mouth, 5–15 milliliters (1 tea-spoonful–1 tablespoonful) as needed.

6. **Docusate** (COLACE, DIALOSE, DIOCTO, DIO-SUL, DISONATE, DOXINATE, MODANE SOFT, REGULAX SS, SURFAK, THER-EVAC, and others): OTC

- Capsules:
Children to 6 years: Use is not recommended.
Children 6 years and older: By mouth, 50–100 milligrams as needed.
- Oral solution (for children):
Children 6 years and older: See *Syrup* (below).
Children to 3 years: By mouth, 1–2 milliliters 1–3 times daily as needed.
Children 3–6 years: By mouth, 2 milliliters 1–3 times daily as needed.
- Syrup:
Children to 3 years: Use is not recommended.
Children 3–6 years: By mouth, 5–15 milliliters (1 teaspoonful–1 tablespoonful) 1–3 times daily as needed.
Children 6–12 years: By mouth, 10 milliliters (2 teaspoonsful) 1–3 times daily as needed.
Rectal suppositories (pediatric): Insert 1 applicatorful rectally as needed.

7. **Glycerin** (FLEET BABYLAX): OTC

- Pediatric suppositories and rectal solution:
Children to 6 years: Insert 1 applicatorful of the rectal solution or 1 pediatric suppository into the rectum as needed.

Children 6 years and older: Insert 1 adult suppository into the rectum as needed.

8. **Magnesium Citrate** (CITROMA, CITRO-NESIA): OTC

- Oral solution:
Children to 2 years: Use is not recommended.
Children 2–6 years: By mouth, 4–12 milliliters as needed.
Children 6–12 years: By mouth, 50–100 milliliters as needed.
Note: Magnesium Citrate solution may be more palatable if refrigerated before use.

9. **Magnesium Hydroxide** (PHILLIPS' MILK OF MAGNESIA): OTC

- Oral suspension:
Children to 2 years: Use is not recommended.
Children 2–6 years: By mouth, 5–15 milliliters (1–3 teaspoonsful) as needed.
Children over 6 years: By mouth, 15–30 milliliters (1–2 tablespoonsful) as needed.
- Tablets:
Children to 6 years: Use is not recommended.
Children over 6 years: By mouth, 3–6 tablets as needed.

10. **Magnesium Hydroxide/Mineral Oil** (HALEY'S M-O): OTC

- Emulsion liquid:
Children to 3 years: Use is not recommended.
Children 3–6 years: By mouth, 5–10 milliliters (1–2 teaspoonsful) as needed.
Children 6–12 years: By mouth, 10–20 milliliters (2–4 teaspoonsful) as needed.

11. **Malt Soup Extract** (MALTSUPEX): OTC

- Oral solution:
Children 1 month to 2 years:
  - Bottle-fed: 5–10 milliliters (1–2 teaspoonsful) in bottle for each feeding, not to exceed 30 milliliters daily as needed.
  - Breast-fed: 5–10 milliliters (1–2 teaspoonsful) in 2–4 ounces of water or fruit juice once or twice daily as needed.
Children over 2 years: By mouth, 15–30 milliliters (1–2 table-

spoonsful) in 8 ounces of water or fruit juice once or twice daily as needed.
- Powder:
Children 1 month to 2 years:
  – Bottle-fed: 1–2 teaspoonsful in bottle for each feeding as needed.
  – Breast-fed: 1–2 teaspoonsful in 2–4 ounces of water or fruit juice once or twice daily as needed.

12. Mineral Oil (AGORAL PLAIN, FLEET MINERAL OIL, KON-DREMUL PLAIN, NEO-CULTOL, PETROGALAR PLAIN, ZYME-NOL, and others): OTC

- Gel and oral suspension:
Children to 6 years: Use is not recommended.
Children over 6 years: By mouth, 5 milliliters (1 teaspoonful) as needed.
- Liquid emulsion:
Children to 6 years: Use is not recommended.
Children over 6 years: By mouth, 5–10 milliliters (1–2 teaspoonsful) as needed.
- Rectal enema:
Children to 2 years: Use is not recommended.
Children over 2 years: Insert rectally, 30–60 milliliters (1–2 ounces) as needed.

13. Phenolphthalein (ALLOPHEN, CORRECTOL, ESPOTABS, EVAC-U-GEN, EX-LAX, FEEN-A-MINT, MODANE, and others): OTC

- Chewable tablets and tablets:
Children to 6 years: Use is not recommended.
Children over 6 years: By mouth, ½–1 tablet depending on the strength.
- Gum:
Children to 6 years: Use is not recommended.
Children over 6 years: Chew ½ tablet as needed.
- Oral solution:
Children to 6 years: Use is not recommended.
Children over 6 years: By mouth, 15 milliliters (1 tablespoonful) in the morning or evening as needed.

- Wafers:
  Children to 2 years: Use is not recommended.
  Children over 2 years: By mouth, ½ wafer as needed.

14. **Polycarbophil** (FIBERCON, MITROLAN): OTC

- Chewable tablets and tablets:
  Children to 2 years: Use is not recommended.
  Children 2–6 years: By mouth, 1 tablet 1–2 times daily as needed.
  Children 6–12 years: By mouth, 1 tablet 1–4 times daily as needed.

15. **Senna** (BLACK-DRAUGHT, FLETCHER'S CASTORIA, SEN-OKOT, X-PREP, and others): OTC

- Granules:
  Children to 6 years: Use is not recommended.
  Children over 6 years: By mouth, ½ teaspoonful in water or other liquid as needed, up to 1 level teaspoonful twice daily.
- Syrup:
  Infants under 1 year: By mouth, 1.25–2.5 milliliters once or twice daily as needed.
  Children 1–5 years: By mouth, 2.5–5 milliliters (½–1 teaspoonful) once or twice daily as needed.
  Children 5–15 years: By mouth, 5–10 milliliters (1–2 teaspoonsful) once or twice daily as needed.
- Tablets:
  Children to 6 years: Use is not recommended.
  Children over 6 years: By mouth, 1 tablet as needed, up to 2 tablets twice daily.

16. **Sodium Phosphate** (FLEET ENEMA, FLEET PHOSPHO-SODA): OTC

- Oral solution:
  Children to 6 years: Use is not recommended.
  Children 6–9 years: By mouth, 5 milliliters (1 teaspoonful) as needed.
- Rectal enema:
  Children to 2 years: Use is not recommended.

Children over 2 years: Squeeze the contents of 1 pediatric unit (60 milliliters) into the rectum as needed.

COMMENTS

For more complete information regarding specific laxative products, parents should read all of the label information provided by the laxative manufacturer or distributor. If there are any questions regarding the use of a specific commercial product, consult with your doctor or pharmacist.

GROUP NAME
NONSTEROIDAL ANTI-INFLAMMATORY ANALGESICS (NSAIDs)

1. IBUPROFEN (ACHES-N-PAIN, ADVIL, EXCEDRIN IB, GENPRIL, IBUPRIN, IBU-TABS, MEDIPREN, MIDOL 200, MOTRIN-IB, NUPRIN, PAMPRIN-IB, PEDIAPROPHEN, TRENDAR, AND OTHERS). 2. NAPROXEN (NAPROSYN). 3. TOLMETIN (TOLECTIN).

USES AND INDICATIONS

Nonsteroidal anti-inflammatory analgesics (NSAIDs) are drugs that are used in treating disorders associated with pain and inflammation. In children, NSAIDs are used in treating acute and chronic arthritis, inflammatory (nonrheumatic) disorders, headache, and other disorders associated with mild to moderate pain, with or without inflammation.

There is an important subgroup of NSAIDs called salicylates (including Aspirin) that do not require a prescription. Because of their wide use, they are discussed under a separate monograph for salicylates (see page 234).

ADVERSE EFFECTS

The frequency of adverse effects with NSAIDs is considerable, and they include fatal allergic reactions and severe gastrointestinal ulceration and bleeding. While the widespread use of these agents in children has not been fully accepted for all of the medications in this group, sufficient experience has been achieved for Ibuprofen, Indomethacin, Naproxen, and Tolmetin. The adverse effects identified do not occur with all the medications in the group. Also, there may be wide variation in the frequency and severity of side effects that do occur. Some of the major side effects include:

- Gastrointestinal: nausea, vomiting, diarrhea, constipation, stomach pains or cramps, dry mouth, swollen tongue, jaundice, belching, and ulceration and bleeding (can be fatal).
- Cardiovascular: high or low blood pressure, water retention, palpitations, and irregular heartbeats.
- Central nervous system: dizziness, nervousness, headache, drowsiness, muscle weakness, tremors, convulsions, numbness of the extremities, difficulty sleeping, confusion, and fever and coma.
- Other: anaphylactic reactions, including asthma, fever, skin rash, skin eruptions, itching, sensation of numbness of the skin, and difficulty breathing.

OVERDOSAGE: The signs of toxicity with NSAIDs include the following: drowsiness, dizziness, mental confusion, nausea, vomiting, severe headache, abdominal pain, blurred vision, sweating, convulsions, numbness of the extremities, ringing in the ears, rapid irregular heartbeats, fall in blood pressure, and seizures. Parents should contact their doctor immediately, as further medical attention may be required.

WARNINGS AND PRECAUTIONS

- Children allergic to one NSAID may be allergic to others as well.
- Anaphylactic reactions may occur in patients allergic to Aspirin. Patients on NSAID therapy should avoid Aspirin-containing products.
- NSAIDs should not be used in patients with bleeding disorders.
- Taking NSAIDs with food or milk or, in some cases, antacids minimizes the possibility of gastrointestinal irritation.

MEDICATION AND FOOD INTERACTIONS

- The use of NSAIDs with the following drugs may increase the risk of gastrointestinal irritation, including bleeding: alcohol, corticosteroids (see Appendix II), and potassium supplements (see Appendix II).
- NSAIDs may decrease the effectiveness of loop diuretics (see Appendix II).
- The concurrent use of NSAIDs and salicylates (see Appendix II)

may result in an increased risk of gastrointestinal irritation and bleeding.

- NSAIDs may increase the risk of toxicity of Colchicine.

Following are monographs for specific NSAID medications.

BRAND NAME(S)

1 . ADVIL   Rx, OTC

(Other brands: **ACHES-N-PAIN, EXCEDRIN IB, GENPRIL, IBUPRIN, IBU-TAB, MEDIPREN, MIDOL 200, MOTRIN-IB, NUPRIN, PAMPRIN-IB, PEDIAPROFEN, TRENDAR,** and others)
See also general information on NSAIDs on page 208.

GENERIC NAME

IBUPROFEN

USES AND INDICATIONS

ADVIL is used in children for the treatment of minor aches and pain associated with colds, headache, toothache, muscle aches and strains, backache, arthritis, and menstrual pain. In children over 12 years, the dosage of ADVIL should be adjusted for each child. ADVIL suspension is used in reducing fever in infants and children over 6 months. Limited studies to date indicate that ADVIL is at least as effective as TYLENOL in reducing fever in children, and may be somewhat more effective in reducing temperatures at or above 102.5 degrees Fahrenheit).

ADVERSE EFFECTS

The adverse effects of ADVIL are consistent with those of other NSAIDs, and in clinical trials using PEDIA-PROFEN (Ibuprofen) suspension, the reported side effects were mild and infrequent. They included vomiting, diarrhea, nervousness, skin rash, and irritability.

OVERDOSAGE: With ADVIL, parents should be aware of the signs of poisoning, which include stomach pain, nausea, vomiting, drowsiness, and lethargy. Breathing difficulty (particularly in children) and coma may occur rarely. If severe symptoms are exhibited, or if a large overdose is suspected, parents should first contact their physician for instructions before inducing vomiting (with Syrup of Ipecac [page 50] or warm salt water), since the use of emetics may interfere with the treatment that may be required if the child is hospitalized due to the Ibuprofen poisoning.

DOSAGE GUIDELINES
- Oral suspension and tablets:
  - Reduce fever: Daily dosage should not exceed 40 milligrams for each 2.2 pounds of body weight.
    - • For temperatures up to 102.5 degrees Fahrenheit:
    Children to 6 months: Use is not recommended.
    Children 6–11 months (or 13–17 pounds): By mouth, 25 milligrams (¼ teaspoonful) every 6–8 hours as needed.
    Children 12–23 months (or 18–23 pounds): By mouth, 50 milligrams (½ teaspoonful) every 6–8 hours as needed.
    Children 2–3 years (or 24–35 pounds): By mouth, 75 milligrams (¾ teaspoonful) every 6–8 hours as needed.
    Children 4–5 years (or 36–47 pounds): By mouth, 100 milligrams (1 teaspoonful) every 6–8 hours as needed.
    Children 6–8 years (or 48–59 pounds): By mouth, 125 milligrams (1¼ teaspoonsful) every 6–8 hours as needed.
    Children 9–10 years (or 60–71 pounds): By mouth, 150 milligrams (1½ teaspoonsful) every 6–8 hours as needed.
    Children 11–12 years (or 72–95 pounds): By mouth, 200 milligrams (2 teaspoonsful) every 6–8 hours as needed.
    Children over 12 years (or 96–154 pounds): By mouth, 200–400 milligrams every 4–6 hours as needed.
    - • For temperatures at or above 102.5 degrees Fahrenheit:
    Children to 6 months: Use is not recommended.
    Children 6–11 months (or 13–17 pounds): By mouth, 50 milligrams (½ teaspoonful) every 6–8 hours as needed.
    Children 12–23 months (or 18–23 pounds): By mouth, 100 milligrams (1 teaspoonful) every 6–8 hours as needed.
    Children 2–3 years (or 24–35 pounds): By mouth, 150 milligrams (1½ teaspoonsful) every 6–8 hours as needed.
    Children 4–5 years (or 36–47 pounds): By mouth, 200 milligrams (2 teaspoonsful) every 6–8 hours as needed.
    Children 6–8 years (or 48–59 pounds): By mouth, 250 milligrams (2½ teaspoonsful) every 6–8 hours as needed.
    Children 9–10 years (or 60–71 pounds): By mouth, 300 milligrams (1 tablespoonful) every 6–8 hours as needed.
    Children 11–12 years (or 72–95 pounds): By mouth, 400 milligrams (4 teaspoonsful) every 6–8 hours as needed.
    Children over 12 years (or 96–154 pounds): By mouth, 200–400 milligrams every 4–6 hours as needed.

– Juvenile arthritis: By mouth, 20–50 milligrams daily for each 2.2 pounds of body weight given in 3–4 divided doses. Usually, 20 milligrams daily for each 2.2 pounds of body weight is sufficient for milder forms of the disease, with 30–40 milligrams daily for each 2.2 pounds of body weight the usual dose for more severe forms.

COMMENTS

ADVIL and other Ibuprofen preparations in strengths of 200 milligrams are available without prescription; higher concentrations, including the PEDIA-PROFEN oral suspension, require a doctor's prescription. PEDIA-PROFEN oral suspension should be shaken well before use, and it should be used only as directed by a physician. As with other pain and fever medications, ADVIL should not be used for extended periods unless as directed by a physician. If pain or fever persist after several days of continuous treatment, your child should be seen by a doctor.

BRAND NAME(S)
2. NAPROSYN   Rx
See also general information on NSAIDs on page 208.

GENERIC NAME
NAPROXYN

USES AND INDICATIONS
NAPROSYN is used in treating juvenile rheumatoid arthritis.

ADVERSE EFFECTS
The following adverse effects supplement those in the general monograph for NSAIDs (page 208): NAPROSYN may cause more pulmonary toxicity than do other NSAIDs, as well as more skin rash and bleeding problems.

WARNINGS AND PRECAUTIONS
The following precaution supplements those noted in the general monograph for NSAIDs (page 208): NAPROSYN should not be used in children with liver disorders.

MEDICATION AND FOOD INTERACTIONS
- The following interaction supplements those noted in the general monograph for NSAIDs (page 208): NAPROSYN tablets and the oral suspension may increase the risk of water retention and high

blood pressure in children who ingest foods, medications, or beverages high in salt (sodium).

DOSAGE GUIDELINES

- Oral suspension and non-sodium-containing tablets: By mouth, 10 milligrams daily for each 2.2 pounds of body weight, given in 2 divided doses.

COMMENTS

Oral suspensions of NAPROSYN should be shaken well before use.

BRAND NAME(S)
3. TOLECTIN   Rx
See also general information on NSAIDs on page 208.

GENERIC NAME
TOLMETIN

USES AND INDICATIONS

TOLECTIN is a NSAID used in treating adult and juvenile rheumatoid arthritis and osteoarthritis.

ADVERSE EFFECTS

The following adverse effects supplement those in the general monograph for NSAIDs (page 208): Water retention, muscle cramps, rapid changes in weight gain or loss, headache, diarrhea, and dizziness may be more common with TOLECTIN than with other NSAIDs.

WARNINGS AND PRECAUTIONS

The following are in addition to those in the general monograph for NSAIDs (page 208):

- TOLECTIN is not recommended for use in children under 2 years.
- Sodium Bicarbonate–containing antacids should not be used to minimize the gastrointestinal irritation of TOLECTIN.

MEDICATION AND FOOD INTERACTIONS

The following interaction is in addition to those noted in the general monograph for NSAIDs (page 208): Milk may decrease the availability of TOLECTIN.

DOSAGE GUIDELINES

- Capsule and tablets:

  Children to 2 years: Dosage has not been established.

  Children 2 years and older: By mouth, 20 milligrams daily for each 2.2 pounds of body weight, given in divided doses. The maintenance dose is 15–30 milligrams daily for each 2.2 pounds of body weight, given in divided doses.

BRAND NAME(S)

PANCREASE   Rx, OTC

(Other brands: **COTAZYM, ILOZYME, KU-ZYME HP, ULTRASE MT, VIOKASE, ZYMASE**)

GENERIC NAME

PANCREALIPASE

USES AND INDICATIONS

PANCREASE is a combination of enzymes that help in the digestion and absorption of fats, proteins, and sugars (carbohydrates). It is used in treating children who are deficient in these enzymes.

ADVERSE EFFECTS

The major adverse effects of PANCREASE are abdominal cramps, nausea, diarrhea, joint pains, bloody urine, swelling of feet or legs, skin rash, nasal congestion, and difficulty breathing.

WARNINGS AND PRECAUTIONS

- PANCREASE powder may irritate the skin or mucous membranes, and it should not be inhaled.
- Children who are allergic to pork should not take PANCREASE.
- PANCREASE tablets should not be chewed, and they should be taken before or with meals in order to be most effective and less irritating to the mouth.
- PANCREASE capsules may be opened and sprinkled on soft foods such as gelatin or applesauce to administer to children.

MEDICATION AND FOOD INTERACTIONS

- PANCREASE may interfere with the absorption of iron preparations.

- Antacids containing calcium or magnesium (see Appendix II) may decrease the effectiveness of PANCREASE, and other antacids should be used if necessary.
- Foods or liquids having a high acidity may inactivate PANCREASE; these foods should be avoided.

DOSAGE GUIDELINES
- Capsules and tablets: By mouth, 1–3 capsules or tablets with meals, adjusting the dosage as necessary.
- Delayed-release capsules: By mouth, 1–2 capsules with meals, adjusting the dosage as necessary. The capsules containing enteric-coated spheres should not be chewed but taken with liquids or soft food.
- Oral powder: By mouth, 700 milligrams with meals, adjusting the dosage as necessary.

GROUP NAME
PEDICULICIDES

1. LINDANE (KILDANE, KWELL, KWILDANE, PMS LINDANE, SCABENE). 2. PERMETHRIN (NIX). 3. PYRETHRINS/PIPERONYL BUTOXIDE (A-200, BLUE, LICETROL, R & C, RID, TISIT, TRIPLE X).

USES AND INDICATIONS
Pediculicides are medications used to relieve the infestations caused by lice and scabies. They destroy head and body lice, including pubic lice (crabs), by stimulating the parasites' central nervous systems to produce convulsions, paralysis, and death. These agents also destroy the female reproductive cells (ova), which become new parasites after they are fertilized. In addition to the use of a pediculicide, treatment also requires thorough laundering of personal clothing and bed linen to prevent reinfestation. Consideration should be given to treating all brothers and sisters and close friends or playmates of the infected child.

COMMENTS
Infestations of head and body lice are usually evident but may be overlooked because the louse is such a tiny parasite. The symptoms of infestation are localized itching and redness in the areas of infestation. On close inspection, the parasites can be seen with the naked eye; and the nits, or eggs, may be attached to hair and may be seen when a fine

comb is passed through the infested hairy area. Usually, infected children require only 1 or 2 treatments to cure the infestation.

BRAND NAME(S)
1. KWELL   Rx
(Other brands: **KILDANE, KWILDANE, PMS LINDANE, SCABENE**)
See also general information on pediculicides on page 215.

GENERIC NAME
LINDANE

USES AND INDICATIONS
KWELL is used to treat both head and body lice (including pubic, or crab, lice), as well as scabies.

ADVERSE EFFECTS
The major adverse effects of KWELL are its central nervous system stimulant effects, which may include dizziness and convulsions, as well as skin rash and itching that were not present before the start of treatment. Other side effects may be nausea, vomiting, muscle cramps, nervousness, and rapid heartbeats.

OVERDOSAGE: The symptoms of toxicity with KWELL usually follow oral ingestion and are exhibited by signs of central nervous system stimulation, such as convulsions. Medical attention should be obtained as soon as possible. If emergency medical aid is not immediately available, and if the child is conscious, give Syrup of Ipecac or warm salt water to induce vomiting. If in doubt as to what to do, contact your nearest poison control center for appropriate instructions (see Appendix IV).

WARNINGS AND PRECAUTIONS

- Do not use KWELL in premature infants who are 1 month old or less, since they are unable to metabolize the medication due to the lack of development of liver function.
- Do not use KWELL in children with seizure disorders.
- Flush with large amounts of water if KWELL comes in contact with the eyes.
- Avoid getting KWELL in any open cuts or skin wounds, as it may cause skin irritation; flush well with water.
- Read the patient instructions carefully before using KWELL, and

adhere to all instructions as well as patient cautions. Keep out of reach of young children.

MEDICATION AND FOOD INTERACTIONS

Oil-based medications applied to the area(s) to which KWELL will be applied may increase its absorption, as well as the possible risk of toxicity. Wash and dry the area(s) well before applying KWELL.

DOSAGE GUIDELINES

- Cream and lotion: Apply a thin coating to the affected area and immediate surrounding area and rub in well; leave on for 8–12 hours, then wash thoroughly and rinse well. If there is still evidence of infestation, repeat treatment again in 7 days.
- Shampoo: Apply 1–2 ounces (depending on hair length) to dry hair and work in thoroughly; allow to stand for 4 minutes, then add a small amount of water to get a good lather. Rinse hair thoroughly and towel briskly. Comb hair with a fine-tooth comb, or use tweezers to remove any remaining nits. If there is still evidence of infestation, repeat treatment again in 7 days.

COMMENTS

KWELL lotion and shampoo should be shaken well before use, and KWELL should only be used externally.

BRAND NAME(S)
2 . NIX   Rx
See also general information on pediculicides on page 215.

GENERIC NAME
PERMETHRIN

USES AND INDICATIONS

NIX is a synthetic pyrethroid used to treat head lice and their ova. It exerts its destructive effect on the parasites by interfering with sodium chemistry in their nerve cells.

ADVERSE EFFECTS

The adverse effects of NIX include skin rash, itching, and a burning or tingling sensation that were not present before the drug was applied. Redness and inflammation of the scalp may also occur.

WARNINGS AND PRECAUTIONS

- NIX is not recommended for use in children under 2 years.
- The use of NIX may increase the redness and swelling often associated with head lice.
- Avoid contact with the eyes or open cuts or wounds; flush well with water.
- All personal clothing and bed linen that may be contaminated should be thoroughly laundered to prevent reinfestation.

DOSAGE GUIDELINES

- Lotion: Shampoo and towel-dry hair before applying NIX. Apply to the head and rub in to wet the hair thoroughly. Allow to remain for 10 minutes, then rinse thoroughly and comb with a fine-tooth comb to remove nits. If there is evidence of continued infestation, repeat the treatment no later than 7 days.

COMMENTS

NIX lotion should be shaken well before use, and it should only be used externally.

BRAND NAME(S)

3. A-200   OTC

(Other brands: **BLUE, LICETROL, R & C, RID, TISIT, TRIPLE X**)
See also general information on pediculicides on page 215.

GENERIC NAME
PYRETHRINS/PIPERONYL BUTOXIDE

USES AND INDICATIONS

A-200 preparations are used to treat head and body lice (including pubic, or crab, lice) and their eggs.

ADVERSE EFFECTS

The adverse effects of A-200 include skin rash and irritation not present before start of treatment. The central nervous system effects from inhaling the vapors may include nausea, vomiting, diarrhea, and muscle paralysis (death has occurred). Contact your doctor immediately if these symptoms are observed. Other side effects may include wheezing, runny nose, and difficulty breathing.

WARNINGS AND PRECAUTIONS

- Children allergic to ragweed, kerosene, or chrysanthemums may be allergic to A-200.
- Avoid contact with the eyes or open cuts or wounds; flush well with water if spilled.
- All personal clothing and bed linen that may be contaminated should be thoroughly laundered to prevent reinfestation.
- Follow all patient instructions carefully. Keep out of reach of children.
- A-200 may be harmful if swallowed; use only externally.

DOSAGE GUIDELINES

- Gel, liquid, and shampoo: Apply to the hair, scalp, or skin, rubbing in well and wetting hair thoroughly. Leave on for 10 minutes, then wash thoroughly with warm water or regular shampoo. Remove dead parasites and nits by combing with a fine-tooth comb. Do not use more than twice in 24 hours. Repeat again in 7–10 days.

GROUP NAME
PENICILLINS

1. Amoxicillin (AMOXIL, LAROTID, POLYMOX, TRIMOX, WYMOX, and others). 2. Amoxicillin/Clavulanate (AUGMENTIN). 3. Ampicillin (OMNIPEN, POLYCILLIN, PRINCIPEN, and others). 4. Bacampicillin (SPECTROBID). 5. Cloxacillin (CLOXAPEN, TEGOPEN). 6. Cyclacillin (CYCLAPEN-W). 7. Dicloxacillin (DYCIL, DYNAPEN, PATHOCIL). 8. Nafcillin (UNIPEN). 9. Penicillin G (BICILLIN, PENTIDS). 10. Phenoxymethyl Penicillin (BEEPEN-VK, BETAPEN-VK, LEDERCILLIN VK, PEN-VEE K, V-CILLIN K, VEETIDS, and others).

USES AND INDICATIONS

Penicillins are antibiotics that share a common chemical structure and similar mechanisms of action. They kill bacteria in higher concentrations and inhibit bacterial growth in lower concentrations. Oral penicillins are used to treat mild to moderately severe infections of the lungs, skin and soft tissues, and urinary and biliary tracts.

ADVERSE EFFECTS

Children with a history of allergies, hay fever, or asthma are more likely to develop allergies to medications, including penicillins. Also, children who are allergic to one type of penicillin may be cross-sensitive to other penicillins as well as cephalosporins (see Appendix II). Serious adverse effects may result from an allergic (anaphylactic) reaction to penicillins, and parents should be familiar with the signs of toxicity should these occur. The symptoms include sneezing, wheezing, itching, skin eruptions, hives, throat spasms, drop in blood pressure, and circulatory collapse (death has occurred). Medical attention should be obtained as soon as possible after any of these symptoms are observed.

Some of the more common adverse effects of penicillins include nausea, vomiting, diarrhea, and skin rash, as well as inflammation of the tongue, mucous membranes of the mouth, and stomach lining; stomach cramps; weight loss; unusual tiredness; and fungal infections.

WARNINGS AND PRECAUTIONS

- Penicillins should be used with caution in children who have experienced an allergic reaction to a penicillin-type medication in the past.
- Children with cystic fibrosis, mononucleosis, or lymphatic leukemia, as well as children taking allopurinol medication, may be more likely to experience allergic rashes when taking penicillins.
- Penicillins should be used with caution in children who are allergic to cephalosporins (see Appendix II).
- In infections caused by streptococcal organisms (e.g., sore throat), penicillins should be used for a minimum of 10 days to prevent the possibility of rheumatic fever or infection of the lining of the heart muscle.
- As with all anti-infective medications, children should receive the medication for the full course of treatment prescribed, even if the child's symptoms have improved.

MEDICATION AND FOOD INTERACTIONS

- The use of Erythromycin or one of the tetracyclines (see Appendix II) may reduce the effectiveness of penicillins.
- ZYLOPRIM may increase the possibility of skin rash when used with Ampicillin.
- CHLOROMYCETIN toxicity may be increased when used with

penicillins, and the effectiveness of penicillins may be decreased as well.

- Neomycin may decrease the absorption of Penicillin V when they are used together.

COMMENTS

Liquid oral penicillin products should be shaken well before use and should be stored in the refrigerator. Unused portions should be discarded at the end of the treatment period prescribed by the physician or at the end of the expiration period indicated on the label. With the exception of SPECTROBID, Amoxicillin, AUGMENTIN, and Penicillin V, all oral penicillins should be taken on an empty stomach, or 1 hour before meals or 2 hours after meals, and may be taken with water.

GENERIC NAME
1 . AMOXICILLIN   Rx
See also general information on penicillins on page 219.

BRAND NAME(S)
AMOXIL, LAROTID, POLYMOX, TRIMOX, WYMOX, and others

USES AND INDICATIONS

Amoxicillin is a penicillin-type antibiotic similar to Ampicillin in its activity and use. Amoxicillin is used to treat infections of the lungs, skin and soft tissues, and middle ear, as well as infections of the urinary tract, including gonorrhea.

ADVERSE EFFECTS

The most common adverse effects from Amoxicillin are diarrhea, nausea, vomiting, rash, itching, and hives. If your child exhibits rash, itching, or hives, stop the medication and contact your doctor immediately. Prolonged use of oral antibiotics may result in diarrhea, with significant loss of body fluid and electrolytes. If this occurs, stop the antibiotic and contact your doctor.

WARNINGS AND PRECAUTIONS

Children who are allergic to other substances should be observed carefully while taking any antibiotic, including Amoxicillin. Do not administer if your child is allergic to penicillin or Ampicillin, or if your child has previously experienced an allergic reaction to Amoxicillin. Serious allergic reactions, including anaphylactic reactions, may result, and they may require immediate medical attention.

MEDICATION AND FOOD INTERACTIONS
ZYLOPRIM may increase the possibility of skin rash when used with Amoxicillin.

DOSAGE GUIDELINES
- Capsules, chewable tablets, oral drops (50 milligrams per milliliter dropper), and oral suspension (125 milligrams per 5 milliliters and 250 milligrams per 5 milliliters):
  Infants to 13 pounds: By mouth, 25–50 milligrams (0.5–1 milliliter) every 8 hours.
  Infants 13–18 pounds: By mouth, 50–100 milligrams (1–2 milliliters) every 8 hours.
  Children 18–44 pounds: By mouth, 6.7–13.3 milligrams for each 2.2 pounds of body weight every 8 hours.
  Children 44 pounds and over: By mouth, 250–500 milligrams every 8 hours.
- Pediatric drops in infants with severe respiratory infections:
  Infants to 13 pounds: 62.5 milligrams (1.25 cubic centimeters) every 8 hours by mouth.
  Infants 13–15 pounds: 87.5 milligrams (1.75 cubic centimeters) every 8 hours by mouth.
  Infants 16–18 pounds: 112.5 milligrams (2.25 cubic centimeters) every 8 hours by mouth.
- For gonorrhea in prepubertal children 2 years and older:
  Children 2 years and older: By mouth, a single dose of 50 milligrams of Amoxicillin for each 2.2 pounds of body weight with 25 milligrams of Probenecid (which enhances the effect of the antibiotics) for each 2.2 pounds of body weight. Probenecid should not be used in children under 2 years.

COMMENTS
If your child experiences shortness of breath, wheezing, rash, itching, or hives, stop the medication and obtain medical attention as soon as possible. Do not stop the antibiotic treatment sooner than the period prescribed by your physician, even though your child no longer exhibits the symptoms of the infection. Liquid suspensions of Amoxicillin should be shaken well before use and should be kept in the refrigerator. Discard any unused Amoxicillin after the expiration date noted on the label.

GENERIC NAME
2. AMOXICILLIN/CLAVULANATE Rx
See also general information on penicillins on page 219.

BRAND NAME(S)
AUGMENTIN

USES AND INDICATIONS
The uses of Amoxicillin/Clavulanate are similar to those for Amoxicillin and Ampicillin. The addition of Clavulanate Potassium to Amoxicillin extends the latter's range of activity and reduces the likelihood that bacterial resistance to the antibiotic will occur.

DOSAGE GUIDELINES
- Chewable tablets and oral suspension:
  Children to 88 pounds:
  - Middle ear infection, pneumonia, and other severe infections: By mouth, 13.3 milligrams for each 2.2 pounds of body weight every 8 hours.
  - Other infections: By mouth, 6.7 milligrams for each 2.2 pounds of body weight every 8 hours.
- Tablets:
  Children 88 pounds and over: By mouth, 250–500 milligrams every 8 hours.

COMMENTS
The adverse effects, warnings and precautions, and medication and food interactions for Amoxicillin/Clavulanate are essentially the same as those for Amoxicillin (page 221).

GENERIC NAME
3. AMPICILLIN   Rx
See also general information on penicillins on page 219.

BRAND NAME(S)
OMNIPEN, POLYCILLIN, PRINCIPEN, AND OTHERS

USES AND INDICATIONS
Ampicillin is a penicillin-type antibiotic used to treat infections of the ear, skin and soft tissues, and urinary tract, as well as bronchitis and pneumonia.

Although Ampicillin is effective against a broader range of bacteria than are Penicillin G and Phenoxymethyl Penicillin, many pediatricians have supplanted its use with Amoxicillin because Amoxicillin is more effective than Ampicillin in infections caused by resistant bacteria. Ampicillin may also be used as a single-dose antibiotic treatment for gonorrhea.

DOSAGE GUIDELINES
- Capsules and oral suspension:
  Children to 44 pounds: By mouth, 12.5–25 milligrams for each 2.2 pounds of body weight every 6 hours.
  Children 44 pounds and over: By mouth, 250–500 milligrams every 6 hours. For gonorrhea, give by mouth 3.5 grams with 1 gram of Probenecid as a single dose.

COMMENTS
The adverse effects, warnings and precautions, and medication and food interactions for Ampicillin are similar to those for Amoxicillin (page 221).

GENERIC NAME
4. BACAMPICILLIN   Rx
See also general information on penicillins on page 219.

BRAND NAME(S)
SPECTROBID

DOSAGE GUIDELINES
- Oral suspension and tablets:
  – Pneumonia:
    Children to 55 pounds: By mouth, 17.5 milligrams for each 2.2 pounds of body weight every 12 hours.
    Children 55 pounds and over: By mouth, 400–800 milligrams every 12 hours.
  – Other infections:
    Children to 55 pounds: By mouth, 8.75–17.5 milligrams for each 2.2 pounds of body weight.

Children 55 pounds and over: By mouth, 400–800 milligrams every 12 hours.

COMMENTS

For information regarding uses and indications, adverse effects, warnings and precautions, and medication and food interactions, see under Ampicillin (page 223).

GENERIC NAME
5. CLOXACILLIN   Rx

See also general information on penicillins on page 219.

BRAND NAME(S)
CLOXAPEN, TEGOPEN

USES AND INDICATIONS

Cloxacillin is used in treating pneumonia, endocarditis, sinusitis, skin and soft tissue infections, infections of the biliary tract, and other infections caused by staphylococcus organisms.

DOSAGE GUIDELINES

- Capsules and oral solution:
  Children to 44 pounds: By mouth, 12.5–25 milligrams for each 2.2 pounds of body weight every 6 hours.
  Children 44 pounds and over: By mouth, 250–500 milligrams every 6 hours, not to exceed 6 grams.

COMMENTS

Cloxacillin oral solution should be shaken well before use and should be stored in the refrigerator. Unused portions should be discarded at the end of the treatment period.

GENERIC NAME
6. CYCLACILLIN   Rx

See also general information on penicillins on page 219.

BRAND NAME(S)
CYCLAPEN-W

USES AND INDICATIONS

For information regarding uses and indications, see the monograph for Ampicillin (page 223).

DOSAGE GUIDELINES
- Oral suspension and tablets (use is not recommended in infants under 2 months):
  - Middle ear infection: By mouth, 16.7–33.3 milligrams for each 2.2 pounds of body weight every 8 hours.
  - Pharyngitis and tonsillitis:
    Children to 44 pounds: By mouth, 125 milligrams every 8 hours.
    Children 44 pounds and over: By mouth, 250 milligrams every 8 hours.
  - Other infections: By mouth, 12.5–25 milligrams for each 2.2 pounds of body weight every 6 hours.

COMMENTS
The dosage of Cyclacillin should be reduced in children with kidney disorders. Oral suspensions of Cyclacillin should be shaken well before use and should be stored in the refrigerator. Unused portions should be discarded at the end of the treatment period.

GENERIC NAME
7. DICLOXACILLIN   Rx
See also general information on penicillins on page 219.

BRAND NAME(S)
DYCIL, DYNAPEN, PATHOCIL

USES AND INDICATIONS
For information regarding uses and indications, see the monograph for Cloxacillin (page 225).

DOSAGE GUIDELINES
- Capsules and oral suspensions:
  Children to 88 pounds: By mouth, 3.125–6.25 milligrams for each 2.2 pounds of body weight every 6 hours.
  Children 88 pounds and over: By mouth, 125–250 milligrams every 6 hours, not to exceed 6 grams daily.

COMMENTS
Dicloxacillin oral suspension should be shaken well before use and should be stored in the refrigerator. Unused portions should be discarded at the end of the treatment period.

GENERIC NAME
8. NAFCILLIN   Rx
See also general information on penicillins on page 219.

BRAND NAME(S)
UNIPEN

USES AND INDICATIONS
Nafcillin is used in treating pharyngitis, as well as skin and soft tissue infections (see under Cloxacillin, page 225).

DOSAGE GUIDELINES
• Capsules, oral solution, and tablets:
  Newborns: By mouth, 10 milligrams for each 2.2 pounds of body weight every 6–8 hours.
  Children 1 month and older: By mouth, 6.25–12.5 milligrams for each 2.2 pounds of body weight every 6 hours.
  – Streptococcal pharyngitis: By mouth, 250 milligrams every 8 hours.

COMMENTS
Nafcillin oral solution should be shaken well before use and should be stored in the refrigerator. Unused portions should be discarded at the end of the treatment period.

GENERIC NAME
9. PENICILLIN G   Rx
See also general information on penicillins on page 219.

BRAND NAME(S)
BICILLIN, PENTIDS

USES AND INDICATIONS
Penicillin G is used in treating infections caused by sensitive staphylococcal, streptococcal, and pneumococcal organisms, e.g., pneumonia, middle ear infections, sinusitis, rheumatic fever, skin and soft tissue infections, erysipelas, pharyngitis, and gingivostomatitis (inflammation of the gums).

DOSAGE GUIDELINES

- Penicillin G Benzathine (BICILLIN) tablets:

    Children to 12 years: By mouth, 4,167–15,000 units for each 2.2 pounds of body weight every 4 hours; or 6,250–22,500 units for each 2.2 pounds of body weight every 6 hours; or 8,333–30,000 units for each 2.2 pounds of body weight every 8 hours.

    Children 12 years and older: By mouth, 400,000–600,000 units every 4–6 hours. For prophylaxis against rheumatic heart disease, the dose is 200,000 units by mouth every 12 hours. The maximum daily dose is 12,000,000 units.

- Penicillin G Potassium (PENTIDS) oral solution and tablets:

    Children to 12 years: See instructions above for Penicillin G Benzathine.

    Children 12 years and older: By mouth, 200,000–500,000 units every 6–8 hours. For prophylaxis against rheumatic heart disease, the dose is 200,000–250,000 units every 12 hours. The maximum daily dose is 12,000,000 units.

COMMENTS

Penicillin G should not be taken with fruit juices or other acidic beverages, as the acidic solution may reduce the effectiveness of the antibiotic. Penicillin G oral solutions should be shaken well before use and should be stored in the refrigerator. Unused portions should be discarded at the end of the treatment period.

GENERIC NAME
10. PHENOXYMETHYL PENICILLIN

Rx

See also general information on penicillins on page 219.

BRAND NAME(S)
BEEPEN-VK, BETAPEN-VK, LEDERCILLIN VK, PEN-VEE K, V-CILLIN K, VEETIDS, AND OTHERS

USES AND INDICATIONS

For information regarding uses and indications, see under Penicillin G (page 227). In addition, Phenoxymethyl Penicillin is also used in treating Lyme disease, anthrax, and actinomycosis.

MEDICATION AND FOOD INTERACTIONS
Neomycin may interfere with the absorption of Phenoxymethyl Penicillin.

DOSAGE GUIDELINES
- Oral solution and tablets:
  Children to 12 years: By mouth, 2.5–9.3 milligrams (4,167–15,000 units) for each 2.2 pounds of body weight every 4 hours; or 3.75–14 milligrams (6,250–22,500 units) for each 2.2 pounds of body weight every 6 hours; or 5–18.7 milligrams (8,333–30,000 units) for each 2.2 pounds of body weight every 8 hours.
  Children 12 years and older: By mouth, 125–500 milligrams (200,000–800,000 units) every 6–8 hours. For prophylaxis against rheumatic heart disease, the dose is 125–250 milligrams (200,000–400,000 units) every 12 hours. The maximum daily dose is 7.2 grams.

COMMENTS
Phenoxymethyl Penicillin oral solution should be shaken well before use and should be stored in the refrigerator. Unused portions should be discarded at the end of the treatment period.

GENERIC NAME
QUINIDINE   Rx

BRAND NAME(S)
CARDIOQUIN, CIN-QUIN, QUINIDEX, QUINORA, SK-QUINIDINE SULFATE

USES AND INDICATIONS
Quinidine is an antiarrhythmic drug that depresses the excitability of the heart, slows the conduction of electrical impulses, decreases the contraction of the heart muscle, and increases the rest period between contractions. Quinidine is used to treat abnormal heartbeats in children.

ADVERSE EFFECTS

The major adverse effects of Quinidine include the following:

- Gastrointestinal: nausea, vomiting, colic, stomach cramps, and diarrhea.
- Central nervous system: headache, mental confusion, excitability, ringing in the ears, and temporary loss of consciousness.
- Cardiovascular: drop in blood pressure and abnormal heartbeats.
- Allergic: skin rash, itching, skin eruptions, increased sensitivity to sunlight, fever, and asthmatic reactions.
- Ophthalmic: blurred vision, increased size of pupils, night blindness, and color disturbances.

WARNINGS AND PRECAUTIONS

- The use of Quinidine is contraindicated in patients allergic to quinine.
- Quinidine should be used with caution in patients with heart or liver disorders.
- Patients on long-term Quinidine therapy should be periodically tested for blood counts, heart function, potassium and Quinidine serum levels, and for liver and kidney functions.
- Taking Quinidine with food may lessen the chance of upset stomach.

MEDICATION AND FOOD INTERACTIONS

- Quinidine may decrease the effects of COUMADIN, resulting in increased risk of bleeding.
- The following drugs may increase the toxic effects of Quinidine: Sodium Bicarbonate, calcium- and magnesium-containing antacids (see Appendix II), and citrates (see Appendix II).
- The following drugs may increase heart toxicity of Quinidine: SERPASIL, INDERAL, and PRONESTYL.
- TAGAMET and potassium-containing products may increase the effects of Quinidine, including possible toxic effects.
- Quinidine may increase the toxicity of LANOXIN.
- The use of Quinine and Quinidine together may increase the risk of toxicity of both medications.
- The following medications may decrease the effects of Quinidine:

alcohol-containing products, TEGRETOL, FULVICIN V, MYSOLINE, RIMACTANE, and corticosteroids (see Appendix II).

DOSAGE GUIDELINES
- Capsules and tablets:
  - Quinidine Gluconate tablets: By mouth, 8.25 milligrams for each 2.2 pounds of body weight, administered in 5 divided doses.
  - Quinidine Sulfate capsules and tablets: By mouth, 6 milligrams for each 2.2 pounds of body weight, administered in 5 divided doses.

BRAND NAME(S)
RITALIN   Rx

GENERIC NAME
METHYLPHENIDATE

USES AND INDICATIONS
RITALIN is a central nervous system stimulant used in treating attention deficit disorders in children. Its action is not clearly understood, but it appears to share a similar action with amphetamines: improving the child's ability to pay attention by affecting the area of the brain that controls movement activities.

ADVERSE EFFECTS
The adverse effects of RITALIN include the following:

- Central nervous system: dizziness, drowsiness, inability to coordinate muscle movements, involuntary rapid muscle movements, insomnia, nervousness, headache, and behavior changes.
- Gastrointestinal: nausea, vomiting, loss of appetite, weight loss, and abdominal cramps.
- Cardiovascular: changes in blood pressure and pulse, palpitations, and rapid irregular heartbeats.
- Dermatological: hair loss on scalp, skin rash, itching, and skin eruptions.

OVERDOSAGE: Parents should be alert for the signs of acute toxicity with RITALIN, which include agitation, tremors, nausea, vomiting, muscle twitching, mental confusion, delirium, euphoria, increase in size of eye pupils, sweating, increase in blood pressure, rapid heartbeats, headache, and convulsions that may be followed by coma. Parents should contact their doctor as quickly as possible for instructions regarding further medical attention that may be required.

WARNINGS AND PRECAUTIONS

- RITALIN should be used with extreme caution in children who have a history of seizure disorders, high blood pressure, or vision disorders.
- Children on long-term therapy should be monitored periodically with complete blood counts, growth assessment (both height and weight), blood pressure checks, and a determination of the need to continue RITALIN therapy.
- RITALIN is not recommended for use in children under 6 years.
- The last dose of RITALIN should be taken as early in the evening as possible to avoid difficulty sleeping.

MEDICATION AND FOOD INTERACTIONS

- RITALIN may decrease the effectiveness of loop diuretics (see Appendix II).
- RITALIN may increase the risk of toxicity of COUMADIN, all anticonvulsants (see Appendix II), and tricyclic antidepressants (see Appendix II).

DOSAGE GUIDELINES

- Extended-release tablets:
  Children to 6 years: Dosage has not been established.
  Children 6 years and older: By mouth, 20 milligrams 1–3 times daily at 8-hour intervals, on an empty stomach.
- Tablets:
  Children to 6 years: Dosage has not been established.
  Children 6 years and older: By mouth, 5 milligrams twice daily before breakfast and lunch; then the dose may be increased, if required, by 5–10 milligrams at 1-week intervals, up to a maximum of 60 milligrams daily.

COMMENTS

As with amphetamines used in attention deficit disorders, the use of RITALIN on a long-term basis may be interrupted by drug-free periods in which the child is on no medication. Dosage guidelines for the treatment of attention deficit disorders may be extremely flexible, and some physicians modify therapy to permit children to "skip" taking doses on weekends, on holidays, during summer vacations, and during school breaks.

RITALIN is classified as a Schedule II Controlled Substance, and its distribution and use are strictly regulated by federal and state laws.

BRAND NAME(S)
ROBITUSSIN   OTC
(Other brands: **ANTI-TUSS, BAYTUSSIN, BREONESIN, CREMACOAT 2, COLREX EXPECTORANT, GEE-GE, GENATUSS, GG-CEN, GLYATE, GLYCOTUSS, GLYTUSS, GUIATUSS, HALOTUSSIN, HUMIBID L.A., HUMIBID SPRINKLE, HYTUSS, HYTUSS-2X, MALOTUSS, MYTUSSIN, NALDECON SENIOR EX, NORTUSSIN, ROBAFEN, SCOT-TUSSIN, S-T EXPECTORANT,** and others)

GENERIC NAME
GUAIFENESIN

USES AND INDICATIONS
ROBITUSSIN is used alone or in combination with other ingredients in cough and cold preparations. It is believed to act as an expectorant by lowering the surface tension between the mucous membranes of the respiratory tract and the mucous accumulated in the tract during infections. ROBITUSSIN is also believed to reduce the "thickness" of the mucous, making it easier to eliminate. ROBITUSSIN is used in treating the symptoms of dry, nonproductive coughs, as well as in aiding the removal of mucous from the lungs.

ADVERSE EFFECTS
The adverse effects of ROBITUSSIN include nausea, vomiting, drowsiness, stomach pain, and diarrhea.

WARNINGS AND PRECAUTIONS

- ROBITUSSIN should not be used for coughs associated with asthma or where excessive secretions occur.
- If cough persists for more than 7 days, or is accompanied by fever, rash, or headache, contact a physician as soon as possible.

DOSAGE GUIDELINES

Some convenient dosage forms of Guaifenesin come in the following strengths:

- Capsules—200 milligrams; oral solution—200 milligrams per 5 milliliters (teaspoonful); syrup—100 milligrams per 5 milliliters (teaspoonful); tablets—100 milligrams and 200 milligrams:
  Children to 2 years: Dose must be individualized for each child.
  Children 2–6 years: By mouth, 50–100 milligrams (½–1 teaspoonful of syrup) every 4 hours as needed, not to exceed 600 milligrams daily.
  Children 6–12 years: By mouth, 100–200 milligrams (½–1 teaspoonful of the oral solution; or 1–2 teaspoonsful of the syrup; or 1–2 of the 100-milligram tablets) every 4 hours as needed, not to exceed 1,200 milligrams (1.2 grams) daily.
  Children over 12 years: By mouth, 200–400 milligrams (1–2 teaspoonsful of the oral solution; or 2–4 of the 100-milligram tablets; or 1–2 of the 200-milligram tablets) every 4 hours as needed, not to exceed 2,400 milligrams (2.4 grams) daily.

GROUP NAME

SALICYLATES

1. ASPIRIN (A.S.A., ASPERGUM, BAYER ASPIRIN, EASPRIN, ECOTRIN, EMPIRIN, MEASURIN, NORWICH ASPIRIN, ST. JOSEPH ASPIRIN, AND OTHERS). 2. BUFFERED ASPIRIN (ASCRIPTIN, BUFFAPRIN, BUFFERIN, AND OTHERS). 3. CHOLINE SALICYLATE (ARTHROPAN). 4. SODIUM SALICYLATE (URACIL).

USES AND INDICATIONS

Salicylates are a subclass of the nonsteroidal anti-inflammatory analgesics (NSAIDs). In addition to their analgesic and anti-inflammatory properties, they also have the ability to decrease body temperature and reduce fever (antipyretic). Salicylates are among the oldest and most widely used of all pharmacological medications, and they are used alone or in combination with other medications. In children, salicylates are used to treat symptoms of various disorders accompanied by mild to moderate pain, inflammation, or fever, e.g., muscle bruises and sprains, arthritis, flu and allergies, headache, athletic injuries, etc.

ADVERSE EFFECTS

Although Aspirin is still the most widely used of all salicylates, its use in infants and children has been largely supplanted by TYLENOL because of Aspirin's tendency to irritate the stomach lining and because of its potential in producing Reye's syndrome, a disorder that may be fatal in infants and children, particularly in illnesses accompanied by high fever, such as in flu and chicken pox.

The adverse effects associated with the use of salicylates include the following: nausea, vomiting, heartburn, stomach discomfort, and loss of appetite. Allergic reactions include the following: skin rash, itching, skin eruptions, runny nose, and anaphylactic reaction (which can be fatal).

OVERDOSAGE: Toxicity resulting from the overuse of salicylates is known as salicylism, or salicylate poisoning, and may be marked by either mild or severe symptoms. Parents should be familiar with the signs of salicylate poisoning and should contact their physician as soon as possible if these signs are observed in their children.

- Salicylism (mild): The symptoms of mild salicylism include ringing in the ears (tinnitus), dizziness or weakness, nausea, vomiting, mental confusion, diarrhea, difficulty breathing, headache, visual difficulties, and increased thirst and sweating.
- Salicylism (severe): The signs of severe salicylate poisoning include severe confusion or excitement, hallucinations, convulsions, fever, shortness of breath, and bloody urine.

For additional information regarding toxicity and adverse effects of salicylates, see under the monograph for Aspirin (page 237).

WARNINGS AND PRECAUTIONS

- Due to the potential risk of Reye's syndrome, salicylates, particularly Aspirin or Buffered Aspirin, should not be used in infants, children, or teenagers who have high fever (such as in flu or chicken pox).
- Long-term use of salicylates may cause ulceration of the gastrointestinal lining, as well as bleeding, and should be avoided.
- In order to minimize irritation to the stomach, salicylates may be taken with food or immediately following meals, or with water or milk.

- Do not use Aspirin products if they have a vinegarlike odor. This is characteristic of Aspirin that has decomposed, and it may not be fully effective.
- Patients who are allergic to one salicylate, or to NSAIDs, may also be allergic to other salicylates.
- If ringing in the ears (tinnitus) occurs, the medication should be stopped at once and your physician consulted.
- Salicylates should be used with caution in children with kidney disorders.

MEDICATION AND FOOD INTERACTIONS

- The long-term use of salicylates with TYLENOL may result in kidney toxicity.
- Ammonium Chloride, Ascorbic Acid, LASIX, and Paraminobenzoic Acid (PABA) may increase salicylate toxicity.
- The use of salicylates with corticosteroids (see Appendix II) may result in decreased effectiveness of salicylates.
- Salicylates may increase the risk of stomach irritation, including ulceration and bleeding, when used with alcohol and NSAIDs (see Appendix II).
- The use of salicylates with Sodium Bicarbonate, citrates (see Appendix II), or antacids containing calcium or magnesium (see Appendix II) may increase the risk of salicylate poisoning.
- The risk of damage to the ears is increased when salicylates are used with LASIX, EDECRIN, or Erythromycin, particularly in children with kidney disorders.
- The use of salicylates, particularly Aspirin, with COUMADIN may increase the risk of bleeding.
- The effectiveness of salicylates may be reduced by laxatives (see Appendix II).
- Salicylates may reduce the effectiveness of Vitamin K products.

COMMENTS

Aspirin should not be used in children for more than 5 days; also, children should not receive more than 5 doses in a 24-hour period, unless as directed by a physician. If a sore throat persists for more than 2 days, contact your child's doctor.

GENERIC NAME
1. ASPIRIN   OTC
See also general information on salicylates on page 234.

BRAND NAME(S)
A.S.A., ASPERGUM, BAYER ASPIRIN,
EASPRIN, ECOTRIN, EMPIRIN,
MEASURIN, NORWICH ASPIRIN, ST.
JOSEPH ASPIRIN, AND OTHERS

USES AND INDICATIONS
Aspirin is used to relieve the symptoms of flu, colds, sprains, bruises, headache, and arthritis, as well as pain in general (either with or without inflammation.

ADVERSE EFFECTS

REYE'S SYNDROME: Reye's syndrome may occur in infants and children (including teenagers), usually between the ages of 6 months and 15 years, following the use of salicylates (primarily Aspirin) in conditions that are accompanied by high fever, such as flu or chicken pox. The symptoms include severe swelling of the head (cerebral edema), confusion, nausea, vomiting, delirium, seizures, and, eventually, coma. There is a high mortality rate if the symptoms are not detected early and if the child is not treated promptly. The use of Acetaminophen or other nonsalicylate medications are suggested as an alternative to Aspirin or other salicylates in treating conditions accompanied by high fever in children and teenagers.

MEDICATION AND FOOD INTERACTIONS
In addition to those noted above under the general monograph for salicylates (page 234), Aspirin may increase the body's elimination of Ascorbic Acid, requiring children on long-term treatment to increase their Ascorbic Acid intake.

DOSAGE GUIDELINES
- Capsules: See below under chewable tablets.
- Delayed-release capsules, chewable tablets, and tablets:
  - Pain/fever:
    Children to 2 years: Dosage must be individualized for each child.

Children 2–4 years: By mouth, 160 milligrams every 4 hours as needed.

Children 4–6 years: By mouth, 240 milligrams every 4 hours as needed.

Children 6–9 years: By mouth, 320–325 milligrams every 4 hours as needed.

Children 9–12 years: By mouth, 320–480 milligrams every 4 hours as needed.

– Arthritis (anti-inflammatory): By mouth, 80–100 milligrams daily for each 2.2 pounds of body weight, given in divided doses as prescribed by a physician.

• Chewing gum (for pain):

Children to 3 years: Dosage must be individualized for each child.

Children 3–6 years: By mouth, 227 milligrams (1 piece); may be repeated up to 3 times daily.

Children 6–12 years: By mouth, 454 milligrams (2 pieces); may be repeated up to 4 times daily.

• Rectal suppositories:

Children to 2 years: Dosage must be individualized for each child.

Children 2–4 years: Insert rectally 160 milligrams every 4 hours as needed.

Children 4–6 years: Insert rectally 240 milligrams every 4 hours as needed.

Children 6–9 years: Insert rectally 325 milligrams every 4 hours as needed.

Children 9–11 years: Insert rectally 325–400 milligrams every 4 hours as needed.

Children 11–12 years: Insert rectally 325–480 milligrams every 4 hours as needed.

GENERIC NAME
2. BUFFERED ASPIRIN   OTC
See also general information on salicylates on page 234.

BRAND NAME(S)
ASCRIPTIN, BUFFAPRIN, BUFFERIN, AND OTHERS

DOSAGE GUIDELINES
- Tablets:
  - Analgesic/antipyretic:

    Children to 2 years: Dosage must be individualized for each child.

    Children 2–4 years: By mouth, ½ of a 325-milligram tablet every 4 hours as needed.

    Children 4–6 years: By mouth, ¾ of a 325-milligram tablet every 4 hours as needed.

    Children 6–9 years: By mouth, 325 milligrams every 4 hours as needed.

    Children 9–11 years: By mouth, 1–1¼ tablets (325 milligrams) every 4 hours as needed.

    Children 11–12 years: By mouth, 1–1½ tablets (325 milligrams) every 4 hours as needed.

  - Arthritis: By mouth, 80–100 milligrams daily for each 2.2 pounds of body weight, given in divided doses as prescribed by a physician.

GENERIC NAME
3. CHOLINE SALICYLATE   OTC
See also general information on salicylates on page 234.

BRAND NAME(S)
ARTHROPAN

DOSAGE GUIDELINES
- Oral liquid (for pain and fever):

  Children to 2 years: Dosage must be individualized.

  Children 2–4 years: By mouth, 217.5 milligrams every 4 hours as needed.

  Children 4–6 years: By mouth, 326.5 milligrams every 4 hours as needed.

  Children 6–9 years: By mouth, 435 milligrams (½ teaspoonful) every 4 hours as needed.

  Children 9–11 years: By mouth, 435–543.8 milligrams every 4 hours as needed.

  Children 11–12 years: By mouth, 435–652.5 milligrams every 4 hours as needed.

GENERIC NAME
4. SODIUM SALICYLATE   OTC
See also general information on salicylates on page 234.

BRAND NAME(S)
URACIL

DOSAGE GUIDELINES
- Delayed-release tablets:
  Children to 6 years: Use is not recommended.
  Children 6 years and older: By mouth, 325 milligrams as needed.
- Tablets:
  - Pain/fever:
    Children to 2 years: Dosage has not been established.
    Children 2–4 years: By mouth, 162.5 milligrams every 4 hours as needed.
    Children 4–6 years: By mouth, 243.8 milligrams every 4 hours as needed.
    Children 6–9 years: By mouth, 325 milligrams every 4 hours as needed.
    Children 9–11 years: By mouth, 325–406.3 milligrams every 4 hours as needed.
    Children 11–12 years: By mouth, 325–487.5 milligrams every 4 hours as needed.
  - Arthritis: By mouth, 80–100 milligrams daily for each 2.2 pounds of body weight, given in divided doses as prescribed by a physician.

GENERIC NAME
SODIUM FLUORIDE   Rx

BRAND NAME(S)
FLUORITAB, FLURA, FLURA-DROPS, FLURA-LOZ, KARIDIUM, LURIDE, LURIDE-SF, PEDIAFLOR, PHOS-FLUR

USES AND INDICATIONS
Sodium Fluoride promotes the development of strong, healthy teeth, and it inhibits the action of bacteria in producing cavities and general tooth decay. Doctors often prescribe fluorides to infants and children in

areas that have less than 0.7 parts per million of fluoride in the drinking water.

ADVERSE EFFECTS

The major adverse effects of Sodium Fluoride include gastrointestinal irritation, weakness, and headache. Hypersensitivity, which is rare, may cause skin rash and itching.

WARNINGS AND PRECAUTIONS

- Sodium Fluoride should be avoided if the drinking water exceeds 0.7 parts per million.
- Excessive ingestion may result in mottling of the teeth.
- Taking fluorides with food or fluids may lessen stomach irritation.

MEDICATION AND FOOD INTERACTIONS

Fluorides are incompatible with aluminum- and calcium-containing medications (i.e., antacids) and with dairy foods that are high in calcium, including milk.

DOSAGE GUIDELINES

- Chewable tablets, oral solution, and tablets:
  - If drinking water contains less than 0.3 parts per million:
    Birth to 2 years: By mouth, 0.25 milligram daily.
    Children 2–3 years: By mouth, 0.5 milligram daily.
    Children 3–13 years: By mouth, 1 milligram daily.
  - If drinking water contains 0.3–0.7 parts per million:
    Birth to 2 years: Fluoride supplement not required.
    Children 2–3 years: By mouth, 0.25 milligram daily.
    Children 3–13 years: 0.5 milligram daily.
  - If drinking water contains more than 0.7 parts per million:
    Fluoride supplements are not required for children of any age, unless prescribed by a doctor.

BRAND NAME(S)
SUDAFED   Rx, OTC
(Other brands: **AFRINOL, CENAFED, CHILDREN'S SUDAFED, DECOFED, DORCOL CHILDREN'S DECONGESTANT, GENAPHED, HALOFED, NEOFED, NOVAFED, PEDIACARE INFANT'S ORAL DECONGESTANT DROPS, PSEUDOGEST, SINUFED, SUDRIN, SUFEDRIN**)

GENERIC NAME
PSEUDOEPHEDRINE

USES AND INDICATIONS
SUDAFED is a nasal decongestant used in the temporary relief of sinus or nasal congestion—either as a single-ingredient medication or in combination with other antihistamine or antihistamine-decongestant-combination products used in treating the symptoms of coughs, colds, flu, hay fever, and allergic disorders affecting the nasal passages.

ADVERSE EFFECTS
The major adverse effects of SUDAFED include the following:

- Central nervous system: hallucinations, convulsions, nervousness, difficulty sleeping, headache, dizziness, trembling, and restlessness.
- Gastrointestinal: nausea and vomiting.
- Cardiovascular: abnormally slow or rapid heartbeats.
- Other: pale skin color, weakness, difficulty breathing, painful urination, and excessive sweating.

WARNINGS AND PRECAUTIONS

- Newborn and premature infants may be particularly sensitive to the adverse effects of SUDAFED.
- SUDAFED should be used with extreme caution in children with heart disorders, high blood pressure, diabetes, glaucoma, or hyperthyroidism.
- Where possible, SUDAFED should be administered a few hours before bedtime to minimize the possibility of insomnia.

MEDICATION AND FOOD INTERACTIONS

- The adverse effects of SUDAFED may be increased by drugs that increase the alkalinity of the urine, such as citrates (see Appendix II).
- SUDAFED may decrease the effectiveness of INDERAL and of loop diuretics (see Appendix II).
- The use of SUDAFED with RITALIN, Epinephrine, ISUPREL, and amphetamines (see Appendix II) may result in increased heart stimulation, irritability, restlessness, and insomnia.

- The use of SUDAFED and thyroid hormones (see Appendix II) may result in the increased toxicity of both medications.

DOSAGE GUIDELINES
- Oral solution, syrup, and tablets: By mouth, 4 milligrams daily for each 2.2 pounds of body weight, given in 4 divided doses.
  Or:
  Children to 4 months: Dose must be individualized for patient.
  Children 4 months–2 years: By mouth, 3.75 milligrams every 4–6 hours as needed.
  Children 2–6 years: By mouth, 15 milligrams every 4–6 hours as needed.
  Children 6–12 years: By mouth, 30 milligrams every 4–6 hours as needed.
  Children 12 years and older: By mouth, 60 milligrams every 4–6 hours, not to exceed 240 milligrams in 24 hours.

GROUP NAME
SULFONAMIDES

1. SULFAMETHOXAZOLE (GANTANOL). 2. SULFAMETHOXAZOLE/TRIMETHOPRIM (BACTRIM, SEPTRA, AND OTHERS). 3. SULFISOXAZOLE (GANTRISIN).

USES AND INDICATIONS
Sulfonamides are antibacterial medications used in treating urinary infections, middle ear infections, toxoplasmosis (a parasitic infection), and other infections caused by susceptible organisms.

ADVERSE EFFECTS
The adverse effects of sulfonamides are many and affect most of the major organ systems.

- Kidneys: Crystallization of sulfonamides may produce painful urination or decrease in urine production.
- Gastrointestinal: nausea, vomiting, diarrhea (may be bloody), stomach pain, loss of appetite, and swelling of tongue.
- Central nervous system: headache, convulsions, loss of muscle coordination, ringing in the ears, hallucinations, difficulty sleeping, drowsiness, hearing loss, vertigo, and mental depression.
- Blood: anemia and bluish color skin or lips (cyanosis).

- Allergic: skin eruptions with or without itching, increased sensitivity to sunlight, joint pains, and anaphylactic reactions.
- Other: fever, chills, increased urination, yellow-colored urine or skin, and, rarely, goiters.

WARNINGS AND PRECAUTIONS

- Sulfonamides should be used cautiously in children who have kidney, liver, or blood disorders.
- Sulfonamides should be used with caution in children who have a history of allergies, asthma, or glucose-6-phosphate dehydrogenase deficiency.
- Long-term sulfonamide therapy should be monitored with frequent complete blood counts and kidney function tests.
- Contact your physician as soon as possible if the following signs are detected: sore throat, fever, chills, shortness of breath, joint pain, cough, and yellow skin color.
- Children who are allergic to LASIX may also be allergic to sulfonamides.

MEDICATION AND FOOD INTERACTIONS

- Sulfonamides may increase the toxicity of Methotrexate.
- Sulfonamides may increase the potential toxicity of COUMADIN.
- Sulfonamides may decrease the absorption of LANOXIN.

GENERIC NAME
1. SULFAMETHOXAZOLE   Rx
See also general information on sulfonamides on page 243.

BRAND NAME(S)
GANTANOL

USES AND INDICATIONS
Sulfamethoxazole is used in treating urinary infections and toxoplasmosis (a parasitic infection).

ADVERSE EFFECTS
The potential for the formation of crystals in the urinary tract is greater with Sulfamethoxazole than with other sulfonamides.

WARNINGS AND PRECAUTIONS

- Children on Sulfamethoxazole therapy should be given plenty of fluids.
- Sulfamethoxazole should not be used in infants under 1 month due to the potential for adverse neurological effects.
- A reduction in dosage may be required in children with kidney disorders.

DOSAGE GUIDELINES
- Oral suspension and tablets:
  Infants to 1 month: Should not be used except as adjunctive treatment for toxoplasmosis.
  Infants 1 month and older: By mouth, 50–60 milligrams for each 2.2 pounds of body weight (maximum 2 grams) initially, then 25–30 milligrams for each 2.2 pounds of body weight every 12 hours. The maximum daily dose for children should not exceed 75 milligrams for each 2.2 pounds of body weight.

COMMENTS
Sulfamethoxazole oral suspension should be shaken well before use.

GENERIC NAME
2. SULFAMETHOXAZOLE/ TRIMETHOPRIM   Rx
See also general information on sulfonamides on page 243.

BRAND NAME(S)
BACTRIM, SEPTRA, AND OTHERS

USES AND INDICATIONS
Sulfamethoxazole/Trimethoprim is an antibacterial agent combination used in treating urinary infections, middle ear infections, and chronic bronchitis. It is also used as an antiprotozoal agent in HIV-related pneumonia.

DOSAGE GUIDELINES
- Oral suspension and tablets:
  - Antiprotozoal:
    Children to 70 pounds: By mouth, 25 milligrams of

Sulfamethoxazole (and 5 milligrams of Trimethoprim) for each 2.2 pounds of body weight every 8 hours.
Children over 70 pounds: By mouth, 25 milligrams of Sulfamethoxazole (and 5 milligrams of Trimethoprim) for each 2.2 pounds of body weight every 6 hours.
– Antibacterial:
Children to 88 pounds: By mouth, 20 milligrams of Sulfamethoxazole (and 4 milligrams of Trimethoprim) for each 2.2 pounds of body weight every 12 hours.
Children 88 pounds and over: By mouth, 800 milligrams of Sulfamethoxazole (and 160 milligrams of Trimethoprim) (4 teaspoonsful) every 12 hours.

COMMENTS

Sulfamethoxazole/Trimethoprim oral suspensions should be shaken well before use.

GENERIC NAME
3. SULFISOXAZOLE   Rx
See also general information on sulfonamides on page 243.

BRAND NAME(S)
GANTRISIN

USE AND INDICATIONS

Sulfisoxazole is an antibacterial medication used in treating urinary and middle ear infections.

DOSAGE GUIDELINES

- Extended-release oral suspension:
Infants to 1 month: Use is contraindicated except as adjunct in treating toxoplasmosis.
Infants 1 month and over: By mouth, 60–75 milligrams for each 2.2 pounds of body weight every 12 hours, not to exceed 6 grams per day.
- Oral suspension and tablets:
Infants to 1 month: Use is contraindicated except as adjunct in treating toxoplasmosis.
Infants 1 month and older: By mouth, 75 milligrams for each 2.2 pounds of body weight initially, then 25 milligrams for each 2.2

pounds of body weight every 4 hours; or 37.5 milligrams for each 2.2 pounds of body weight every 6 hours.

COMMENTS

Sulfisoxazole should be taken with plenty of fluids, and the oral suspensions should be shaken well before use.

BRAND NAME(S)
TAGAMET   Rx

GENERIC NAME
CIMETIDINE

USES AND INDICATIONS

TAGAMET belongs to the group of medications known as the histamine H2-receptor antagonists, or H2 antagonists. TAGAMET reduces acid secretions by competing with the chemical histamine at specific receptor sites (H2) in the body. TAGAMET is used in treating disorders of the gastrointestinal tract, including gastric and duodenal ulcers, gastrointestinal bleeding, and disorders associated with excessive acid secretions.

ADVERSE EFFECTS

The adverse effects of TAGAMET include the following:

- Gastrointestinal: mild to severe diarrhea; inflammation of the pancreas.
- Central nervous system: mental confusion, headache, dizziness, delirium, and hallucinations.
- Other: fever, breathing difficulty, skin rash, urinary retention, and hair loss.

WARNINGS AND PRECAUTIONS

- TAGAMET may alter the effects of many medications (see *Medication and Food Interactions,* below).
- TAGAMET should be used with caution in children with liver or kidney disorders due to the decreased rate of elimination from the body (a reduction in dosage may be necessary).
- TAGAMET should be taken with meals, or immediately following meals, and at bedtime.

248 THE CHILDREN'S MEDICINE CHEST

Medication and Food Interactions

- Because TAGAMET interacts with many medications, parents should minimize, if possible, other medications their children receive while on TAGAMET therapy, including nonprescription products.
- TAGAMET may increase the toxicity of ALUPENT, FLAGYL, DILANTIN, PRONESTYL, INDERAL, COUMADIN, tricyclic antidepressants (see Appendix II), benzodiazepines (see Appendix II), and xanthine bronchodilators (see Appendix II).

Dosage Guidelines

- Oral solution and tablets: By mouth, 20–40 milligrams daily for each 2.2 pounds of body weight, given 4 times daily, with meals and at bedtime. In children with kidney disorders, the dose should be reduced to 10–15 milligrams daily for each 2.2 pounds of body weight, given every 8 hours.

GROUP NAME
Thyroid Hormones

1. Levothyroxine (LEVOTHROID, LEVOXINE, SYNTHROID).
2. Liotrix (EUTHROID, THYROLAR). 3. Thyroid.

Uses and Indications

Thyroid hormones are naturally occurring substances secreted by the thyroid gland, which not only controls the body's metabolism and tissue growth, but also affects every body system. Thyroid hormones are especially important in the development of the central nervous system in newborns and infants. A deficiency of thyroid hormones results in reduced mental and physical (particularly bone) development. Although thyroid hormones are available as the naturally occurring products, the synthetically produced thyroid preparations are preferred because they are more uniform in their thyroid content. Thyroid hormones are used in treating hypothyroidism (including cretinism), goiter, and cancer of the thyroid gland.

ADVERSE EFFECTS

The adverse effects of thyroid hormones occur rarely, and they are essentially the signs of overdosage (hyperthyroidism). They include the following:

- Gastrointestinal: diarrhea, appetite changes, nausea, vomiting, and weight loss.
- Central nervous system: headache, tremors, nervousness, difficulty sleeping, and irritability.
- Allergic: skin rash, hives, itching, and fever.
- Other: sensitivity to sunlight, sweating, rapid irregular heartbeats, difficulty breathing, and chest pain.

WARNINGS AND PRECAUTIONS

- Thyroid hormones should be used with extreme caution in children with heart disorders, diabetes, pituitary or adrenocortical insufficiency, a history of hyperthyroidism, thyrotoxicosis, or malabsorption disorders.
- Children being treated for thyroid deficiency disorders should be monitored periodically for thyroid determinations, for bone and growth development, and for signs of irregular heartbeats.
- Parents should advise their doctor of all other medications their child is taking while on thyroid hormone therapy, because thyroid hormones may be affected by many other medications. Also, many medications may alter the results of thyroid function tests.
- Thyroid hormone therapy requires close supervision of a child by his or her doctor; all dosages must be determined for the individual child based upon the results of thyroid function tests and the child's clinical response.

MEDICATION AND FOOD INTERACTIONS

- The following may alter the results of thyroid function tests: VALIUM, Insulin, DILANTIN, INDERAL, corticosteroids (see Appendix II), salicylates (see Appendix II), and thiazide diuretics (see Appendix II).
- Thyroid hormones may increase the effects of Epinephrine and tricyclic antidepressants (see Appendix II).
- The effectiveness of LANOXIN, INDERAL, and COUMADIN may be decreased by thyroid hormones.

COMMENTS

The following table illustrates the approximate dosage equivalents for the various thyroid hormones, or commercial thyroid products.

PRODUCT	EQUIVALENT DOSE (APPROXIMATE)
Levothyroxine	0.1 milligrams
Liotrix	0.6 milligrams

GENERIC NAME
1 . LEVOTHYROXINE   Rx
See also general information on thyroid hormones on page 248.

BRAND NAME(S)
LEVOTHROID, LEVOXINE, SYNTHROID

USES AND INDICATIONS

Levothyroxine is the most widely used thyroid hormone for hypothyroidism in children.

DOSAGE GUIDELINES

- Tablets:
    Premature infants (under 4.4 pounds): By mouth, 25 micrograms daily, increased to 50 micrograms daily in 4–6 weeks.
    Children to 6 months: By mouth, 5–6 micrograms daily for each 2.2 pounds of body weight, or 25–50 micrograms daily as a single dose.
    Children 6–12 months: By mouth, 5–6 micrograms daily for each 2.2 pounds of body weight, or 50–75 micrograms daily as a single dose.
    Children 1–5 years: By mouth, 3–5 micrograms daily for each 2.2 pounds of body weight, or 75–100 micrograms daily as a single dose.
    Children 6–10 years: By mouth, 4–5 micrograms daily for each 2.2 pounds of body weight, or 100–150 micrograms daily as a single dose.
    Children over 10 years: By mouth, 2–3 micrograms daily for each 2.2 pounds of body weight, or up to 200 micrograms daily as a single dose.

GENERIC NAME
2. LIOTRIX
Rx
See also general information on thyroid hormones on page 248.

BRAND NAME(S)
EUTHROID, THYROLAR

USES AND INDICATIONS
Liotrix is a synthetic product composed of 2 thyroid components, Liothyronine and Levothyroxine. Liotrix is used in treating hypothyroidism in children.

DOSAGE GUIDELINES
* Tablets:
    Hypothyroidism (without myxedema): By mouth, initially, 50 micrograms of Levothyroxine (and 12.5 micrograms of Liothyronine) daily, or 60 micrograms of Levothyroxine (and 15 micrograms of Liothyronine) daily, with increases of the same amounts at monthly intervals until the desired response is obtained.

    Severe cretinism or hypothyroidism with heart disease: By mouth, 12.5 micrograms of Levothyroxine (and 3.1 micrograms of Liothyronine) daily, with increases of the same amount at intervals of 2–3 weeks until the desired response is obtained.

GENERIC NAME
3. THYROID
Rx
See also general information on thyroid hormones on page 248.

USES AND INDICATIONS
Thyroid, a naturally occurring hormone, does not maintain a uniform concentration of the thyroid hormone, which may result in an uneven clinical response in children being treated for hypothyroidism.

DOSAGE GUIDELINES
* Tablets:
    Hypothyroidism (without myxedema): By mouth, initially, 32 milligrams daily, increasing in increments of 32 milligrams every 1–2 weeks until the desired results are obtained. The usual daily maintenance dose is 65–160 milligrams.

BRAND NAME(S)
TIGAN   Rx
(Other brands: **TEBAMIDE, TEGAMIDE, T-GEN**)

GENERIC NAME
TRIMETHOBENZAMIDE

USES AND INDICATIONS
TIGAN is used in the treatment of nausea and vomiting. While its mode of action is not well understood, it is thought to depress the action of chemical receptors that initiate nausea and vomiting.

ADVERSE EFFECTS
The adverse effects of TIGAN include the following:

- Gastrointestinal: diarrhea.
- Central nervous system: mental depression, dizziness, blurred vision, headache, convulsions, drowsiness, and unusual tiredness.
- Other: tremors, back pain, sore throat and fever, and muscle cramps.

WARNINGS AND PRECAUTIONS
TIGAN should be used with caution, particularly in children who have high fever or who are dehydrated.

MEDICATION AND FOOD INTERACTIONS
The use of TIGAN with the following CNS depressant medications may increase the risk of sedation and other adverse effects: alcohol-containing products, tricyclic antidepressants (see Appendix II), antihistamines (see Appendix II), and benzodiazepines (see Appendix II).

DOSAGE GUIDELINES

- Capsules: By mouth, 15 milligrams daily for each 2.2 pounds of body weight, given in 3–4 doses; or for children weighing 33–99 pounds, 100–200 milligrams 3–4 times daily as needed.
- Rectal suppositories:
  Children to 33 pounds: Insert rectally, 100 milligrams 3–4 times daily as needed.
  Children 33–99 pounds: Insert rectally, 100–200 milligrams 3–4 times daily as needed.

BRAND NAME(S)
TYLENOL OTC
(Other brands: **ACETA, ANACIN-3, APAP, DATRIL, DOLANEX, DORCOL, FEVERALL SPRINKLE, LIQUIPRIN, NEOPAP, GRAPHEN-PD, PANADOL, PANEX, PEEDEE, PHENAPHEN, SK-APAP, SNAPLETS-FR, ST. JOSEPH'S ASPIRIN-FREE, TEMPRA, VALDOL,** and others. Also available in prescription and OTC combination products.)

GENERIC NAME
ACETAMINOPHEN

USES AND INDICATIONS
TYLENOL is used to relieve mild to moderate pain, as well as to reduce the fever associated with flu, colds, and other infections.

ADVERSE EFFECTS
Administering TYLENOL in high doses over a long period may result in serious adverse effects, particularly in infants and newborns. If your child experiences rash or itching while taking TYLENOL, stop the medication. If your child becomes weak or lethargic, if the eyes and skin become yellowish, or if your child has a sore throat, fever, or bleeding, stop the medication immediately and call your physician. Some children may experience dizziness during the early period of treatment, which should disappear with continued use.

WARNINGS AND PRECAUTIONS
Do not use TYLENOL if your child has a kidney or liver disorder or if your child has viral hepatitis.

MEDICATION AND FOOD INTERACTIONS

- TYLENOL may increase the toxicity of CHLOROMYCETIN.
- DILANTIN may increase the liver toxic effects of TYLENOL.

DOSAGE GUIDELINES
Both oral and rectal doses of TYLENOL should be administered every 4–6 hours as needed. Children should not be given more than 5 doses orally, or 6 doses rectally, over a 24-hour period, and it should not be given for more than 5 days. *Parents should remember that the concentrations of TYLENOL drops (40 milligrams per 0.4 milliliter and 80 milligrams*

per 0.8 milliliter) and the elixir (160 milligrams per 5 milliliters or 1 tea-spoonful) are not the same, and that one may be substituted for the other only after appropriate dosage calculations are made.

- For available forms of TYLENOL, see *Comments* (below).

    Infants to 3 months: By mouth, 20–40 milligrams (halfway between the dropper tip and the 0.4-milliliter mark on the dropper, to the 0.4 milliliter mark on the dropper) every 4–6 hours as needed.

    Children 4–11 months: By mouth, 80 milligrams (0.8-milliliter mark on the dropper) every 4–6 hours as needed.

    Children 12–24 months: By mouth, 120 milligrams every 4–6 hours as needed.

    Children 2–3 years: By mouth, 160 milligrams (2 droppersful using the 0.8-milliliter mark; or 1 teaspoonful using the elixir; or 2 chewable tablets every 4–6 hours as needed.

    Children 4–5 years: By mouth, 240 milligrams (3 droppersful using the 0.8-milliliter mark; or 1½ teaspoonsful using the elixir; or 3 chewable tablets) every 4–6 hours as needed; rectally, 120 milligrams every 4–6 hours as needed.

    Children 6–8 years: By mouth, 320 milligrams (4 droppersful using the 0.8-milliliter mark; or 2 teaspoonsful using the elixir; or 4 chewable tablets) every 4–6 hours as needed; rectally, 325 milligrams every 4–6 hours as needed.

    Children 9–10 years: By mouth, 400 milligrams (5 droppersful using the 0.8-milliliter mark; or 2½ teaspoonsful of the elixir; or 5 chewable tablets) every 4–6 hours as needed; rectally, 325 milligrams every 4–6 hours as needed.

    Children 11–12 years: By mouth, 480 milligrams (6 droppersful using the 0.8-milliliter mark; or 1 tablespoonful of the elixir; or 6 chewable tablets) every 4–6 hours as needed; rectally, 325 milligrams every 4–6 hours as needed.

COMMENTS

TYLENOL is available as follows: chewable tablets (80 milligrams; 160 milligrams), effervescent granules (80 milligrams per packet), oral powder (80 milligrams and 160 milligrams in capsule forms), oral solution (80 milligrams per 0.8 milliliter dropperful; 80 milligrams per tea-spoonful; 120 milligrams per teaspoonful; 160 milligrams per tea-spoonful; 325 milligrams per teaspoonful), oral suspension (120 milligrams per ½ teaspoonful), suppository (120 milligrams; 325 milligrams), and tablet (160 milligrams; 325 milligrams).

Although toxicity from TYLENOL use is not very common, TYLE-

NOL products are widely used in children, and parents should know what the toxic signs are. The early signs are nausea, vomiting, profuse sweating, and loss of appetite. These symptoms persist for about 24 hours, followed by apparent improvement over the next 48 hours or so. Parents should not be fooled by the child's apparent improvement, because there may be liver damage that will worsen if the child is not treated as soon as possible. Contact your doctor immediately, and if your doctor is not available, take your child to the hospital or emergency treatment center. If your doctor is not available and there is no hospital or emergency treatment center nearby, call the nearest regional poison control center to get instructions (see Appendix IV).

The use of Syrup of Ipecac or warm salt water is effective in inducing vomiting to eliminate any TYLENOL remaining in the body. If your child has accidentally swallowed TYLENOL, take the container with any remaining medication with you so that appropriate treatment may be determined by hospital personnel.

GROUP NAME
VITAMINS

1. ASCORBIC ACID, OR VITAMIN C (CECON, CE-VI-SOL, FLAVORCEE, SUNKIST, AND OTHERS). 2. IRON SUPPLEMENTS (FERROUS GLUCONATE [FERGON], FERROUS SULFATE [FEOSOL, FER-IN-SOL]). 3. VITAMIN A (AQUASOL A AND OTHERS). 4. VITAMIN D ANALOGS (CALCIFEDIOL [CALDEROL], CALCITRIOL [ROCALTROL], DIHYDROTACHYSTEROL [HYTAKEROL], ERGOCALCIFEROL [DRISDOL]). 5. VITAMIN K ANALOGS (MENADIOL [SYNKAVITE], PHYTONADIONE [MEPHYTON]).

Vitamins are substances required by the body in order to perform and maintain its various functions. Although not a vitamin, iron is also included in this section with vitamins because of its widespread use and common association with nutrition and vitamins in general. Most or all of the vitamins and minerals required by humans are obtained through a normal, well-balanced diet, so that there is little need to take supplemental vitamins except where specific deficiencies exist; in situations where well-balanced diets are not possible due to deficiencies resulting from birth defects or illnesses; or in children whose parents are unable to provide adequate nutrition.

The following table shows the Recommended Dietary Allowances (RDA) for selected vitamins, and is a modified table reproduced from

Recommended Dietary Allowances (9th edition), with permission of the National Academy of Sciences, Washington, D.C., 1980.

VITAMIN	To 13 POUNDS	To 20 POUNDS	To 29 POUNDS	To 44 POUNDS	To 62 POUNDS	To 99 POUNDS
Ascorbic Acid	35 mg*	35 mg	45 mg	45 mg	45 mg	50 mg
Iron	10 mg	15 mg	15 mg	10 mg	10 mg	18 mg
Vitamin A	2,100 IU**	2,000 IU	2,000 IU	2,500 IU	3,500 IU	5,000 IU
Vitamin D	400 IU	400 IU	400 IU	400 IU	400 IU	400 IU

*mg = milligrams.
**IU = international units.

In the following monographs, the uses and indications, adverse effects, warnings and precautions, medication and food interactions, and dosage guidelines will be discussed for each vitamin or vitamin group.

GENERIC NAME
1. ASCORBIC ACID, OR VITAMIN C
OTC

See also general information on vitamins on page 255.

BRAND NAME(S)
CECON, CE-VI-SOL, FLAVORCEE, SUNKIST, AND OTHERS

USES AND INDICATIONS

Although Ascorbic Acid is an essential and widely used vitamin in humans, and it is abundantly available in fresh fruits and vegetables, its precise biological function is not known. Ascorbic Acid is a water-soluble vitamin involved in various oxidation-reduction chemical reactions in the body. Inconclusive studies have demonstrated a possible value in reducing the frequency and severity of cold and flu infections and their associated symptoms. A deficiency of Ascorbic Acid is known as scurvy, a disease characterized by the destruction of bones, capillaries, and connective tissues; at one time it was a disease common to seamen, who were deprived of fresh fruit for long periods while at sea. Scurvy is characterized by generalized weakness, spongy gums, bleeding of the gums and other areas of the mucous membranes, anemia, and a bow-legged appearance.

Although Ascorbic Acid deficiency is rare in healthy humans living on a well-balanced diet, certain diseases and conditions deplete Ascorbic Acid, thereby increasing Ascorbic Acid requirements: cancer, extensive burns, severe diarrhea and other gastrointestinal disorders, tuberculosis, and other disorders. In addition to its use in specific Vitamin C–deficient states, Ascorbic Acid is also used to acidify the urine and to aid in treating toxicity resulting from the chronic ingestion of iron.

ADVERSE EFFECTS

The adverse effects of Ascorbic Acid are few and usually related to the ingestion of high doses; they include nausea, vomiting, stomach cramps, flushing, increased urination, pain in the lower back or side, and formation of kidney stones.

WARNINGS AND PRECAUTIONS

- Ascorbic Acid should be used with caution in children with diabetes, sickle cell anemia, a history of kidney stones, or iron deficiencies.
- The excessive use of chewable Ascorbic Acid tablets may cause dental problems in children.
- The use of Ascorbic Acid in children with glucose-6-phosphate dehydrogenase (G6PD) deficiency may result in anemia.
- The use of high doses (megadoses, or doses that are 10 times the normal) in children should be discouraged, since there is a lack of evidence as to their effectiveness.

MEDICATION AND FOOD INTERACTIONS

The effectiveness of Ascorbic Acid may be decreased by salicylates (see Appendix II).

DOSAGE GUIDELINES

- Chewable tablets, oral solution, syrup, and tablets:
  Nutritional supplement (vitamin) for infants and children under 4 years: By mouth, 20–50 milligrams daily.
  Vitamin C deficiency: By mouth, 100–250 milligrams 1–3 times daily.

GROUP NAME AND GENERIC NAMES
2. IRON SUPPLEMENTS (FERROUS GLUCONATE, FERROUS SULFATE)
See also general information on vitamins on page 255.

BRAND NAMES
FERGON (FERROUS GLUCONATE); FEOSOL, FER-IN-SOL (FERROUS SULFATE)

USES AND INDICATIONS
Iron, a necessary mineral component of red blood cells, is responsible for transporting oxygen in the blood and muscles. Approximately 30% of the body's iron is stored in the bones, liver, and spleen. Deficiencies of iron in the body result in iron deficiency anemia.

ADVERSE EFFECTS
The adverse effects of excessive iron ingestion include nausea, vomiting, diarrhea, constipation, stomach cramps, bloody or tarry stools, throat or chest pain from iron irritation, staining of teeth (temporary), dark-colored urine, and heartburn.

OVERDOSAGE (ACUTE TOXICITY):   The *early* signs of acute toxicity from iron-containing preparations include severe nausea and vomiting (may be bloody), diarrhea (may be bloody), fever, and stomach cramps. The *late* signs of acute toxicity include drowsiness or tiredness; blue-colored lips, palms, and fingernails; pale, clammy skin; weak but rapid heartbeat; and seizures. The late signs may also include a significant drop in blood pressure and circulatory collapse. Medical attention should be obtained as quickly as possible. If medical care is not available and if the child is conscious, induce vomiting with Syrup of Ipecac or warm salt water to empty the stomach of unabsorbed iron.

WARNINGS AND PRECAUTIONS

- Iron is contraindicated in certain blood disorders and in children with peptic ulcers and ulcerative colitis.
- In order to avoid temporary staining of teeth from liquid iron preparations, the iron preparation should be diluted in water or juice, and a straw used to drink the liquid.
- Iron preparations should be used with caution in children with kidney or liver disorders, arthritis, or asthma.

MEDICATION AND FOOD INTERACTIONS

- The use of iron with calcium-containing antacids (see Appendix II), and dairy foods high in calcium may result in a decrease in the absorption of iron. Administer a dose 1 hour before or 2 hours after ingestion of any of the above.
- Iron may decrease the effectiveness of oral tetracyclines (see Appendix II).
- The following may decrease the effectiveness of iron products: PANCREASE and Vitamin E.
- Parents should be aware of the potential for iron toxicity in children who may be receiving excessive amounts of iron over a long-term period, particularly in children who *do not* have an iron deficiency.
- Iron should be administered at least 1 hour before or 2 hours after coffee, tea, dairy products, and whole-grain cereals and breads.

DOSAGE GUIDELINES
Following are the most commonly used iron preparations in children:

Ferrous Gluconate (FERGON): OTC
- Elixir and tablets:
  - • Therapeutic:
    Children to 2 years: Dosage must be individualized.
    Children 2 years and older: By mouth, 16 milligrams 3 times daily for each 2.2 pounds of body weight.
  - • Prophylactic:
    Children to 2 years: Dosage must be individualized.
    Children 2 years and older: By mouth, 8 milligrams daily for each 2.2 pounds of body weight.

Ferrous Sulfate (FEOSOL, FER-IN-SOL): OTC
- Elixir, oral solution (drops), and tablets:
  Children's dose: By mouth, 10 milligrams 3 times daily for each 2.2 pounds of body weight as a therapeutic dose. The prophylactic dose is 5 milligrams daily for each 2.2 pounds of body weight.

COMMENTS
There are numerous vitamin preparations containing iron that have not been discussed here. But the reader should be aware that many multi-

ple-vitamin preparations with iron usually contain less of it than the amount required to treat iron deficiency disorders. *Remember, children who are being treated for an iron deficiency and are also receiving daily supplemental iron without their doctor's knowledge may be at increased risk of iron toxicity.*

Iron products contain varying amounts of iron. The following table shows the iron contents of the different salts of iron:

IRON SALT	IRON CONTENT
Ferrous Gluconate	11.6%*
Ferrous Sulfate	20

*The above percentages are approximate.

GENERIC NAME
3. VITAMIN A   Rx, OTC
See general information on vitamins on page 255.

BRAND NAME(S)
AQUASOL A AND OTHERS

USES AND INDICATIONS
Vitamin A is a fat-soluble vitamin used in the treatment and prevention of Vitamin A deficiencies. In healthy children, Vitamin A is readily available in a normal diet.

ADVERSE EFFECTS
Because Vitamin A is fat-soluble, it accumulates in the body, and long-term use of Vitamin A (as well as Vitamins D and E) may result in toxicity, both from chronic use and from ingestion of a large dose.

TOXICITY: The effects of chronic poisoning from long-term use of Vitamin A include generalized weakness, bone and joint pain, dry skin, stomach pain, loss of appetite, loss of hair, nausea and vomiting, headache, fever, and yellow discoloration of skin on the lips, nose, hands, and feet. The symptoms of acute poisoning may also include diarrhea, double vision, dizziness, tiredness, sore or bleeding gums, severe vomiting, irritability, headache, and seizures.

WARNINGS AND PRECAUTIONS
- Children are especially sensitive to the effects of Vitamin A, particularly high doses.
- Vitamin A should be used with caution in children with kidney disorders.
- Vitamin A oral solution may be dropped into the mouth or mixed in food or juice.
- Infants who are on special diets, i.e., milk substitutes or unfortified skim milk, may require Vitamin A supplements.

MEDICATION AND FOOD INTERACTIONS

- The following may interfere with the absorption of Vitamin A: QUESTRAN, COLESTID, Mineral Oil, MYCIFRADIN, CARAFATE, and aluminum-containing antacids (see Appendix II).
- Vitamin A may increase the risk of bleeding when used with COUMADIN.

DOSAGE GUIDELINES
- Capsules, oral solution (drops), and tablets:
  Vitamin A deficiency: By mouth, 5,000 units (0.1-milliliter dropper) daily for each 2.2 pounds of body weight.

GROUP NAME AND GENERIC NAMES
4. VITAMIN D ANALOGS (CALCIFEDIOL, CALCITRIOL, DIHYDROTACHYSTEROL, ERGOCALCIFEROL)
See general information on vitamins on page 255.

BRAND NAME(S)
CALDEROL (CALCIFEDIOL), ROCALTROL (CALCITRIOL), HYTAKEROL (DIHYDROTACHYSTEROL), DRISDOL (ERGOCALCIFEROL)

USES AND INDICATIONS
Vitamin D analogs are fat-soluble vitamins derived from fish-liver oils and other foods. Vitamin D assists in controlling the body's metabolism of calcium and phosphorous, and to a lesser extent, magnesium. Deficiencies of Vitamin D may lead to hearing loss, rickets in children, and

loss of bone calcium and phosphorous, resulting in softening of the bones. Vitamin D preparations are used clinically in the treatment of rickets, Vitamin D deficiency, familial hypophosphatemia, hypocalcemia, and hypoparathyroidism.

ADVERSE EFFECTS

The adverse effects of Vitamin D analogs usually result from excessive use over a long period, with an accumulation of Vitamin D in the body. The earlier symptoms include nausea, vomiting, unusual weakness or drowsiness, metallic taste, achy bones or joints, muscle pain, constipation, and dry mouth. The later side effects not only include the above symptoms, but may also include increased urination (with cloudy urine), appetite and weight loss, seizures, abnormal heartbeats, high blood pressure, severe abdominal pain, behavioral changes, increased sensitivity to sunlight, and itchy skin.

WARNINGS AND PRECAUTIONS

- Vitamin D preparations are contraindicated in children with hypercalcemia who are allergic to Vitamin D, and in children with malabsorption disorders.
- Vitamin D preparations should be used with caution in children with heart or kidney disorders.
- The use of calcium is essential for children on Vitamin D therapy, and it should be carefully monitored.
- The ingestion of foods high in Vitamin D should be carefully monitored to prevent hypercalcemia.
- Serum phosphate and calcium levels should be periodically checked.
- Tablets of Vitamin D preparations should be swallowed whole, not crushed or chewed.

MEDICATION AND FOOD INTERACTIONS

- Mineral Oil, QUESTRAN, COLESTID, CARAFATE, and aluminum-containing antacids (see Appendix II) may decrease the absorption of Vitamin D.
- The use of Vitamin D preparations with the excessive ingestion of medications or foods high in calcium and/or phosphorous, or calcium-containing antacids (see Appendix II), may result in hypercalcemia.

- The effects of Vitamin D may be decreased by MYSOLINE and by hydantoin anticonvulsants (see Appendix II).

Dosage Guidelines

Calcifediol (CALDEROL): Rx
- Capsules:
  Children to 2 years: By mouth, 20–50 micrograms daily.
  Children 2–10 years: By mouth, 50 micrograms daily.
  Children 10 years and older: By mouth, 300–350 micrograms (0.3–0.35 milligrams) per week, given in divided doses once daily or on alternate days. If necessary, the dosage may be increased at 4-week intervals.

Calcitriol (ROCALTROL): Rx
- Capsules:
  Rickets: By mouth, initially 0.25 micrograms daily, with the dosage being increased, if necessary, in increments of 0.25 micrograms daily at 2–4 week intervals, up to 1 microgram daily. The daily dose may be given as a single daily dose or in 2–3 divided doses.
  Hypoparathyroidism: By mouth, initially 0.25 micrograms daily, with the dosage being increased, if necessary, in increments of 0.25 micrograms daily at 2–4 week intervals, up to 0.08 micrograms daily for each 2.2 pounds of body weight. The daily dose may be given as a single daily dose or in 2–3 divided doses.

Dihydrotachysterol (HYTAKEROL): Rx
- Capsule, oral solution, and tablets:
  Hypophosphatemia: By mouth, initially, 0.5–2 milligrams daily, then may be adjusted to 0.2–1.5 milligrams daily as a maintenance dose.
  Hypoparathyroidism: By mouth, initially, 1–5 milligrams daily for 4 days, then may be continued or adjusted to ¼ of the dose, then further adjusted until a daily maintenance dose of 0.5–1.5 milligrams is reached.

Ergocalciferol (DRISDOL): Rx, OTC
- Capsule, oral solution (drops), and tablets:
  Osteomalacia: By mouth, 1,000 units (5 drops) daily.
  Vitamin D deficiency: By mouth, 1,000–4,000 units (5–20 drops)

daily, then may be adjusted to 400 units (2 drops) daily as directed by a physician.

Hypoparathyroidism: By mouth, 50,000–200,000 units daily.

Vitamin D–dependent rickets: By mouth, 3,000–10,000 units daily, then may be adjusted, if necessary, up to 50,000 units daily.

GROUP NAME AND GENERIC NAMES
5. Vitamin K Analogs (Menadiol, Phytonadione)
See general information on vitamins on page 255.

BRAND NAME(S)
SYNKAVITE (MENADIOL), MEPHYTON
(PHYTONADIONE)

USES AND INDICATIONS
The Vitamin K preparations are used in treating blood coagulation disorders. Vitamin K preparations are also used in malabsorption disorders resulting in Vitamin K deficiency.

ADVERSE EFFECTS
There are relatively few side effects with the Vitamin K analogs, but they do include allergic reaction, which, although rare, has resulted in death for highly sensitive children. The potential for serious adverse effects is greater for premature and newborn infants due to their undeveloped liver function. The more common adverse effects include skin rash, redness and itching, flushing, and unpleasant taste.

WARNINGS AND PRECAUTIONS

- Menadiol should not be administered to infants due to their inability to metabolize the drug.
- Vitamin K analogs should be used with caution in children with liver disorders or with glucose-6-phosphate deficiency.
- Parents should advise their child's new physician or dentist if their child is on Vitamin K therapy.
- Children on Vitamin K therapy should be monitored periodically for blood coagulation function (prothrombin time).

Medication and Food Interactions

- The absorption of Vitamin K analogs may be decreased by Mineral Oil and aluminum-containing antacids (see Appendix II).
- The need for Vitamin K may be increased in patients taking Quinidine, salicylates (see Appendix II), or sulfonamides (see Appendix II).

Dosage Guidelines

Menadiol (SYNKAVITE): Rx
Nutritional supplement: By mouth, 5–10 milligrams daily.

Phytonadione (MEPHYTON): Rx
Nutritional supplement: By mouth, 5–10 milligrams daily.

BRAND NAME(S)
ZANTAC   Rx

GENERIC NAME
RANITIDINE

Uses and Indications

ZANTAC is an H-2 antagonist used in treating peptic ulcers and other conditions associated with stomach acids and gastrointestinal bleeding. Much of the same information known about TAGAMET also applies to ZANTAC, including uses and indications, adverse effects, warnings and precautions, and medication and food interactions. The major differences between the two medications are their dosages and dosage frequencies, with ZANTAC requiring fewer daily doses.

In children, ZANTAC is used in treating ulcers and stress-related damage to the lining of the gastrointestinal tract; for excessive acid secretions, and for regurgitation of stomach contents.

Adverse Effects

In general, the adverse effects, warnings and precautions, and medication and food interactions of ZANTAC are similar to those of TAGAMET. For more information, see the monograph for TAGAMET (page 247).

DOSAGE GUIDELINES
- Oral solution and tablets: By mouth, 2–4 milligrams daily for each 2.2 pounds of body weight, administered every 12 hours.

COMMENTS
In patients with impaired kidney function, a decrease in dosage and/or frequency may be required.

BRAND NAME(S)
ZOVIRAX   Rx

GENERIC NAME
ACYCLOVIR

USES AND INDICATIONS
ZOVIRAX is an antiviral medication used in treating various forms of herpes and varicella infections, including fever blisters, chicken pox, and shingles.

ADVERSE EFFECTS
Adverse effects related to ZOVIRAX include nausea, vomiting, diarrhea, headache, dizziness, irritability, depression, fatigue, skin rash, acne, hair loss, loss of appetite, water retention, sore throat, leg pain and muscle cramps, fever, joint pain, and palpitations.

DOSAGE GUIDELINES

- Ointment: Apply to affected skin area, covering lesions well, every 3 hours, 6 times a day for 1 week.
- Capsules and tablets: By mouth, 200 milligrams every 4 hours while awake, 5 times a day for 10 days. If infection recurs or persists, your child's doctor may continue intermittent treatment for up to 6 months.

COMMENTS
Parents should keep the affected areas clean and dry, and loose clothing should be worn to minimize irritation of the skin lesions.

APPENDIX I

GLOSSARY

Acute. Pertaining to a brief but severe period of illness or disease.

Anaphylaxis. A severe allergic reaction to a medication, resulting in nasal congestion, wheezing, difficulty breathing, hives, itching, loss of consciousness, and circulatory collapse; may be fatal.

Anemia. A deficiency in red blood cells.

Antiarrhythmic. A medication used to correct irregular or abnormal heartbeats.

Anticholinergic. A medication that inhibits the action of the parasympathetic nervous system.

Anticoagulant. A medication that prevents blood clotting.

Antidote. A substance that counteracts the effects of a medication or poison.

Antiemetic. A medication that prevents nausea and vomiting.

Arrhythmia. Abnormal or irregular heartbeats.

Ataxia. Lack of muscle coordination.

Beta blocker. An adrenergic medication that reduces blood pressure, prevents chest pains, slows the heart rate, and relieves migraine.

Blood count. A laboratory determination of the number of white and red cells, platelets, and other components of the blood.

Bronchial constriction. A narrowing or closing of the bronchial tubes.

Bronchodilator. A medication that causes a widening or opening of the bronchial tubes.

Cholinergic (or parasympathomimetic). A medication or chemical that mimics the effects of Acetylcholine.

Cirrhosis. A disorder in which the liver is scarred and destroyed.

CNS. Pertaining to the central nervous system.

Contraindication. A condition or situation in which a specific medication should not be used.

Convulsions. Violent, uncontrolled contractions of the voluntary muscles of the body.

Decongestant. A medication that relieves congestion or stuffiness in the upper respiratory tract.

Delirium. A state of extreme excitement characterized by unconnected acts or ideas.

Dilation. A widening or enlargement of an opening (i.e., as with a vasodilator, bronchodilator, etc.).

Diuretic. A medication used to increase urination.

Divided doses. The number of times a given amount of medication is to be administered over a specific period of time (usually 24 hours), as specified by a physician. For example, a total daily dose of 1,000 milligrams given in 4 divided doses is 250 milligrams given every 6 hours; or a total daily dose of 500 milligrams given in 2 divided doses is 250 milligrams given every 12 hours.

Drug interaction. The effect in the body when two or more medications are taken together, causing a change in the effect of one or more of the medications.

Eczema. A skin disorder characterized by itching, runny blisters, and abnormal pigmentation (or coloring) of the skin.

Electrocardiogram (ECG, EKG). A recording of the electrical potentials of the heart; used to determine if the heart is functioning properly.

Electroencephalogram (EEG). A recording of electrical impulses in the brain; used to determine if the brain is functioning properly.

Embolism. An artery that is blocked by a clot or other foreign substance, preventing normal blood circulation.

Emetic. A medication or substance that causes vomiting.

Emphysema. A chronic breathing difficulty due to an inability to effectively release air from the lungs.

Enzyme. A proteinlike substance found in the body; aids the body in its various chemical reactions.

Epilepsy. A chronic disorder of the central nervous system characterized by convulsions and/or periods of unconsciousness.

Extrapyramidal effects. Involuntary spasms of the neck, back, and jaw; rolling of the eyes; convulsions; and difficulty breathing.

Gastritis. Inflammation of the stomach.

Gland. A specialized group of cells in the body that manufactures substances that are excreted or secreted, and utilized by other parts of the body.

Glaucoma. An ophthalmic disorder in which there is increased pressure inside the eye.

Glucose-6-phosphotransferase (G6PT). An enzyme used in the body's metabolism of carbohydrates.

Hemoglobin. A pigment found in red blood cells; responsible for carrying oxygen to other cells of the body.

Hemorrhage. Excessive bleeding.

Hepatitis. A disorder of the liver in which its cells are inflamed and damaged.

Histamine. A chemical released from body cells when a foreign substance is introduced into the body.

Histamine reaction. Symptoms resulting from histamine release, including difficulty breathing, fall in blood pressure, increased heart rate, and skin eruptions.

Hives. Elevated skin eruptions that are itchy and that may be red or pale in color.

Hormone. A chemical produced in the body to regulate other body functions or activities.

Hypercalcemia. An abnormally high calcium level in the blood.

Hyperglycemia (diabetes). An abnormally high sugar (glucose) level in the blood.

Hyperkalemia. An abnormally high potassium level in the blood.

Hyperlipidemia. Excessive cholesterol and/or triglyceride levels in the blood.

Hyperphosphatemia. An abnormally high phosphate level in the blood.

Hypoacidity. A deficiency of acid in the stomach.

Hypocalcemia. An abnormally low calcium level in the blood.

Hypoglycemia. An abnormally low sugar (glucose) level in the blood.

Hypokalemia. An abnormally low potassium level in the blood.

Hyponatremia. An abnormally low sodium level in the blood.

Hypophosphatemia. An abnormally low phosphate level in the blood.

Immunity. Resistance to a specific infection.

Lupus erythematosus. A serious disorder involving connective tissue; characterized by skin eruptions, lowered immune system response, joint pain, and damage to one or more organs.

Megadose. An abnormally large dose of a medication; a dose at least 10 times the normal dose.

Metabolism. The chemical reactions involved in the body's absorption and utilization of medications, and in their elimination from the body.

Monoamine oxidase (MAO) inhibitor. A medication that exerts its effect by interfering with the activity of monoamine oxidase enzymes in the body.

Narcolepsy. Attacks marked by an uncontrolled desire to sleep.

Osteoporosis. Softening of the bones due to a deficiency of calcium and other chemicals required for normal bone growth and development.

Palpitations. Rapid heartbeats that may be felt by a patient.

Pancreatitis. Serious inflammation of the pancreas, resulting in abdominal pain.

Parkinson's disease. A disorder of the central nervous system characterized by a slow gait, muscle tremors, a fixed facial expression, slow movements, and muscle weakness.

Pituitary gland. A gland, located at the base of the brain, that controls growth and stimulates other glands.

Platelet. A component of the blood responsible for blood clotting.

Porphyria. An inherited disorder characterized by changes in the kidneys and in the central nervous system.

Potassium. An important electrolyte found in body cells; plays an important role in cardiac function.

Prothrombin. A substance necessary in the formation of blood clots.

Pruritis. Itching.

Psoriasis. A chronic, inherited skin disorder characterized by itching and sores (lesions) having silvery scales.

Raynaud's phenomena. A rare disorder characterized by inadequate blood flow to the toes and fingers, and sometimes to the nose and ears; caused by exposure to cold or by emotional situations.

Reye's syndrome. A rare disorder in children characterized by damage to the liver and brain, and which is often fatal.

Seizure. A brain disorder characterized by erratic brain impulses (which cause changes in consciousness) and convulsions.

Smooth muscle relaxant. A medication that relaxes the muscles lining the bronchi, stomach, bladder, etc.

Spasms. Violent, involuntary muscle contractions.

Stupor. A state of near-consciousness.

Sublingual. Under the tongue.

Symptom. A sign that indicates a change in appearance or function in relation to a disease.

Tachycardia. Abnormally rapid heartbeats.

Tardive dyskinesia. Involuntary movements of the tongue, lips, or jaw, resulting from a medication reaction or adverse effect.

Therapeutic. Pertaining to the ability to cure or heal.

Thrombophlebitis. Inflammation of a vein caused by a blood clot.

Thyroid gland. A gland, located in the neck, that is responsible for body metabolism.

Tremor. An involuntary trembling.

Urticaria. An itchy skin rash or hives.

APPENDIX II

MEDICATION GROUPS

The following is an alphabetical list of medication groups used in this book. Each group name is shown in bold type. Within each "group" are listed the "generic" medications in regular type, with the more popular brands for each generic medication listed in parenthesis, in capital letters. Please keep in mind that the medication groups listed are not complete, that they may not include all of the generic medications belonging to the groups shown, and that they also may not contain all of the brands that are commercially available for each generic medication. In general, the specific brands listed are those that have commercially available dosage forms that are suitable for use in children.

Amphetamines: Amphetamine; Dextroamphetamine (DEXEDRINE); Methamphetamine (DESOXYN).

Anesthetics, Local or Topical: Benzocaine (AMBESOL, CHLORASEPTIC, ORAJEL, NUM-ZIT); Dibucaine (NUPERCAINAL); Dyclomine (SUCRETS); Lidocaine (XYLOCAINE).

Antacids: Aluminum Carbonate (BASALJEL); Aluminum Hydroxide (ALTERNAGEL, AMPHOJEL); Aluminum Hydroxide/Magnesium Carbonate (GAVISCON [liquid]); Aluminum Hydroxide/Magnesium Trisilicate (GAVISCON [tablets]); Aluminum/Magnesium Hydroxide (ALUDROX, AMPHOJEL, CREAMALIN, MAALOX); Aluminum/ Magnesium Hydroxide with Simethicone (AMPHOJEL PLUS, DI-GEL, GELUSIL, MAALOX PLUS, MYLANTA II); Aluminum/Magnesium with Calcium Carbonate (CAMALOX); Calcium Carbonate/

Magnesium Hydroxide (BISODOL, DI-GEL, ROLAIDS SODIUM FREE); Magaldrate (RIOPAN); Magaldrate/Simethicone (RIOPAN PLUS); Magnesium Hydroxide (PHILLIPS' MILK OF MAGNESIA); Magnesium Trisilicate with Aluminum/Magnesium Hydroxides (MAGNATRIL).

Anthelmintics: Mebendazole (VERMOX); Niclosamide (NICLOCIDE); Praziquantel (BILTRICIDE); Pyrantel (ANTIMINTH); Quinacrine (ATABRINE); Thiabendazole (MINTEZOL).

Antiarrhythmic Drugs: Digoxin (LANOXIN); Procainamide (PRONES-TYL); Propranolol (INDERAL).

Anticoagulants, Oral: Warfarin (COUMADIN).

Anticonvulsants, Barbiturate: Mephobarbital (MEBARAL); Phenobarbital (BARBITAL, SOLFOTON).

Anticonvulsants, Benzodiazepines: Clonazepam (KLONOPIN); Clorazepate (TRANXENE); Diazepam (VALIUM, VAZEPAM).

Anticonvulsants, Dione: Paramethadione (PARADIONE); Trimethadione (TRIDIONE).

Anticonvulsants, Hydantoin: Ethotoin (PEGANONE); Mephenytoin (MESANTOIN); Phenytoin (DILANTIN).

Anticonvulsants, Succinimide: Ethosuximide (ZARONTIN); Methsuximide (CELONTIN); Phensuximide (MILONTIN).

Anticonvulsants, Miscellaneous: Carbamazepine (TEGRETOL); Phenacemide (PHENURONE); Primidone (MYIDONE, MYSOLINE); Valproic Acid Derivatives (DEPAKENE, DEPAKOTE).

Antidepressants, Tricyclic: Amitriptyline (AMITRIL, ELAVIL, EMI-TRIP, ENDEP); Desipramine (NORPRAMIN, PERTOFRANE); Imipramine (TOFRANIL).

Antidiarrheal Preparations: Bismuth Subsalicylate (PEPTO-BISMOL); Kaolin/Pectin (KAOPECTATE); Loperamide (IMODIUM, IMODIUM A-D).

Antifungal Agents: Clioquinol (VIOFORM); Clioquinol/Hydrocortisone (VIOFORM-HC); Clotrimazole (LOTRIMIN, MYCELEX); Flucytosine (ANCOBON); Griseofulvin (FULVICIN P/G, FULVICIN U/F, GRIFULVIN V, GRISACTIN, GRISACTIN ULTRA, and others); Nystatin (MYCOSTATIN, NILSTAT); Nystatin/Triamcinolone (MYCO II, MYCOBIOTIC II, MYCOGEN II, MYCOLOG II, MYCO-TRIACET,

MYTREX, and others); Tolnaftate (AFTATE, GENASPORE, NP-27, TINACTIN, TING, ZEASORB-AF).

Antihistamines: Brompheniramine (DIMETANE); Chlorpheniramine (ALLER-CHLOR, CHLOR-TRIMETON, PEDIACARE ALLERGY FORMULA); Cyproheptadine (PERIACTIN); Dimenhydrinate (DRAMAMINE, MOTION-AID); Diphenhydramine (BENADRYL, BENYLIN COUGH); Diphenylpyraline (HISPRIL); Doxylamine (UNISOM NIGHTTIME SLEEP AID); Hydroxyzine (ATARAX, VISTARIL); Promethazine (PHENERGAN); Pyrilamine (DORMAREX); Trimeprazine (TEMARIL); Tripelennamine (PBZ); Triprolidine (ACTIDIL, ALLERACT).

Antihistamine/Decongestant/Analgesic Combinations: Chlorpheniramine/Phenylephrine with Acetaminophen (ADVANCED FORMULA DRISTAN); Chlorpheniramine/Phenylpropanolamine with Acetaminophen (ALLEREST HEADACHE STRENGTH, CORICIDIN 'D' DECONGESTANT, CORICIDIN DEMILETS, SINAREST, TYLENOL COLD MEDICATION); Chlorpheniramine/Pseudoephedrine with Acetaminophen (CHILDREN'S COTYLENOL, MAXIMUM STRENGTH TYLENOL ALLERGY SINUS); Chlorpheniramine/Phenylpropanolamine with Aspirin (SINE-OFF SINUS MEDICINE).

Antihistamine/Decongestant Combinations: Brompheniramine/Phenylpropanolamine (BROMATAP, DIMETAPP); Brompheniramine/Pseudoephedrine (BROMFED, BROMFED-PD, DRIXORAL); Carbinoxamine/Pseudoephedrine (CARBODEC, CARDEC-S, RONDEC); Chlorpheniramine/Pseudoephedrine (CO-PYRONIL 2 PEDIATRIC, DECONAMINE, DORCOL CHILDREN'S COLD FORMULA, DURATAP PD, FEDAHIST, KRONOFED-A JR., PEDIACARE COLD FORMULA, RYNA, SUDAFED PLUS, T-DRY JUNIOR); Diphenhydramine/Pseudoephedrine (BENYLIN DECONGESTANT); Phenylephrine/Brompheniramine (DIMETANE DECONGESTANT); Phenylephrine/Chlorpheniramine (COLTAB CHILDREN'S, NOVAHISTINE); Phenylephrine/Chlorpheniramine with Pyrilamine (R-TANNATE, RYNATAN); Phenylephrine/Phenylpropanolamine with Pyrilamine/Chlorpheniramine (HISTALET FORTE); Phenylpropanolamine/Chlorpheniramine (ALLEREST, A.R.M. MAXIMUM STRENGTH, CORSYM, DEMAZIN, GENAMIN, MYMINIC, NORAMINIC, SNAPLETS-D, TRIAMINIC ALLERGY, TRIAMINIC CHEWABLES, TRIAMINIC COLD, TRIND); Phenylpropanolamine/Pheniramine with Pyrilamine (TRIAMINIC ORAL INFANT DROPS);

Phenylpropanolamine/Phenylephrine with Phenyltoloxamine/ Chlorpheniramine (AMARIL D, NALDECON, NEW-DECONGEST, TRI-PHEN-CHLOR); Phenylpropanolamine/Phenyltoloxamine with Pyrilamine/Pheniramine (POLY-HISTINE-D PED); Promethazine/ Phenylephrine (PHENERGAN VC, PROMETH VC PLAIN); Triprolidine/Pseudoephedrine (ACTIFED).

Antithyroid Agents: Methimazole (TAPAZOLE); Propylthiouracil.

Benzodiazepines: Chlordiazepoxide (LIBRIUM); Clonazepam (KLO-NOPIN); Clorazepate (TRANXENE); Diazepam (VALIUM).

Bronchodilators, Adrenergic: Albuterol (PROVENTIL, VENTOLIN); Ephedrine; Epinephrine (ADRENALIN, ASTHMAHALER, ASTH-MANEFRIN, BRONITIN, BRONKAID, MEDIHALER-EPI, PRI-MATENE, VAPONEFRIN); Isoproterenol (AEROLONE, ISUPREL, MEDIHALER-ISO, VAPO-ISO); Metaproterenol (ALUPENT, METAPREL).

Bronchodilators, Xanthine: Aminophylline (PHYLOCONTIN, SOMOPHYLLIN, TRUPHYLLINE); Oxtriphylline (CHOLEDYL); Theophylline (AEROLATE, ASMALIX, BRONKODYL, ELIXOMIN, ELIXOPHYLLIN, LANOPHYLLIN, LIXOLIN, SLO-BID, SLO-PHYL-LIN, SOMOPHYLLIN-CRT, SOMOPHYLLIN-T, THEOBID JR., THE-OCLEAR L.A., THEO-DUR, THEOLAIR, THEOSPAN-SR, THE-OVENT LONG-ACTING, THEO-24, TRUXOPHYLLIN).

Cephalosporins: Cefaclor (CECLOR); Cefadroxil (DURICEF, UL-TRACEF); Cefixime (SUPRAX); Cefuroxime (CEFTIN); Cephalexin (KEFLEX); Cephradine (ANSPOR, VELOSEF).

Corticosteroids: Oral Inhalation Corticosteroids (Beclomethasone [BECLOVENT, VANCERIL], Dexamethasone [DECADRON RESPI-HALER], Flunisolide [AEROBID], Triamcinolone [AZMACORT]); Nasal Corticosteroids (Beclomethasone [BECONASE, BECONASE AQ, VANCENASE, VANCENASE AQ], Dexamethasone [DE-CADRON TURBINAIRE], Flunisolide [NASALIDE]); Topical Corticosteroids (Amcinonide [CYLCOCORT], Betamethasone [DIPROSONE, UTICORT, VALISONE, and others], Desonide [DESOWEN, TRIDESILON], Desoximetasone [TOPICORT], Dexamethasone [AEROSEB-DEX, DECADERM, DECADRON, DECASPRAY], Diflorasone [FLORONE, MAXIFLOR, PSORCON], Fluocinolone [FLUROSYN, SYNALAR, and others], Fluocinonide [FLUOCIN, LIDEX, and others], Flurandrenolide [CORDRAN, CORDRAN SP], Halcinonide [HALOG, HALOG-E], Hydrocortisone [AEROSEB-HC,

ALLERCORT, BACTINE, CETACORT, CORTAID, CORT-DOME, CORTICAINE, CORTRIL, DERMICORT, HYTONE, LANACORT, LOCOID, NUTRACORT, TEXACORT, WESTCORT, and others], Methylprednisolone [MEDROL], Triamcinolone [ARISTOCORT, FLUTEX, KENALOG, TRIACET, and others]).

Cough and Cold Preparations: See Chapter 5, pages 148–190.

Decongestant/Analgesic Combinations: Phenylephrine/Acetaminophen (CONGESPIRIN FOR CHILDREN); Phenylpropanolamine/Acetaminophen (CONGESPIRIN FOR CHILDREN Solution).

Diuretics, Loop: Ethacrynic Acid (EDECRIN); Furosemide (LASIX, MYROSEMIDE).

Histamine H2-Receptor Antagonists (or **H2 Antagonists**): Cimetidine (TAGAMET); Famotidine (PEPCID); Ranitidine (ZANTAC).

Laxatives: Bisacodyl (CARTER'S LITTLE PILLS, DACODYL, DEFICOL, DULCOLAX, and others); Casanthrol (BLACK DRAUGHT); Casanthrol/Docusate (DIALOSE PLUS, DISANTHROL, PERI-COLACE, and others); Cascara Sagrada (Aromatic Cascara Fluidextract); Castor Oil (NEOLOID); Docusate (COLACE, DIALOSE, DIOCTO, DIOSUL, DISONATE, DOXINATE, MODANE SOFT, REGULAX SS, SURFAK, THERAVAC, and others); Glycerin (FLEET BABYLAX); Magnesium Citrate (CITROMA, CITRO-NESIA); Magnesium Hydroxide (PHILLIPS' MILK OF MAGNESIA); Magnesium Hydroxide/Mineral Oil (HALEY'S M-O); Malt Soup Extract (MALTSUPEX); Mineral Oil (AGORAL PLAIN, FLEET MINERAL OIL, KONDREMUL PLAIN, NEO-CULTOL, PETROGALAR PLAIN, ZYMENOL, and others); Phenolphthalein (ALOPHEN, ESPOTABS, EVAC-U-GEN, EX-LAX, FEEN-A-MINT, MODANE, CORRECTOL, and others); Polycarbophil (FIBERCON, MITROLAN); Senna (BLACK DRAUGHT, FLETCHER'S CASTORIA, SENOKOT, X-PREP, and others); Sodium Phosphate (FLEET ENEMA, FLEET PHOSPHO-SODA).

Nonsteroidal Anti-Inflammatory Analgesics (NSAIDs): Ibuprofen (ACHES-N-PAIN, ADVIL, EXCEDRIN IB, GENPRIL, IBUPRIN, IBU-TABS, MEDIPREN, MIDOL 200, MOTRIN-IB, NUPRIN, PAM-PRIN-IB, PEDIAPROPHEN, TRENDAR, and others); Naproxen (NA-PROSYN); Tolmetin (TOLECTIN).

Pediculicides: Lindane (KILDANE, KWELL, KWILDANE, PMS LINDANE, SCABENE); Permethrin (NIX); Pyrethrins/Piperonyl Butoxide (A-200, BLUE, LICETROL, R & C, RID, TISIT, TRIPLE X).

Penicillins: Amoxicillin (AMOXIL, LAROTID, POLYMOX, TRIMOX, WYMOX, and others); Amoxicillin/Clavulanate (AUGMENTIN); Ampicillin (OMNIPEN, POLYCILLIN, PRINCIPEN, and others); Bacampicillin (SPECTROBID); Cloxacillin (CLOXAPEN, TEGOPEN); Cyclacillin (CYCLAPEN-W); Dicloxacillin (DYCIL, DYNAPEN, PATHOCIL); Nafcillin (UNIPEN); Penicillin G (BICILLIN, PENTIDS); Phenoxymethyl Penicillin (BEEPEN-VK, BETAPEN-VK, LEDERCILLIN VK, PEN-VEE K, V-CILLIN K, VEETIDS, and others).

Potassium Supplements: Potassium Bicarbonate (KLOR-CON/EF, K-LYTE); Potassium Chloride (CENA-K, GEN K, KAOCHLOR, KAY CIEL, KAON-CL, K-LOR, KLOR-CON, KLORVESS, K-LYTE/CL); Potassium Gluconate (KAON); Potassium Gluconate/Potassium Chloride (KOLYUM); Potassium Gluconate/Potassium Citrate (TWIN-K).

Salicylates: Aspirin (A.S.A., ASPERGUM, BAYER ASPIRIN, EASPRIN, ECOTRIN, EMPIRIN, MEASURIN, NORWICH ASPIRIN, ST. JOSEPH ASPIRIN, and others); Buffered Aspirin (ASCRIPTIN, BUFFAPRIN, BUFFERIN, and others); Choline Salicylate (ARTHROPAN); Sodium Salicylate (URACIL).

Sulfonamides: Sulfamethoxazole (GANTANOL); Sulfamethoxazole/Trimethoprim (BACTRIM, SEPTRA, and others); Sulfisoxazole (GANTRISIN).

Tetracyclines: Chlortetracycline (AUREOMYCIN); Demeclocycline (DECLOMYCIN); Doxycycline (DORYX, VIBRAMYCIN); Minocycline (MINOCIN); Oxytetracycline (TERRAMYCIN); Tetracycline (ACHROMYCIN V, PANMYCIN, ROBITET, SUMYCIN, TETRACYN).

Thyroid Hormones: Levothyroxine (LEVOTHROID, LEVOXINE, SYNTHROID); Liotrix (EUTHROID, THYROLAR); Thyroid.

Vitamins: Ascorbic Acid, or Vitamin C (CECON, CE-VI-SOL, FLAVORCEE, SUNKIST, and others); Iron Supplements (Ferrous Gluconate [FERGON], Ferrous Sulfate [FEOSOL, FER-IN-SOL]); Vitamin A (AQUASOL A and others); Vitamin D Analogs (Calcifediol [CALDEROL], Calcitriol [ROCALTROL], Dihydrotachysterol [HYTAKEROL], Ergocalciferol [DRISDOL]); Vitamin K Analogs (Menadiol [SYNKAVITE], Phytonadione [MEPHYTON]).

GENERAL MEDICATION TIPS

Following are some everyday, commonsense suggestions about medications.

1. Tell your child's doctor what prescription and nonprescription medications your child is taking.

2. Tell your child's doctor if your child has an allergy, or if your child has experienced any hypersensitivity reactions to particular foods or medications.

3. When buying over-the-counter medication, read the entire label and pay close attention to warnings, side effects, contraindications, and dosage instructions.

4. Don't share your child's prescription medication with other children, even though the symptoms are similar, unless this has been approved by your doctor.

5. Don't give your child medication prescribed for someone else, even if the symptoms are similar.

6. Check your home medication supplies regularly and dispose of all expired medication.

7. Store all medications in a relatively cool, dry place, protected from light and out of reach of children.

8. Keep all household cleaners, insecticides, and other potentially

toxic substances out of your child's reach; lock them in a drawer or cabinet.

9. Never mix different medications together in one container, even if it means you have to carry several containers.

10. Never remove the label from a prescription container or household product.

11. Discard any unused medication once the condition being treated has been cured or alleviated, or if the medication has expired.

12. Do not replace childproof container tops with tops that are easier to remove, just for the sake of convenience.

13. If you have any question regarding a medication, do not use it until you have discussed it with your doctor or pharmacist.

14. If you feel that the cost of your child's medication is too high, ask your child's doctor if a generic brand is available, or if a less expensive alternative medication may be used instead.

15. Ask your child's doctor or your pharmacist to advise you of specific foods or drugs to avoid while taking the prescribed medication, or if there are any special instructions to be followed, such as the need to avoid exposing the child to sunlight; the need to take the medication with meals; the need to take the medication one hour before meals, etc.

16. Prescription medication should be taken (or administered) as close to the prescribed times as possible, and at the same time each day, unless you are otherwise instructed.

17. If a dose is missed, call your child's doctor or your pharmacist for instructions before taking (or administering) another dose.

18. If your child experiences adverse effects, such as nausea, vomiting, skin rash or eruptions, mood or behavior changes, fever, or other detectable changes, or if your child complains of discomfort, contact your child's doctor for further instructions.

19. Try to anticipate your child's prescription-medication needs by renewing prescriptions before the medication runs out.

20. Avoid using Aspirin or other salicylates in a child or teenager who has a high fever (e.g., flu or chicken pox); use Acetaminophen or Ibuprofen instead.

21. Alcohol-containing medications, such as cough and cold preparations, liquid vitamin preparations, and other oral liquids, should be avoided when taking certain medications; consult your doctor or pharmacist.

22. Caffeine-containing medications, such as pain and cold preparations, as well as soft drinks and other foods, should be avoided when taking certain medications; consult your doctor or pharmacist.

23. Place the telephone numbers of your pediatrician, the nearest emergency room, and the nearest poison control center (see Appendix IV) near your telephone.

24. Ask your child's doctor how long your child should take a medication, and if prescribed medications can be refilled. (Antibiotics should be used for the full course of treatment, even though a child's symptoms have improved.)

25. If your child requires medication doses while in school, be sure that your child knows when doses should be taken, or that a school nurse or homeroom teacher is able to assist your child.

26. If your child is unable to take the prescribed medication, ask your child's doctor if there are other dosage forms of the same medication available, or if a different medication can be used. (Sometimes, bad-tasting medications may be made more acceptable to a child by crushing a tablet, or by sprinkling the contents of a capsule on applesauce or other food product.)

POISON CONTROL CENTERS

Regional poison control centers are certified by the American Association of Poison Control Centers, and provide information related to accidental or intentional poisoning. A center is usually part of a hospital or medical facility, and has staff who are trained to provide specific poison information. The following poison control centers are open twenty-four hours, and are supervised by a qualified staff available to answer questions. **Place the telephone number of the nearest center by your telephone with other emergency numbers.** When traveling with a child, take along the number of the center nearest to your destination.

POISON CONTROL CENTERS IN THE UNITED STATES

Alabama:
Children's Hospital of Alabama
Regional Poison Control Center
(205) 939-9201
(800) 292-6678

Alaska:
Anchorage Poison Control Center
(907) 261-3193
(800) 478-3193

Arizona:
Arizona Poison and Drug Information Center
(800) 362-0101 (Ariz. only)
(602) 626-6016

Samaritan Regional Poison Center
(602) 253-3334

Arkansas:
University Hospital Poison Control Center
(501) 661-6161

California:
Fresno Regional Poison Control Center
(209) 445-1222
(800) 346-5922

Santa Clara Valley Medical Regional Poison Control Center
(408) 299-5112
(800) 662-9886

L.A. County Medical Association Regional Poison Control Center
(213) 484-5151
(800) 777-6476 (Calif. only)

UCDMC Regional Poison Control Center
(916) 453-3692
(800) 342-9293 (N. Calif. only)

San Diego Regional Poison Center
(619) 543-6000
(800) 876-4766 (619 area code only)

San Francisco Bay Area Regional Poison Control Center
(415) 821-5524
(800) 523-2222 (Bay Area only)

Colorado:
Rocky Mountain Poison Center
(303) 629-1123
(800) 332-3073 (Colo. only)

District of Columbia:
National Capital Poison Center
(202) 625-3333
(202) 4660 (TTY for deaf)

Florida:
Florida Poison Information Center
(800) 282-3171 (Fla. only)
(813) 253-4444

University Hospital of Jacksonville Clinical Toxicology Service
(904) 350-6899

Georgia:
Georgia Regional Poison Control Center
(800) 282-5846 (Ga. only)
(404) 589-4400
(404) 525-3323 (TTY)

Indiana:
Indiana Poison Center
(800) 382-9097
(317) 929-2323

Kentucky:
Kentucky Regional Poison Center of Kosair Children's Hospital
(800) 722-5725 (Ky. only)
(502) 629-7275

Maryland:
Maryland Poison Center
(800) 492-2414 (Md. only)
(301) 232-2120

Massachusetts:
Massachusetts Poison Control System
(800) 682-9211 (Mass. only)
(617) 232-2120

Michigan:
Poison Control Center
(800) 462-6642 (Mich. only)
(313) 745-5711

Blodgett Regional Poison Center
(800) 632-2727 (Mich. only)
(616) 774-7854
(800) 356-3232 (TTY deaf)

Minnesota:
Minnesota Regional Poison Center
(612) 221-2113

Hennepin Regional Poison Center
(612) 337-7474 (TTY for deaf)
(612) 347-3141

Missouri:
Cardinal Glennon Children's Hospital Regional Poison Center
(800) 366-8888
(314) 772-5200

Nebraska:
The Poison Center
(402) 390-5400
(800) 642-9999 (Nebr. only)
(800) 228-9515 (adjacent states)

New Jersey:
New Jersey Poison Information and Education System
(800) 962-1253 (N.J. only)
(201) 926-7443

New Mexico:
New Mexico Poison and Drug Information Center
(800) 432-6866 (N. Mex. only)
(505) 843-2551

New York:
Long Island Regional Poison Control Center
(516) 542-2323

N.Y.C. Poison Control Center
(212) POISONS
(212) 340-4494

Ohio:
Regional Poison Control Center
(513) 558-5111
(800) 872-5111

Central Ohio Poison Center
(800) 682-7625 (Ohio only)
(614) 228-1323
(614) 228-2272 (TTY for deaf)

Pennsylvania:
Pittsburgh Poison Center
(412) 681-6669

The Poison Control Center
(215) 386-2100

Rhode Island:
Rhode Island Poison Center
(401) 277-8062

Texas:
North Texas Poison Center
(800) 441-0040 (Tex. only)
(214) 590-5000

Utah:
Intermountain Regional Poison Control Center
(800) 662-0062 (Utah only)
(800) 581-7504

West Virginia:
West Virginia Poison Center
(800) 642-3625 (W. Va. only)
(304) 348-4211

POISON CONTROL CENTERS IN CANADA
Newfoundland and Labrador:
Provincial Poison Control Centre
(709) 722-1110

Western Memorial Hospital
(709) 637-5263
(709) 637-5264

James Paton Memorial Hospital
(709) 256-5552
(709) 651-2500 (switchboard)

Central Newfoundland Hospital
(709) 292-2134

Capt. Wm. Jackman Memorial Hospital
(709) 944-2632

St. Anthony Charles S. Curtis Memorial Hospital
(709) 454-3333, ext. 364

Prince Edward Island:
Queen Elizabeth Hospital
(902) 566-6250

Prince County Hospital
(902) 436-9131, ext. 175

Nova Scotia:
Izaak Walton Killam Hospital for Children
(902) 428-8161

Highland View Regional Hospital
(902) 667-3361, ext. 122

Antigonish St. Martha's Hospital
(902) 863-2830, ext. 122

Dawson Memorial Hospital
(902) 543-4603

Dartmouth General Hospital
(902) 465-8333
(902) 465-8300 (Emerg. Dept.)

Victoria General Hospital Emergency Department
(902) 428-2043

Blanchard-Fraser Memorial Hospital
(902) 678-7381, ext. 215

Aberdeen Hospital
(902) 752-8311

Sydney City Hospital
(902) 539-6400, ext. 118

Yarmouth Regional Hospital
(902) 742-3541, ext. 111

New Brunswick:
Chaleur General Hospital
(506) 546-4666

Campbellton
Hotel-Dieu St. Joseph
(506) 753-5212

Edmundston
Hotel-Dieu St. Joseph
(506) 735-7384

Dr. Everett Chalmers Hospital
(506) 452-5400
911 (Fredericton area only)

Moncton Hospital
(506) 857-5555
911 (Moncton area only)

Saint John Regional Hospital
(506) 648-7111
911 (Saint John area only)

Quebec:
Poison Control Centre of Quebec
656-8090 (Quebec City only)
(800) 463-5060 (province only)
(418) 656-8090 (all others)

Quebec City
(418) 654-2254

Ontario:
Hospital for Sick Children
(416) 598-5900 (416 area and 807 collect calls)
(800) 268-9017 (other Ont.)

Children's Hospital of Eastern Ontario
(613) 737-1100
(800) 267-1373 (other Ont.)

Brantford General Hospital
(519) 752-7871

Kingston General Hospital
(800) 267-1373

Kirkland & District Hospital
(705) 567-5251

Kitchener-Waterloo Hospital
(519) 749-4220

St. Mary's General Hospital
(519) 744-4121

Victoria Hospital
(519) 667-6565

St. Catherines General Hospital Poison Control Centre
(416) 684-7271, ext. 461

Sarnia General Hospital
(519) 336-6311

St. Joseph's Hospital
(519) 336-3111

Plummer Memorial Public Hospital
(705) 759-3800

Norfolk General Hospital
(519) 428-0750, ext. 212

McKellar General Hospital
(807) 623-5561

Port Arthur General Hospital
911 (Thunder Bay area only)
(807) 344-6621 (outside)
(416) 598-5900 (health prof.)

East General and Orthopaedic Hospital
(416) 469-6245

Hotel-Dieu de St. Joseph
(519) 973-4400

Manitoba:
Provincial Poison Information Centre
(204) 787-2591

Saskatchewan:
Regina General Hospital
(306) 359-4545

Saskatchewan University Hospital Poison Control Centre
(306) 966-1010

Alberta:
Poison and Drug Information Service
(800) 332-1414 (Alta. only)
(403) 270-1414 (Calgary area)

British Columbia:
B.C. Drug and Poison Information Centre
(604) 682-5050
(604) 682-2344, ext. 2126 (M.D.)

Royal Jubilee Hospital Emergency Department
(604) 595-9211

Northwest Territories:
Fort Smith Health Centre
(403) 872-2713, ext. 211 (ask for Poison Control)

Baffin Regional Hospital
(819) 979-5231, ext. 268

H. H. Williams Memorial Hospital
(403) 874-6512

Inuvik General Hospital
(403) 979-2955

Stanton Yellowknife Hospital
(403) 920-4111

Yukon Territory:
Whitehorse General Hospital
(403) 668-9444, ext. 226

BIBLIOGRAPHY

American Academy of Pediatrics. "Anticonvulsants and Pregnancy." *Pediatrics* 63, no. 2 (February 1979).

————. *Generic Prescribing, Generic Substitution, and Therapeutic Substitution.* Elk Grove, Ill.: 1987.

————. " 'Inactive' Ingredients in Pharmaceutical Products." *Pediatrics* 76, no. 4 (October 1985).

————. "Medication for Children with an Attention Deficit Disorder." *Pediatrics* 80, no. 5 (November 1987).

————. *Report of Committee on Infectious Disease.* 20th ed. Elk Grove, Ill.: 1986.

————. *Substance Abuse: A Guide for Health Professionals.* Elk Grove Village, Ill.: 1988.

————. "The Transfer of Drugs and Other Chemicals into Human Breast Milk." *Pediatrics* 73, no. 3 (September 1983).

————. "Use of Codeine- and Dextromethorphan-Containing Cough Syrups in Pediatrics." *Pediatrics* 62, no. 1 (July 1978).

————. "Vitamin and Mineral Supplement Needs in Normal Children in the United States." *Pediatrics* 66, no. 6 (December 1980).

American Society of Hospital Pharmacists. *American Hospital Formulary Service Drug Information.* Bethesda, Md.: 1990.

———. *Medication Teaching Manual*. 4th ed. Bethesda, Md.: 1987.

———. *The New Consumer Drug Digest*. Bethesda, Md.: 1985.

Besunder, J. B.; Reed, M. D.; and Blumer, J. L. "Principles of Drug Biodisposition in the Neonate." *Clinical Pharmacokinetics* 14, no. 4 (April 1988).

Bullock, B. L., and Rosendahl, P. P. *Pathophysiology, Adaptations and Alterations in Function*. 2nd ed. Glenview, Ill.: Scott Foresman/Little Brown College Division, 1988.

Compendium of Drug Therapy. 1988–89 ed. New York: McGraw-Hill Book Company, 1988.

Consumer Guide, Prescription Drugs. New York: Beekman House, 1988.

Consumers Union. *The Medicine Show*. 5th ed. New York: Mount Vernon, 1980 (*Consumer Reports* book; updated January 1983).

Drug Facts and Comparisons. 1990 ed. Hagerstown, Md.: J. B. Lippincott Company, 1990.

Florida Pharmacy Association. *Medicine Do's and Dont's*. Tallahassee, Fla.: 1988.

Friel, John P., ed. *Dorland's Illustrated Medical Dictionary*. 26th ed. Philadelphia, Penn.: W. B. Saunders Company, 1985.

Gilman, J. T. "Pediatric Considerations in Drug Therapy." *Florida Journal of Hospital Pharmacy* 7 (1987).

Gossel, T. A. "OTC Nasal and Ophthalmic Decongestants." *U.S. Pharmacist,* July 1988.

Graedon, J. *The People's Pharmacy*. New York: St. Martin's Press, 1986.

Griffith, H. W. *Complete Guide to Prescription and Non-Prescription Drugs*. 5th ed. Los Angeles: The Body Press, 1988.

Harkness, R. *OTC Handbook: What to Recommend and Why*. 2nd ed. Oradell, N.J.: Medical Economics Company, 1983.

Lebhar-Friedman, Inc. "Drug Store News/Inside Pharmacy." *1990 Pharmacist's Reference to Patient Counseling* 5, no. 2 (February 1990).

Libert, I. "Modifying Therapy for the Young." *Drug Therapy*, April 1976.

Love, N. C.; Lamy, P. P.; and Riley, A. N. "The Pediatric Medical Triangle." *Drug Intelligence and Clinical Pharmacy* 10 (September 1976).

Ludwikowski, K. K. "PPA: An Innocent Over-the-Counter Drug?" *Pediatric Nursing,* November/December 1984.

Masaki, B. W. "Physiologic Basis for Pediatric Drug Therapy." *U.S. Pharmacist,* November/December 1978.

McKenzie, M. W. "The Effect of Food on the Bioavailability of Selected Drugs: Considerations for Pediatric Patients," *Florida Journal of Hospital Pharmacists* 9 (April/May 1989).

————. "Oral Medication Administration in Infants and Children." *Florida Journal of Hospital Pharmacists* 9 (April/May 1989).

Medical Economics Company. "Interactions by OTC Product Type." *Drug Topics Red Book.* Oradell, N.J.: 1988.

————. *Drug Interactions and Side Effects Index.* 42nd ed. Oradell, N.J.: 1988.

————. *Physicians' Desk Reference.* 44th ed. Oradell, N.J.: 1990.

————. *Physicians' Desk Reference for Nonprescription Drugs.* 10th ed. Oradell, N.J.: 1989.

Mellooni, B. J.; Dox, I.; and Eisner, G. M. *Mellooni's Illustrated Medical Dictionary.* Baltimore: The Williams and Wilkins Company, 1979.

Pagliaro, L. A., and Pagliaro, A. M. *Problems in Pediatric Drug Therapy.* 2nd ed. Hamilton, Ill.: Drug Intelligence Publications, Inc., 1987.

Reid, J. D. "Effects of Selected OTC Medications on the Unborn and Newborn." *Nurse Practitioner,* September 1983.

Rowe, P. C. *The Johns Hopkins Hospital/The Harriett Lane Handbook.* 11th ed. Chicago: Year Book Medical Publishers, 1987.

Shirkey, Y. C. *Pediatric Dosage Handbook.* Washington, D.C.: American Pharmaceutical Association, 1980.

Simon, G. I., and Silverman, H. M. *The Pill Book.* 3rd ed. New York: Bantam Books, 1986.

Stewart, C. F., and Hampton, E. M. "Effect of Maturation on Drug Disposition in Pediatric Patients." *Clinical Pharmacy* 6 (July 1987).

Stile, I. L.; Hegyi, T.; and Hiatt, I. M. *Drugs Used with Neonates and During Pregnancy.* 2nd ed. Montvale, N.J.: Medical Economics Books, 1984.

United States Pharmacopeial Convention. *USP DI: Advice for the Patient.* 9th ed. Rockville, Md.: 1989.

————. *USP DI: Drug Information for the Health Care Professional.* Vols. 1A and 1B. Rockville, Md.: 1989.

INDEX OF BRAND NAMES AND GENERIC NAMES

Sudafed, Children's, 241–43
Sudafed DM, 183
Sudafed Plus, 108
Sudrin, 241–43
Sufedrin, 241–43
Sulfamethoxazole, 244–45
Sulfamethoxazole/Trimethoprim, 245–46
Sulfisoxazole, 246–47
Sunkist, 256–57
Suprax, 133
Surfak, 204
Symmetrel, 83, 191
Synalar, 147
Synkavite, 265
Synthroid, 79, 250
Syracol, 183

Tagamet, 70, 83, 115, 126, 127, 198, 230, 247–48
Tapazole, 114, 141
Tartrazine, 193
T-Dry Junior, 108
Tebamide, 252
Tegamide, 252
Tegopen, 225
Tegretol, 57, 70, 73, 75–77, 81, 83, 194, 231
Temaril, 101
Tempra, 253–55
Tetracycline, 200, 202, 220
Texacort, 147
T-Gen, 252
Theo-24, 129–30
Theobid Jr., 129–30
Theoclear L.A., 129–30
Theo-Dur, 129–30
Theolari, 129–30
Theolari-SR, 129–30
Theon, 129–30
Theophyl, 129–30
Theophylline, 70, 77, 129–30
Theophyl-SR, 129–30
Theospan SR, 129–30
Theovent Long-Acting, 129–30
Therevac, 204
Thiabendazole, 62
Thyroid, 251
Thyrolar, 251
Tigan, 252
Tinactin, 95–96

Ting, 95–96
Tisit, 218–19
T-Koff, 184
Tofranil, 84–85
Tolectin, 213–14
Tolmetin, 213–14
Tolnaftate, 95–96
Tolu-Sed, 184
Tolu-Sed DM, 184
Topicort, 147
Tranxene, 66, 116
Trendar, 210–12
Triacet, 148
Triacin C, 184
Triamcinolone, 139, 143, 148
Triaminic, 184–85
Triaminic Allergy, 110–11
Triaminic Chewables, 110–11
Triaminic Cold, 110–11
Triaminic-DM, 184
Triaminic Expectorant w/Codeine, 185
Triaminic Night Light, 185
Triaminicol Multi-Symptom Relief, 185
Triaminic Oral Infant Drops, 111
Tricodene #1, 186
Tricodene Forte, 185
Tricodene NN, 185–86
Tricodene Pediatric, 186
Tridesilon, 147
Tridione, 68
Trifed-C, 186
Trimedine, 186
Trimeprazine, 97, 101
Trimethadione, 68
Trimethobenzamide, 252
Trimox, 221–23
Trind, 110–11
Trind DM, 186
Tripelennamine, 97, 101
Tri-Phen-Chlor, 111–12
Triphenyl, 186
Triple X, 218–19
Triprolidine, 97, 101–2
Triprolidine/Pseudoephedrine, 112
Truphylline, 126–27
Truxophyllin, 129–30
Tuiatuss, 233–34
Tusquelin, 187
Tussafed, 187
Tussanil DH, 187

INDEX OF DRUG TYPES